Early Records
of
Cumberland County
New Jersey

Compiled by
Charlotte D. Meldrum

HERITAGE BOOKS
2011

HERITAGE BOOKS
AN IMPRINT OF HERITAGE BOOKS, INC.

Books, CDs, and more—Worldwide

For our listing of thousands of titles see our website
at
www.HeritageBooks.com

Published 2011 by
HERITAGE BOOKS, INC.
Publishing Division
100 Railroad Ave. #104
Westminster, Maryland 21157

Copyright © 1998 Charlotte Meldrum

All rights reserved. No part of this book may be reproduced or transmitted in any form or by any means, electronic or mechanical, including photocopying, recording or by any information storage and retrieval system without written permission from the author, except for the inclusion of brief quotations in a review.

International Standard Book Numbers
Paperbound: 978-1-58549-457-6
Clothbound: 978-0-7884-8868-9

CONTENTS

Introduction v

Cohansey Baptist Church 1

Deerfield Presbyterian Church 8

German Presbyterian Church, Cohansey 33

    Baptisms of Children Over Age of 13 Years 44

    Burials in Old Cohansy German Presbyterian Graveyard

    at Cohansey 45

    Immigrants Living at Cohansey 47

Methodist Epispocal Church of Port Elizabeth 51

Marriages Performed by the Ministers of the Methodist Church

    in Salem Circuit 52

Maurice Monthly Meeting 53

Fairton Presbyterian Church 56

Cumberland County Marriages 63

Combined Register of the Moravian Missionaries in West New Jersey,

    1742-1762 75

New England Town Burying Ground, Fairton 84

Baptist Church at Dividing Creek 87

Greenwich Presbyterian Church Records 92

Marriage Licenses from [published] New Jersey Archives 110

Index 77

INTRODUCTION

Cumberland County was formed from Salem County by the act of 19 January 1748. Maurice River Township was in Cape May County until 1710, then in Salem County until 1748, and then in Cumberland County. The early settlers of the county were largely persons from New England and Long Island, mostly Presbyterians. A large number of Baptists moved into the county from other colonies.

BAPTISTS

COHANSIE BAPTIST CHURCH

According to notes by Rev. Robert Kelsay, in 1755, the Baptist Church at Cohansie was constituted in the year 1690 by a colony of Irish Baptists from Tipperary. It was established by Thomas Killingsworth and met in a log house in Beck Neck on the south side of the Cohansey. Mr. Killingsworth labored in the work of the ministry at Cohansie, Salem and Pens-Neck until his death in 1709 along with Mr. Timothy Brooks from New England. Records were kept by both men and after the death of Mr. Killingsworth were combined, Mr. Brooks continuing in the ministry until his death.

After the death of Mr. Brooks the church requested and obtained assistance from the church at Cape May once a month. Mr. William Butcher from Chester County, Pennsylvania, became minister until his death only two years from his ordination. Mr. Nathaniel Jenkins came from Cape May to minister for several years before he moved to Cohansie. The church at Cohansie grew under the ministry of Mr. Nathaniel Jenkins with several branches at Piles-grove, Allowes-Creek and Great Egg-Harbour. Job Sheppard and Robert Kelsay were both licensed to preach at the branches of the church.

DIVIDING CREEK BAPTIST CHURCH

A log meeting house was built by this congregation in 1751. The church minutes run from 1761. A lists of baptisms, beginning in 1765, was compiled and published in the Vineland Histrocial Magazine, Vol. 30, No. 1 and 2.

WEST CREEK BAPTIST CHURCH was founded in 1792 in Maurice

River Township. Records begin in 1810.

PRESBYTERIANS

Fairfield Presbyterian Church, known as Christ Church of Fairfield, was an independent church from about 1680. By 1697 they had a log church and cemetery on Back Neck Road near Fairton on the south bank of the Cohansey River. Fairfield became a member of the Presbytery of Philadelphia in 1708. A new church was built in 1780 at New England Crossroads, later becoming an historic landmark. The church registers contains session minutes from 1759, baptisms from 1762, deaths form 1773 and marriages from 1794. The original records are held by the Presbyterian Historical Society at Philadelphia.

A Presbyterian church was built at Greenwich in 1717. Session records begin in 1766 and include baptisms, marriages, deaths and names of members. A transcription of the records, 1757-1828, was done by Charles E. Sheppard of Bridgeton and published in the *Vineland Historical Magazine*, Vol. 27-1:298 (January 1942).

With the sale of land at Deerfield, many Presbyterians of Fairfield moved into the area and established a church. Beginning in 1732 they met at a log school and in 1737 built a log church. Existing records are held by the church with copies at the Presbyterian Historical Society and the Historical Society of Pennsylvania. A copy of the vital records from these records is held by the library of the Vineland Historical and Antiquarian Society. The records include baptisms, 1771-1776 and 1794-1806. Deaths are covered, 1771-1776 and 1795-1801. Marriages are covered 1771-1776 and 1796-1806. Session minutes are covered, 1779-1827.

The First Presbyterian Church of Bridgeton was formed in 1791; however it was one session with Greenwich Church until 1824 and hence their records prior to this date would be with the Greenwich or Fairfield Church.

German Presbyterian Church, Cohansey. This church was founded in 1760 by German settlers in Upper Hopewell Township near Cohansey. Shirley Garton Straney in Church Archives in Cumberland County New Jersey - An Inventory, states "The church stood until 1840, and the cemetery, still receiving burials until 1860, is still visible on a hill in that place (two miles from Friesburg). ... Members of this church appear to have alternately attended the Lutheran church at Friesburg." The records were translated in 1936 by Charles C. D. Baker or Danzenbaker.

METHODISTS
The Methodist Church of Port Elizabeth was founded in 1785. The oldest book was copied in 1934 by Herbert W. Vanaman. The book has been lost; the transcript is held by Vineland Historical Society and included marriages, 1797-1806, baptisms, 1798-1801 and a list of trustees. That portion of the marriages and baptisms through 1800 is included in this work.

ANGLICANS
St. Stephen's Episcopal Church was founded in 1729, now located on Commerce Street, Bridgetown. No records appear to exist for the 1700s.

SEVENTH DAY BAPTISTS
Shiloh Seventh Day Baptist Church was organzied in 1737 near Bowentown; they met in the log meeting house of the regular Baptists until they built their own meeting house in 1739 at Cohansey Corners (now Shiloh). Records begin in 1737. They are held by the church historian.

UNITED BRETHREN SWEDISH-MORAVIAN CHURCH
The records are held by the Moravian Archives, Bethlehem, Pennsylvania. Those records for the period, 1744-1798, have been published in the *Genealogical Magazine of New Jersey*, Vol. 13-1:20.
The following was taken from the "Journal of the Rev. Abraham Reinke* among the Swedes of West Jersey, 1745", published in *Pennsylvania Magazine of History and Biography*, Vol. 33.

Raccoon, Mar. 31: -Visited Matthew Gill, an awakened Irishman.
April 1:-Gerred van Nimmen, one of the principal men among the Swedes in Penn's Neck. John van Nimmen and his son went with us seven miles to the church of Penn's Neck. Van Nimmen's family is very numerous and lives in the neighborhood, the emigrant was from Holland; the Gracebergs, an Irish family, also live nearby.
April 3-4: -Set out early this morning with Andreas Holstein for Morris River, 40 miles from Raccoon. ---In the evening came to old George Keen's who has one son Eric, who with his family lives

with him. Old George, a widower, desires to marry a widow of about 50 years ---(See marriage record above).

April 5: --Visited in the neighborhood, Nicholas Hoffman and wife Catharine ----Crossed the creek to the church begun some years ago by the Moravians ---thence to old John Hopman's who looks like an Indian, and met his wife and the wife of William Cobb; thence to Joseph and Abraham Johnson's.

April 8:---came to Samuel Cobb's, who married a daughter of George Keen. . . I found in this country scarcely one genuine Swede left, the most of them are either in part or in whole on one side or the other descended from English or Dutch parents, some of them have had a Dutch German, or English father, others a Swedish mother, and others a Dutch, or English mother and a Swedish father. Many of them can just recollect that their grand-fathers or mothers were Swedish. . The English are evidently swallowing up the people, and the Swedish language is so corrupted that if I did not know the English, it would be impossible to understand the language of my dear Sweden.

* He was born at Stockholm in 1712, educated at the University of Jena, entered the Moravian ministry, and came to Pennsylvania in 1744.

QUAKERS

Maurice Monthly Meeting was formed in 1804 at Port Elizabeth in 1804. An indulged meeting was formed here in 1693 by Salem Quarterly Meeting by which the friends about Cohansey were allowed to worship separate from the Salem Meeting. The records of births and deaths exist from 1728.

MARRIAGE RECORDS

In 1918 the recorded marriages (Book A) of the county clerk were compiied by Frank H. Stevens and later the records were copied by H. Stanly Craig and published by him in 1932. Shown in this work is Stevens' copy; major variances by Craig are shown in brackets [].

MARRIAGE LICENSES

Those marriage licenses in the New Jersey Archives (published) in which one of the parties is shown from Cumberland County, are shown in this book.

BIOGRAPHY

Craig, H. Stanley. *Cumberland County New Jersey Genealogical Data. Records Pertaining to Persons Residing in Cumberland County Prior to 1800.* Author: Merchantville, N.J. (1930s). Currently published by The Gloucester County Historical Society, P.O. Box 409.

Craig, H. Stanley. *Genealogical Data From Cumberland County New Jersey Wills.* Author: Merchantville, N.J. (1930s). Currently published by The Gloucester County Historical Society, P.O. Box 409.

Craig, H. Stanley. *Cumberland County (New Jersey) Marriages.* Author: Merchantville, N.J. (1932). Currently published by The Gloucester County Historical Society, P.O. Box 409.

Straney, Shirley Garton. *Church Archives in Cumberland County New Jersey.* Genealogical Society of New Jersey: New Brunswick (1982).

COHANSEY BABTIST (BAPTIST) CHURCH

A list of names of the members of the Church of Christ at Cohansie baptised on profession of their faith as of Jan. 1757:

Robert Kelsay, minister.	Mary Bacon
Jonadab Sheperd, elder.	Ann Shepherd
Seth Brooks, elder.	Mary Shepherd
Ashbury Smith, elder.	Miriam Kelsay
Obadiah Robins, deacon.	Sarah Harris
Samuel Harris, deacon.	Tabitha Dowdney
Stephen Mulford, deacon - d. July 13, 1763.	Hanah Wheaton
	Deborah Davis
John Dowdney	Hester Pooler
Abraham Smith	Phebe Smith
Seth Bowen	Eleanor Brooks
David Jenkins	Phebe Westcoat
Philip Vickers	Ruhanna Auston
Daniel Bowen	Patience Pauling
Stephen Shepherd	Rachel Loring
Philip Shepherd	Rebekah Boon
John Remington - d. Nov. 13, 1761.	Richard Langley
	Daniel Johnson
Isaac Wheaton - d. Feb. 16, 1762.	Elizabeth Remington
Eldad Cook	Hester Perry
Benjamin Bacon	Grace Long
Benjamin Mulford	Martha Leek
Joseph Goldan	Sarah Shepherd
Enoch Shepherd	Mary Bacon
John Lloyd	Elizabeth Wheaton
Jeremiah Bacon	Rachel Hood
David Shepherd	Hanah Mulford
Alexander Coningham	Martha Swinney
John Shepherd	Ann Jenkins
William Newcomb	Rhoda Johnson
David Shepherd	Ann Sirak
Nathan Miller	Ruth Shepherd
Jonathan Rumford	Eleanor Shepherd
Alplan Simkins	Eve Sackwell
Mary Fithian	Phebe Barns
Mary Bowen	Lydia Bateman

Mary Walling

Members living near Pilesgrove:
Henry Pauling
John Mayhew
William Brick
John Mayhew, Jr.
Onifornus Seagraves
David James
Kathrine Harker
Jemina Garrison
Esther Hews
Mary Willson
Jedidia Hudson
Mary Dickenson
Rebekah Hewett

William Paling
Samuel Morgan
Jacob Elwell
Samuel Harker, Jr.
John Dickenson
Jona Mayhew
Elonar Nealson
Hannah Elwell
Mary Hendrickson
Susannah Duvall
Martha Wallace
Sarah Seagraves
Rachel Brick

Members living in Great Egg Harbour:
John English
Nehemiah Nicheson
Peter Scull
Hannah Scull
Mary Blackman

John Goldan
Isaiah Counover
Desire Nicheson
Rebekah Goldan
Sephiah Smith

Persons baptised by the Rev. Robert Kelsay:
David Sayres bapt. Sept. 4, 1757,
   d. April 12, 1767.
Jonathan Bowen, Jr., bapt. Sept.
   4, 1757.
Ephraim Brooks bapt. Sept. 4,
   1757.
David Long bapt. Sept. 4, 1757.
Jonathan Bowen, Jr., bapt. Sept.
   4, 1757.
Ephraim Brooks bapt. Sept. 4,
   1757.
David Long bapt. Sept. 4, 1757.
Isaac Mulford bapt. Jul, 1758.
Abel Shepherd bapt. Aug. 1759.
Burgan Ayars bapt. Dec. 15, 1759.
Nathan Bacon bapt. Sept. 1760.

David Bown bapt. Sept. 1760.
Dickenson Shepherd bapt. Oct.
   15, 1760.
Richard Richardson bapt. 1761.
Henry Jelley bapt. 1761.
Joseph Shepherd bapt. Nov. 1761.
Hannah Brooks, bapt. Oct. 1757,
   d. July 24, 1763.
Mary Perry bapt. Sept. 1758, d.
   April 14, 1767.
Mary Parry, widow, bapt. Sept.
   1758.
Margaret Smith bapt. Nov. 2,
   1758.
Eleanor Dare bapt. Sept. 12, 1759.
Mary Fithian bapt. July 1760.

COHANSEY BAPTIST CHURCH

Mary Richardson bapt. May 1761.
Rachel Bacon bapt. Aug. 1761.
Sarah Bowen bapt. Aug. 1761.
Lydia Wethman bapt. Oct. 1761.
Susanna Oliver bapt. Oct. 1761.
Sarah Coffin bapt. Nov. 1761.
Sarah Miles bapt. May 1762.
Mary Bowen bapt. Nov. 1765.
Eunice Mulford bapt. Nov. 1765.
Jonathan Bowen bapt. Jun, 1765.
Joseph Shepherd bapt. Jun, 1765.
Samuel Harris, Jr., bapt. July 1765.
Elijah Bowen bapt. July 1765.
Rachel Bowen bapt. July 1765.
Susannah Harris bapt. July 1765.
Mary Bowen bapt. July 1765.
David Mayhew bapt. Aug. 1765.
Nathan Shepherd bapt. Aug. 1765.
Samuel Brick bapt. Nov. 1765.
Isaac Smith bapt. Nov. 1765.
Samuel Wood bapt. Dec. 1765.
Elezabeth Wood bapt. Dec. 1765.
Ruth Jarman bapt. Dec. 1765, d. Jan. 8, 1804.
Providence Ludlam bapt. Dec. 1765.
Sarah Ludlam bapt. Dec. 1765.
Elezabeth Lee bapt. Dec. 1765.
Daniel Harris bapt. Dec. 1765.
Mary Harris bapt. Dec. 1765.
Alpheus Brooks bapt. Dec. 1765.
Martha Brooks bapt. Dec. 1765.
Ephraim Russal bapt. Dec. 1765.
Sarah Russal bapt. Dec. 1765.
Abegail Brooks bapt. Dec. 1765.
Sarah Wheaton bapt. Dec. 1765.
Joseph Norberry bapt. Jul, 1766.
Abraham Smith, Jr., bapt. Jul, 1767.

Ebenezer Howel bapt. April 1769.
Cornelius Austen bapt. April 1769.
Philip Bacon bapt. Sep, 1770, d. July 1, 1808.
Jacob Brown bapt. May 1771.
Richard Richardson bapt. May 1771.
Mary Richardson bapt. May 1771.
Levi Heaton bapt. Aug. 1781.
James Shepherd bapt. Aug. 1781.
Enos Bacon bapt. Aug. 1781.
Ephraim Brick bapt. Aug. 1781.
David Shepherd bapt. Aug. 1781.
Catharine Pauling bapt. Aug. 1781.
Ami Parrey bapt. Aug. 1781.
Mary Shepherd bapt. Aug. 1781.
Jeremiah Brooks bapt. Aug. 1781.
Samuel Bowen bapt. Nov. 1781.
Ephraim Shepherd bapt. Nov. 1781.
Moses Bowen bapt. Nov. 1781.
Sarah Rieley bapt. Nov. 1781.
Martha Aarons bapt. Aug. 1765.
Rhoda Iszard bapt. Aug. 1765.
Sarah Miller bapt. Aug. 1765.
Sarah Ward bapt. Aug. 1765.
Phebe Nelson bapt. Sep, 1765.
Rachel Smith bapt. Sep, 1765.
Rachel Brick bapt. Sep, 1765.
Hephzibah Wheaton bapt. Oct. 1765.
Prudence Shepherd bapt. Oct. 1765.
Lucy Bowen bapt. Oct. 1765.
Sarah Shepherd bapt. Nov. 1765.
Elezabeth Robenson bapt. Jul, 1767.
Mary Shepherd bapt. Sept. 1768.

David Elwell of Pittsgrove bapt. Mar, 1775.
Sarah Elwell of Pittsgrove bapt. Mar, 1775.
Mary Shepherd bapt. Sep, 1774.
Elezabeth Brown bapt. Oct. 1774.
Synthche Smith bapt. Oct. 1775.
David Long and wife bapt. Dec. 1777.
Rev. P. Peterson Vanhorn bapt. Jul, 1777.
Andrew Padget bapt. May 1781.
Mary Padget bapt. May 1781.
Ruth Brick bapt. May 1781.
Rachel Simpkins bapt. May 1781.
Elesabeth Russal bapt. May 1781.
William Pauling bapt. Jun, 1781.
Abigail Johnson bapt. Oct. 1781.
Thomas Rementon bapt. Oct. 1781.
Ann Dickson bapt. Oct. 1781.
Margaret Harris bapt. Oct. 1781.
Ann Hudson bapt. Oct. 1781.
Dorcas Brooks bapt. Oct. 1781.
Achjah Russal bapt. Nov. 1781.
Hannah Shepherd bapt. Nov. 1781.
Sarah Coals bapt. Nov. 1781.
Elesabeth Bacon bapt. Nov. 1781.
Phebe Shepherd bapt. Nov. 1781.
Mary Harris bapt. Dec. 1781.
Moses Harris bapt. Dec. 1781.
Richard Barker bapt. Feb. 1782.
David Bown bapt. Feb. 1782.
Keziah Shepherd bapt. Feb. 1782.
Letitia Plotts bapt. Feb. 1782.
Prudence Robenson bapt. Feb. 1782.
Mary Ireland bapt. Feb. 1782.
Moses Crosley bapt. Mar, 1782.
David Gilmon bapt. Mar, 1782.
Robert Harris bapt. Mar, 1782.
William Branagan bapt. Mar, 1782.
John Royal bapt. Mar, 1782.
Henry Mulford bapt. Mar, 1782.
Lydia Gilmon bapt. Mar, 1782.
Milicent Shepherd bapt. Mar, 1782.
Damaras Dare bapt. Mar, 1782.
Hannah Leek bapt. Mar, 1782.
Mary Barber bapt. May 1782, d. Sept. 27, 1805.
Deborah Davis bapt. May 1782.
Lydia Shepherd bapt. May 1782.
Ruth Shepherd bapt. May 1782.
Sarah Fithian bapt. May 1782.
Sarah Shepherd bapt. May 1782.
Phebe Harris bapt. May 1782.
Amos Simpkins bapt. Jul, 1782.
Rebeca Simpkins bapt. Jul, 1782.
George Fithian bapt. Aug. 1782.
Elnathan Shepherd bapt. Aug. 1782.
Hannah Kimsey bapt. Aug. 1782.
Phebe Smith bapt. Sep, 1782.
Abnar Simpkins bapt. Sep, 1782.
Obed Hodson bapt. Sep, 1782.
Rachel Moore bapt. Sep, 1782.
Sarah Wheaton bapt. Oct. 1782.
Jacob Harris bapt. Oct. 1782.
Rachel Harris bapt. Oct. 1782.
Hannah Ewing bapt. Oct. 1782.
Cornelius Elwell bapt. Oct. 1782.
Epheraim Heaton bapt. Nov. 1782.
Mary Heaton bapt. Nov. 1782.
John Kelsay bapt. Nov. 1782.
Sarah Kelsay bapt. Nov. 1782.
Anne Garrison bapt. Nov. 1782.
Miriam Bowen bapt. Nov. 1782.

Hannah Shepherd bapt. Dec. 1782.
Hope Shepherd bapt. Dec. 1782.
Zebulun Brooks bapt. April 1783.
Lucy Mulford bapt. April 1783.
Elesabeth Bishop bapt. May 1783.
Dorcas Long bapt. Jun, 1783.
Sarah Nickels bapt. Jun, 1784.
David Platts bapt. Jul, 1784, d. July 9, 1805.
Mary Williams bapt. Jul, 1784.
Philip Westcoat bapt. Oct. 1784.
David Bowen bapt. Oct. 1785.
Elesabeth Smith bapt. Oct. 1785.
Charity Bowen bapt. May 1786.
Malichia Long bapt. Nov. 1785.
Philothea James bapt. Nov. 1785.
Henry Westcoat bapt. Jan. 1788.
Cornelius Elwell bapt. Jan. 1788.
David Elwell bapt. Feb. 1789.
Sarah Elwell bapt. Feb. 1789.
Sarah Coles bapt. Jan. 1791.
Jacob Brown bapt. April 1791.
James Dare bapt. Nov. 1791.
Martha Edwards bapt. Dec. 1791.
Sarah Beacon bapt. Dec. 1791.
Ann Dixson bapt. Dec. 31, 1791.
William Kelsay bapt. Jan. 19, 1792.
Hannah Elwell bapt. May 18, 1792.
Providence Ludlam bapt. July 5, 1792.
Abraham Smith's wife bapt. Oct. 15, 1792.
Elizabeth Sayre bapt. Oct. 1795.
Richard Barker bapt. Nov. 1795.
Ann Jenkins bapt. Nov. 1795.
Henry Westcoat bapt. Dec. 28, 1796.
Philip Shepherd bapt. Jan. 5, 1797.
Sarah Shepherd bapt. Dec. 1797.
Isaac Wheaton bapt. May 19, 1790.
Martha Shepherd bapt. May 19, 1790.
Francis Dixson bapt. Aug. 2, 1790.
Nicholas Johnson bapt. May 19, 1790.
Joseph Smith bapt. May 19, 1790.
Daniel Harris bapt. May 19, 1790.
Mary Harris, his wife bapt. May 19, 1790.
Soviah Bowen bapt. May 19, 1790.
Rebecah Wheaton bapt. May 19, 1790.
Sarah Glaspy bapt. May 19, 1790.
Elezebeth Sayre bapt. May 19, 1790.
Ruth Dare bapt. May 19, 1790.
Catharine Thomson bapt. May 19, 1790.
John Siffin bapt. Aug. 28, 1790.
Ruben Wheaton bapt. Aug. 28, 1790.
David Dare bapt. Aug. 28, 1790.
Philothea Bacon bapt. Aug. 28, 1790.
Phebe Mulford bapt. Nov. 6, 1790.
Howel Watson bapt. June 4, 1791.
Sarah Watson bapt. June 4, 1791.
Hannah Bacon bapt. June 4, 1791.
Sarah Bacon bapt. June 4, 1791.
Marget Solley bapt. June 4, 1791.
Dorcas Smith bapt. Aug. 6, 1791.
Susannah Right bapt. Aug. 6, 1791.
James Dear bapt. Sept. 13, 1791.
Platts Veal bapt. Sept. 13, 1791.

Marion Dear bapt. Sept. 13, 1791.
Sarah Cownover bapt. Sept. 13, 1791.
Jane Potter bapt. Aug. 16, 1794.
David Westcoat bapt. Nov. 6, 1791.
Phebe Westcoat bapt. Nov. 6, 1791.
Isaac Shepherd bapt. Nov. 6, 1791.
Sarah Shepherd bapt. Nov. 6, 1791.
Mary Dear bapt. March 31, 1792.
Joel Clark bapt. May 5, 1792.
Bathsheba Clark bapt. May 5, 1792.
Phebe Shepherd bapt. May 5, 1792.
Hannah Stackhouse bapt. May 5, 1792.
Eunice Cook bapt. Aug. 4, 1792.
Stephen Mulford bapt. Sept. 1, 1792.
Owen Shepherd bapt. Sept. 1, 1792.
Deborah Shepherd bapt. Sept. 1, 1792.
Abba Hall bapt. Sept. 29, 1792.
Hope Mulford bapt. Sept. 29, 1792.
Nathan Davis bapt. Nov. 3, 1792.
Ruth Shepherd, afterward Bateman, bapt. Nov. 3, 1792, d. July 29, 1806.
William Davis bapt. Dec. 1, 1792.
Eunice Davis bapt. Dec. 1, 1792.
Yocominetie Elwell bapt. Dec. 1, 1792.
Thomas Smith bapt. Aug. 3, 1793.
Sylvena Tubman bapt. at Dividing Creek (no date).
Theodosia Tubman bapt. at Dividing Creek (no date).
Mary Sowders bapt. at Dividing Creek (no date)
Eleanor Garrison bapt. at Dividing Creek (no date).
William Mason bapt. at Dividing Creek (no date).
Rhoda Worthington bapt. at Broad Neck (no date).
Ami Davis bapt. Dec. 1793.
Elizabeth Davis bapt. June 6, 1795.
Joel Robertson bapt. Jul, 1795.
Rachel Robertson bapt. Jul, 1795.
Hezia Kelsay bapt. July 7, 1797.
Kesiah Kelsay bapt. July 7, 1799.
Sarah Mattison bapt. Aug. 3, 1799.
Susannah Poor bapt. Aug. 3, 1799.
Abel Bacon bapt. May 31, 1800.
Rebecca Bacon bapt. May 31, 1800.
Rachel Cook bapt. May 31, 1800.
Harvey Shepherd bapt. May 31, 1800.
John Robertson bapt. May 31, 1800.

Deaths of members from Oct. 1, 1790 to May 1800:
Moses Bowen, d. Dec. 1789.
Mary Shepherd, d. Jan. 22, 1790.
Phebe Smith, d. Jan. 29, 1790.
Thomas Reamington d. June 17, 1790.
Jacob Harris d. Feb. 13, 1798.
Nathan Miller d. Feb. 19, 1798.

Phebe Shepherd d. Jan. 23, 1799.
Mary Shepherd, dau. of Philip
 Shepherd d. May 17, 1799.
Francis Dixon d. July 5, 1799.
Mary Harris, wife of Robert
 Harris d. Sept. 1, 1799.

Philip Husted d. 1800.
Tabitha Bacon d. 1800.
Thomas Smith d. 1800.
David Elwell d. May 4, 1800.

DEERFIELD PRESBYTERIAN CHURCH, 1746-1806

As published in the *Journal of the Presbyterian Historical Society*, Vol. IX.

Ministers of Deerfield:
Rev. Andrew Hunter the ordained paster of Greenwich and Deerfield Sept. 4, 1746 6-1760. Died July 31, 1775 age 60.
Mr. Simon Williams (supply) 1764-1766.
Enoch Green, pastor June 9, 1767. Died Dec. 2, 1776 age 41.
John Brainerd, pastor in 1777, died March 18, 1781.
Simeon Hyde pastor June 25, 1783, d. Aug. 10, 1783.
William Pickles, paster Jun, 1786. Dismissed and suspended Nov. 24, 1787.
John Davenport, pastor Aug. 12, 1795. Dismissed Oct. 16, 1805.

Ruling Elders:
Arthur Davis
Jeremiah Foster
John Garrison
Thomas Reed
William Tullis ordained by Mr. Brainerd March 1779, d. Dec. 9, 1796.
Ezekiel Foster, 1779.
Recompence Leake, also a Deacon, ordained by Mr. Brainerd March 1779, d. March 4, 1801.
William Smith, also a Deacon, ordained by Mr. Pickles April 1786.
John Stratton, also a Deacon, ordained by Mr. Pickles Oct. 1786.
William Garrison, also a Deacon, ordained by Dr. Robert Smith Sep, 1790.
Abner Smith, also a Deacon, ordained by Dr. Robert Smith Sep, 1790.
Joseph Moore ordained by Mr. Davenport Oct. 15, 1797.
Ebenezer Loomis ordained by Mr. Davenport Oct. 15, 1797.
Dr. Joseph Brewster ordained by Mr. Davenport Oct. 15, 1797.
Nathaniel Diament ordained by Mr. Davenport Aug. 18, 1801.
Ebenezer Harris ordained by Mr. Davenport Aug. 18, 1801.
Ephraim Loomis first chosen a ruling elder at Bridgeton and ordained by Mr. Davenport.

DEERFIELD PRESBYTERIAN CHURCH

Deacons:
Recomenpence Leake ordained by Dr. Robert Smith Sept. 1790.
William Garrison ordained by Dr. Robert Smith Sept. 1790.
John Stratton ordained by Mr. Davenport May 13, 1798.
Abner Smith set apart by Mr. Davenport April 10, 1803.
Ephraim Loomis set apart by Mr. Davenport April 10, 1803.

Members

Men received by Rev. Andrew Hunter:
William Tullis
Daniel Ogden
Recompence Leake

Received from the time of Mr. Hunter's dismission to installment of Mr. Green by Mr. Ramsey:
Jacob Jocelin
Othaniel David
Jonathan Ogden
Jonathan Garrison

Received by Rev. E. Green:
Broadway Davis
Samuel Jocelin
Elijah Davis
Joseph Moore by certificate from Greenwich.
Isaac Jessup - dismissed.

Females received by Rev. Andrew Hunter:
Patience James
Elizabeth Leake

Received from the time of Mr. Hunter's dismission to installment of Mr. Green:
Elizabeth Davis, widow rec'd by Mr. Hunter.
Patience Davis rec'd by Mr. Hunter.
Hannah Foster rec'd by Mr. Hunter.
Mary Garrison rec'd by Mr. Hunter.
Susannah Ogden.

Received by Rev. E. Green:
Rebecca Ingersoll, w.
Rachel Biggs, w. dismissed.
Jane Jocelin
Abigail Smith
Athele Fithian, w.
Mary Moore, w.
Anne Jessup-dismissed
Temperance Ogden, w.

Received by Rev. J. Brainerd:
William Smith
William Garrison - dismissed.
Ebenezer Harris
Abner Smith
Ezekiel Foster - dismissed.

Received into full communion from the time of Mr. Brainerds' death to the installment of Mr. Hyde:
Preston Hannah - by Mr. Hollinshead - dismissed.
Uriah Davis by Mr. Hollinshead.

Received by the Rev. S. Hyde:
John Brooks - removed
Jack ? - dismissed.

Received from the time of Mr. Hyde's death to time of Mr. Pickles' installment:
John Stratton by certficate from Fairfield - dismissed.

Females received by Rev. J. Brainerd:
Ester Davis, w. by certificate from Fairfield.
Ruth Garrison
Jemima Smith
Sarah Davis

Received into full communion from the time of Mr. Brainerds' death to the installment of Mr. Hyde:
Thomazine (or Tamsin) James, w. - by Mr. Hollinshead.
Amey Moore - by Mr. Hollinshead
Mary Paris by Mr. Schenck.

DEERFIELD PRESBYTERIAN CHURCH 11

Hannah Foster, wife of Ezekiel by certificate from Fairfield - dismissed.

Received from the time of Mr. Hyde's death to time of Mr. Pickles' installment:
Lydia Logan - by Mr. Hollinshead.
Eleanor Stratton by certificate from Fairfield.
Mabal Leake by certificate from Greenwich.
Males:
Ebenezer Loomis by Rev. W. Pickles.

Received from the time of Mr.Pickles' dismission to the time of Mr. Davenport's installment:
George Paris by Mr. Faitonte June 10, 1789.
Levi Leake by Dr. Robert Smith, May 1791.
James Davis by Dr. Robert Smith.
Benjamin Kenard by Dr. Robert Smith who has since joined the Methodists.
John Garrison by Mr. Foster, Nov. 9, 1793 - dismissed.

Received by Rev. J. Davenport:
Nathaniel Diament by certificate from Fairfield.
David Weeks by certificate from Pittsgrove - dismissed.
James Park by certificate from Greenwich - dismissed.
Joseph Brewster by certificate from Greenwich - dismissed.
David James by certificate from Greenwich - dismissed.
Daniel Davis by certificate April 3, 1796.
John Lawrence by certificate April 3, 1796.
Benjamin Davis by certificate April 3, 1796.
Broadway Davis, Jr., by certificate April 3, 1796.
Samuel Thompson by certificate May 7, 1797.
Uriah Davis by certificate Aug. 5, 1798.
Jonathan Smith by certificate Dec. 9, 1798.
Joel Berriman by certificate April 6, 1800.

Females received by Rev. W. Pickles:
Lydia Loomis by certificate from Fairfield.

Received from the time of Mr. Pickles dismission to the time of Mr. Davenport's installment:
Hannah Davis by Dr. R. Smith April 1790.
Hannah Dare, widow by certificate from Fairfield.

Rhoda Davis by certificate from Fairfield

Females received by Rev. J. Davenport:
Elizabeth Davenport by certificate from Bedford, State of New York.
Polly Baker by certificate from Bedford, State of New York.
Hannah Barker by certificate from Bedford, State of New York.
Priscilla Diament by certificate from Fairfield - dismissed.
Mary Weeks by certificate from Pittsgrove.
Phebe Murphy by certificate from Pittsgrove.
Sarah Buck by certificate from Pittsgrove.
Lucinda Brewster by certificate from Greenwich.
Phebe Park by certificate from Greenwich - dismissed.
Anne Ambler by certificate from Greenwich - dismissed.
Elizabeth Albertson by certificate from Pittsgrove.
Elizabeth Nelson, widow, received May 17, 1795.
Susannah Duffel received Sept. 29, 1795.
Bathsheba Hannah received Dec. 20, 1795 - dismissed.
Margaret Peck received April 3, 1796.
Jemima Avery received April 3, 1796.
Rebecca Reeves received April 3, 1796.
Hannah Harris received May 7, 1797.
Ruth Thompson received Aug. 20, 1797.
Eleanor Harris received May 4, 1798.
Mary Husted, widow received Aug. 5, 1798 - dismissed.
Reumah (?) Davis received Sept. 16, 1798.
Juliana Reeves, widow, received Dec. 9, 1798.
Christiana Garrison received Aug. 4, 1799.
Ruth Davis received Aug. 4, 1799.
Sally Moore received Aug. 4, 1799.
Lydia Foster received Aug. 4, 1799 - dismissed.
Mary O'Hara received April 6, 1800.
Rebecca Berriman received April 6, 1800.
Jemima Stratton received April 12, 1801.
Eunice Davis received April 12, 1801.
Ester Heritage received Aug. 2, 1801.
Mary Jocelin received Aug. 2, 1801.
Phebe Jocelin received Aug. 2, 1801.
Ruth Dare, widow, received Dec. 6, 1801.
Phebe Stratton received Dec. 6, 1801.
Lovisa Loomis by certificate from Bridgetown.
Elizabeth Richmond received Oct. 1, 1802.

Ruth Howard received Oct. 1, 1802.
Hannah Garrison received Oct. 1, 1802.
Martha Reeve received Oct. 3, 1802.
Ruth Ryal received Oct. 3, 1802.
Bathsheba Long received April 1, 1803.
Phebe Davis received Dec. 11, 1803.

Members in full communion with the Church in Deerfield
June 6, 1801

Broadway Davis
Samuel Jocelin
Othniel Davis
Daniel Davis
Elijah Davis
William Smith
Jonathan Ogden
Isaac Jessup - dismissed
Nathaniel Diament
Uriah Davis
William Garrison - dismissed
George Paris
Ebenezer Loomis
John Stratton - dismissed.
Levi Leake
Ebenezer Harris
David Weeks - dismissed
Abner Smith
Jonathan Garrison
John Brooks - dismissed
David James
Joseph Brewster
Benjamin Davis
Samuel Thompson
Uriah Davis, Jr.
Jonathan Smith
Broadway Davis, Jr.
Joel Berriman
Jack ? - dismissed.

Tom - a black man
Jedidiah Jocelin
Jonathan Jocelin
Ephraim Loomis
David Ryal
John Davis
John Leake
John Garrison - dismissed
Noah Harris
David Garrison
Rebecca Ingersoll, w.
Patience James
Elizabeth Davenport
Elizabeth Leake, w.
Jane Jocelin
Rachel Reeve - dismissed
Esther Davis, w.
Abigail Smith
Elizabeth Nelson, w.
Susannah Ogden
Juliana Reeves, w.
Athele Fithian, w.
Temperance Ogden, w.
Hannah Foster, w.
Patience Davis
Rhoda Davis
Sarah Davis
Priscilla Diament
Mary Weeks - dismissed

14 EARLY RECORDS OF CUMBERLAND CO.

Eleanor Stratton
Hannah Harris
Phebe Murphy
Anna Jessup - dismissed
Lydia Loomis, w.
Sarah Buck
Jemima Smith
Amey Moore
Thomazine (or Tamsin) James, w.
Mabal Leake
Mary Barker
Susannah Duffel
Anne Ambler - dismissed
Mary Paris
Hannah Barker
Lucinda Brewster
Reumah Davis
Rebecca Reeves
Christiana Garrison
Jemima Avery
Eleanor Harris

Jemima Stratton
Elizabeth Albertson
Eunice Davis
Ruth Davis
Sarah Moore
Esther Heritage
Mary O'Hara
Rebecca Berriman
May Jocelin
Phebe Jocelin
Ruth Dare, w.
Phebe Stratton
Lovisa Loomis
Lydia Moore
Elizabeth Richmond
Ruth Heuard
Hannah Garrison
Ruth Ryal
Martha Reeve
Bathsheba Long
Phebe Davis

Deaths while Mr. Davenport was pastor from 1795-1806:

Hannah Dare, w.
Moses Moore
Mary Foster
John Lawrence
William Tullis
Daniel Ogden
Jacob Jocelin
Elizabeth Davis, w.
Ruth Garrison
Margaret Peck
Mary Garrison, w.
James Davis
Hannah Davis
Phebe Garrison
Mary Moore, w.
Lydia Logan
Ruth Thompson
Daniel Garrison

Joseph Moore
Lydia Moore
Recompence Leake
Athele Fithian, w.
Ebenezer Loomis
Jonathan Garrison
Susannah Ogden
Rebecca Reeves
Ruth Dare, w.
Lovisa Loomis
Phebe Jocelin
Hannah Harris
Thomasin James
Uriah Davis
Ruth Davis
Temperance Ogden
Daniel Davis
William Smith

DEERFIELD PRESBYTERIAN CHURCH 15

Suspension of members:
John Ambler - suspended Dec. 18, 1781 for adhering to the Methodists.
Levi Riley - suspended Dec. 18, 1781 for adhering to the Methodists.
Sarah Stratton suspended Dec. 18, 1781 for adhering to the Methodists.
Levi Garrison suspended March 11, 1782 for adhering to the Methodists.
Priscilla Tarble suspended March 11, 1782 for adhering to the Methodists.
David James suspended April 25, 1805 for intemperance.
Names of other members who have joined the Methodists:
Fithian Stratton
Abraham Tarble
Sarah Foster, w.
Phebe Swain
Benjamin Kenard

Dismissions:
John Stevens
Esther Ireland, w.
Elizabeth Stratton, w.
Judah Brooks
Ezekiel Foster
Hannah Foster
James Park
Phebe Park
Preston Hannah
Bathsheba Hannah
John Garrison (stratched out)
Lydia Foster

Mary Husted
John Garrison (stratched out)
David Weeks
Mary Weeks
John Stratton
John Brooks - removed
Jack
Rachel Reeve
Isaac Jessup
Anne Jessup
Anne Ambler

Baptisms by the Rev. Enoch Green 1771:
John, son of William Garrison, bapt. June 9, 1771.
Hannah, dau. of Joseph Smith, bapt. June 16, 1771.
John Applin, son of Noah Harris, bapt. June 23, 1771.
David, son of John Teiler, bapt. June 23, 1771.
Jonathan, son of Jonathan Stratton, bapt. June 30, 1771.
Judith, wife of John Jessup, bapt. July 14, 1771.
Dau. of Benjamin Mall, bapt. July 14, 1771.
Phebe, dau. of Jonathan Garton, bapt. July 21, 1771.
Lydia, wife of Abraham Garrison, bapt. Aug. 11, 1771.
Wife of Jonathan Nichols, bapt. Aug. 11, 1771.
Ruhannah, dau. of James Clark, bapt. Sept. 1, 1771.

Hannah, a grand-dau. of Robert Dare, Sr., bapt. Sept. 1, 1771.
Butler, son of Newcomb Thompson, bapt. Oct. 25, 1771.
Rhoda., dau. of Levi Garrison, bapt. Oct. 27, 1771.
William, son of Jeremiah Biggs, bapt. Dec. 1, 1771.
Rachel, dau. of Eleazer Smith, bapt. Dec. 15, 1771.
Hannah, dau. of Constant Peck, bapt. March 8, 1772.
Elijah, son of Daniel Davis, bapt. April 12, 1772.
Jacob, son of William Casto, bapt. April 27, 1772.
Susannah, dau. of Samuel Jocelin, bapt. May 8, 1772.
Stephen Garrison, bapt. May 17, 1772.
Phebe, dau. of John Stevens, bapt. May 31, 1772.
William, son of Rev. Enoch Green, bapt. May 31, 1772.
Stephen, son of John Jessup, bapt. June 7, 1772.
Elizabeth Davis, widow, bapt. June 7, 1772.
William, son of Widow Jocelin, bapt. June 7, 1772.
Dau. of Daniel Garrison, bapt. July 12, 1772.
Lois, dau. of John Moore, bapt. July 12, 1772.
Sarah, grand-dau. of Abner Smith, bapt. Aug. 16, 1772.
Damaris, dau. of Uriah Davis, bapt. Sept. 13, 1772.
Hannah, dau. of John Ambler, bapt. Sept. 20, 1772.
Four children of the widow Damaris Daniel, bapt. Oct. 4, 1772.
William, son of William Smith, bapt. Nov. 1, 1772.
Sarah, dau. of Jonathan Harris, bapt. Dec. 6, 1772.
Rachel, dau. of John Jessup, bapt. Jan. 10, 1773.
Hannah, dau. of Robert Dare, bapt. Feb. 28, 1773.
Noah, son of Noah Harris, bapt. April 11, 1773.
John, son of John Harris, bapt. April 11, 1773.
Powel, son of William Garrison, bapt. April 25, 1773.
Hannah, dau. of Ephraim Foster, bapt. June 6, 1773.
William, son of Jacob Jocelin, bapt. June 13, 1773.
Ephraim, son of Nathan Leake, bapt. July 18, 1773.
Abigail, dau. of Jonathan Stratton, bapt. Aug. 18, 1773.
Jeremiah, son of Adam Terril, bapt. Aug. 22, 1773.
Hannah, dau. of Levi Garrison, bapt. Aug. 22, 1773.
Lewis James, bapt. Sept. 26, 1773.
Phebe, dau. of Broadway Davis, bapt. Oct. 17, 1773.
William, son of Newcomb Thompson, bapt. Oct. 22, 1773.
Aaron, son of Jeremiah Biggs, bapt. Oct. 22, 1773.
Lot, son of Amos Davis, bapt. Oct. 30, 1773.
Ruth, dau. of John Moore, bapt. Jan. 2, 1774.
Hannah, dau. of Eleazer Smith, bapt. Feb. 27, 1774.

DEERFIELD PRESBYTERIAN CHURCH 17

Ephraim, son of Ephraim Loomis, bapt. April 3, 1774.
Ruth, dau. of Jonathan Ogden, bapt. April 10, 1774.
Rachel, dau. of Constant Peck, bapt. May 1, 1774.
Phebe, dau. of Daniel Davis, bapt. May 1, 1774.
Gartey, dau. of Michael Kelsey, bapt. June 12, 1774.
Ann, dau. of Rev. E. Green, bapt. by Rev. A. Hunter at Greenwich June 21, 1774.
Daniel and Lewis, sons of Malachi Ogden, bapt. June 26, 1774.
Susy, dau. of --- Souders, bapt. July 3, 1774.
David, son of Jonathan Garton, bapt. July 17, 1774.
Hannah, dau. of Samuel Jocelin, bapt. July 18, 1774.
Samuel, son of David Moore, bapt. July 24, 1774.
Son of Daniel Garrison, bapt. July 24, 1774.
Israel, son of Daniel Garton, bapt. July 24, 1774.
Asa, son of William Smith, bapt. Dec. 4, 1774.
John, son of Uriah Davis, bapt. Dec. 18, 1774.
Joel, son of Jonathan Harris, bapt. Jan. 29, 1775.
James, son of widow Amy Boyd, bapt. March 12, 1775.
Ruth Peck and David Hannah, her son, bapt. March 19, 1775.
Elizabeth dau. of William Garrison, bapt. April 16, 1775.
Fithian, Aaron and Joel, sons of Ephraim Stratton, bapt. April 30, 1775.
David and Holmes, sons of Abraham Tarble, bapt. April 30, 1775.
Robert, son of Robert Dare, bapt. April 30, 1775.
Abraham Loper and Levi Riley, bapt. May 7, 1775.
Nathaniel, son of Ephraim Foster, bapt. May 7, 1775.
Judith, dau. of --- Jessup, bapt. June 18, 1775.
Rachel Brazier and Sarah Brazier, bapt. June 25, 1775.
Phebe, dau. of David Garrison, bapt. Dec. 10, 1775.
David, son of Jonathan Ogden, bapt. Dec. 17, 1775.
Phebe, dau. of John Ambler, bapt. Jan. 7, 1776.
Levi, son of Levi Garrison, bapt. Jan. 14, 1776.
Ebenezer, son of Jonathan Foster, bapt. Jan. 28, 1776.
Ruth, dau. of Adam Tyrell, bapt. Feb. 11, 1776.
Mary, dau. of Jacob Fries, bapt. March 1, 1776.
Elizabeth, dau. of Josiah Harris, bapt. March 3, 1776.
Abigail, dau. of Amos Davis, bapt. March 10, 1776.
Dau. of Daniel Davis, bapt. March 10, 1776.
Charles, son of Rev. E. Green, bapt. by the Rev. J. Brainerd March 27, 1776.
Laurania, dau. of Isaac Jessup, bapt. April 10, 1776.
Mary, dau. of Jonathan Garton, bapt. April 21, 1776.

Benaiah Parvin and Rebecca, his dau., bapt. May 5, 1776.
Abel Whitaker and Sarah, his dau., bapt. May 5, 1776.
Silas Seeley, son of Rhoda Reynolds, bapt. May 17, 1776.
Phebe, dau. of Newcomb Thompson, bapt. May 19, 1776.
Mary, dau. of of John Moore, bapt. May 19, 1776.
Hannah, dau. of Abraham Tarbell, bapt. May 19, 1776.
Levi, son of Arthur Davis, Jr., bapt. May 26, 1776.
Ephraim, son of Jacob Jocelin, bapt. June 2, 1776.
Sarah, dau. of John Stevens, bapt. June 2, 1776.
Hannah, wife of Ebenezer Harris and Sarah, his dau., bapt. June 30, 1776.
Ruth, dau. of Nathan Leake, bapt. July 28, 1776.
Nancy, dau. of Broadway Davis, bapt. Sept. 1, 1776.
Phebe, dau. of Joseph Moore, bapt. Sept. 1, 1776.
Elizabeth, dau. of Jonathan Harris, bapt. Sept. 22, 1776.
Lydia, dau. of widow Garrison, bapt. Oct. 17, 1776.

Baptisms by Mr. Davenport 1795:
Ezekiel, son of Ezekiel and Hannah Foster, b. Aug. 18, 1794, bapt. May 3, 1795.
Elijah Davis, son of Daniel and Priscilla Riley, aged 7, Dec. 6, 1794, bapt. May 10, 1795.
Lewis, son of Levi and Mabal Leake b. Nov. 11, 1794, bapt. May 16, 1795.
Elisabeth Nelson, widow aged 54 July 19, 1794, bapt. May 17, 1795.
Susannah, wife of John Duffel and children: William, aged 12, Dec. 28, 1794, John aged 1, Sept. 3, 1795, bapt. Sept. 20, 1795.
Rebecca, dau. of John and Anne Ambler, aged 1, March 10, 1795, bapt. Dec. 18, 1795.
Ruth, dau. of Joseph and Lucinda Brewster, b. Feb. 14, 1796, bapt. Ap 3, 1796.
Esther Preston, aged 7, Feb. 18, 179- and Jane, aged 4, May 21, 1795 daus of Benjamin and Thomazine Davis bapt. April 3, 1796.
Anne, aged 15, March 4, 1796; Charles, aged 13, July 23, 1795; Nathan, aged 11, March 23, 1796; Samuel and Simeon, twins aged 9, Jan. 13, 1796; John, aged 7, Jan. 17, 1796, children of Charles and Jemima Avery bapt. May 1, 1796.
Harriet, dau. of James and Ruth Davis, b. March 5, 1796, bapt. May 8, 1796.
Elizabeth, dau. of Adam and Elizabeth Shute, b. Oct. 1, 1795, bapt. May 8, 1796.

Asa, aged 6, July 31, 1795; Sally aged 5, Dec. 8, 1795, children of John and Sarah Lawrence, bapt. Dec. 8, 1795.

Lewis, son of George and Mary Paris b. Aug. 20, 1796, bapt. Oct. 23, 1796.

Daniel, son of Ezekiel and Hannah Foster, b. Oct. 19, 179-, bapt. March 12, 1797 by Rev. Ethan Osborn.

Alderman, son of Jonathan and Rachel Smith, b. Aug. 29, 1796, bapt. March 26, 1797.

Israel Moore, aged 16 Nov. 4, 1796; Susannah Royal, aged 14, Jan. 27, 1797; Lydia Moore, aged 9, March 5, 1797; Phebe Shoemaker, aged 3, April 21, 1796; David Shute, b. Oct. 17, 1796, children of Andrew and Margaret Peck, bapt. March 26, 1797.

Mary, dau. of Ebenezer and Hannah Harris aged 5, July 31, 1796, bapt. April 30, 1797.

Samuel, aged 5, Nov. 28, 1796; Mary Dare aged 4, June 10, 1796; Ruth, aged 3, June 2, 1797, children of Samuel and Ruth Thompson, bapt. June 2, 1797.

Rebecca, dau. of Broadway Davis, Jr., and Ruth, b. Sept. 21, 1797, bapt. Nov. 26, 1797.

Mary, dau. of Henry and Sarah Buck, b. Sept. 30, 1797, bapt. Dec. 10, 1797.

Eleanor, wife of Joel Harris, aged 25 Oct. 15, 1797, bapt. March 4, 1798.

Charles, son of Adam and Elizabeth Shute, aged 1 Feb. 24, 179-, bapt. April 29, 1798 by Rev. Mr. Clarkson.

Thomas, son of John and Anne Ambler, aged 1 June 7, 1798, bapt. Aug. 3, 1798

Judah, son of Joel and Eleanor Harris, b. April 22, 1798, bapt. Aug. 3, 1798.

Hannah, aged 9, Aug. 14, 1798; Aaron, aged 5 Nov. 25, 1797; Phebe, b. July 29, 1798, children of Uriah and Reumah Davis bapt. Sept. 16, 1798.

Ruth, dau. of of George and Mary Paris, b. Nov. 20, 1798, bapt. March 31, 1799.

William Garrison, son of Abner and Jemima Smith, b. Jan. 21, 1799, bapt. April 5, 1799.

Newcomb, son of Samuel and Ruth Thompson, b. March 13, 1799; bapt. June 9, 1799.

Sarah, dau. of of James and Phebe Park, aged 8 Feb. 3, 1799, bapt. July 14, 1799 at Milville.

Richard, son of Benjamin and Ruth Davis, b. May 4, 1799, bapt. July 28, 1799.

Rebecca, wife of Joel Berriman, aged 26, July 4, 1799, bapt. April 6, 1800.
Thomas, aged 5, Sept. 11, 1799; Hannah, aged 2, May 27, 1799, children of Joel and Rebecca Berriman, bapt. April 13, 1800.
Sarah, aged 11, May 24, 1800; Phebe, aged 8, Sept. 9, 1799; William, aged 6, Dec. 24, 1799; David, aged 4, March 28, 1800, Eliza, aged 1, Sept. 10, 1799, children of Joel and Christiana Garrison, bapt. Aug. 1, 1800.
Samuel, son of Joseph and Lucinda Brewster, b. Aug. 18, 1800, bapt. Dec. 21, 1800.
Alfred, son of Benjamin and Ruth Davis, b. Aug. 22, 1800, bapt. Nov. 2, 1800.
Thomas, son of Joel and Eleanor Harris, b. Aug. 26, 1800, bapt. Nov. 2, 1800.
James, son of Joel and Rebecca Berriman, b. Sept. 27, 1800, bapt. Jan. 18, 1801.
Susannah, dau. of Uriah Davis, Jr., and Reumah, b. Nov. 10, 1800, March 1, 1801.
Maria, dau. of Broadway Davis, Jr., and Ruth, b. Jan. 15, 1801, bapt. April 10, 1801.
Lydia, dau. of Samuel and Mary Moore, b. Jan. 27, 1801, bapt. April 10, 1801.
Susannah, dau. of Henry and Sarah Buck, b. Jan. 18, 1801, bapt. April 10, 1801.
Phebe, dau. of Samuel and Ruth Thompson, b. April 24, 1801, bapt. July 12, 1801.
John, son of Joel and Christiana Garrison, b. Sept. 15, 1800, bapt. June 7, 1801.
Ruth, dau. of John and Anne Ambler, aged 1, Oct. 30, 1800, bapt. July 31, 1801.
Asa, son of Jonathan and Rachel Smith, bapt. July 31, 1801.
Mary, wife of Jedidiah Jocelin, aged 32 May 26, 1801, bapt. Aug. 2, 1801.
Phebe, wife of Jonathan Jocelin aged 27, Aug. 10, 1800, bapt. May 26, 1801.
Elizabeth, dau. of George and Mary Paris, bapt. Aug. 16, 1801.
Sarah, aged 12 Nov. 25, 1800; Hannah, aged 9, March 14, 1801; Jane, aged 7 Nov. 9, 1800; Jonathan Worrel, aged 5, Feb. 23, 1801; Samuel, aged 1, Nov. 3, 1800, children of Jedidiah and Mary Jocelin, bapt. Aug. 20, 1801.
Daniel, aged 7, April 7, 1801; Hosea, aged 5, Jan. 2, 1801; Phebe, b. May 16, 1801, children of Jonathan and Phebe Jocelin, bapt. Aug. 20, 1801.

DEERFIELD PRESBYTERIAN CHURCH 21

Rebecca, aged 4, Aug. 18, 1801; Hannah, aged 1, April 21, 1801 children of William and Jemima Stratton, bapt. Aug. 30, 1801.
Hannah, wife of Jonathan Thompson Garrison, aged 23, Feb. 7, 1802, bapt. Oct. 1, 1802.
Martha, wife of John Reeve, aged 42, April 9, 1802, bapt. Feb. 3, 1802.
Ruth, wife of David Ryal, aged 28, May 5, 1802, bapt. Feb. 3, 1802.
John Nichols, son of Jonathan and Phebe Jocelin, b. Oct. 25, 1802, bapt. Feb. 11, 1803.
Phebe Garrison, dau. of Abner and Jemina Smith, b. Dec. 8, 1802, bapt. Jan. 31, 1802.
Elizabeth, dau. of Samuel and Ruth Thompson, b. Dec. 8, 1802, bapt. June 19, 1803.
William, son of Joseph and Lucinda Brewster, b. Jan. 11, 1803, bapt. June 19, 1803.
Bathsheba Long, bapt. April 1, 1803.
Elizabeth, dau. of Joel and Christiana Garrison, b. Dec. 8, 1802, bapt. July 24, 1803.
Isaac, aged 8 May 1, 1803; Elizabeth aged 6, May 9, 1803; Sarah, aged 4, May 1, 1803, Lydia aged 1, Dec. 26, 1802, children of Ephraim and Ruth Heward, bapt. July 24, 1803.
Susannah, 13, April 15, 1803; Joel, aged 11, Oct. 29, 1802; Phebe, aged 5, May 25, 1803; Polly, aged 2, Oct. 16, 1802; John, b. May 31, 1803, children of David and Ruth Ryal, bapt. July 31, 1803.
Elizabeth, aged 5, Aug. 27, 1803; Daniel Davis, aged 1, Nov. 24, 1802, children of David and Sarah Garrison, bapt. Sept. 4, 1803.
Rachel, aged 9, June 4, 1803, dau. of James and Mary Meek, bapt. Sept. 4, 1803.
Child of Henry and Elizabeth Redmond, bapt. Dec. 11, 1803.
Maria, aged 14, Nov. 8, 1803; Benjamin, aged 11, June 2, 1803; Enoch, aged Sept. 2, 1803, children of Forman and Esther Heritage, bapt. Dec. 11, 1803.
Gilbert, son of Broadway Davis, Jr., and Ruth, b. Feb. 16, 1804, bapt. May 20, 1804 by Rev. Mr. Harris.
Hosea, son of Abner and Jemima Smith, b. Jan. 9, 1804, bapt. July 3, 1804.
Emily, aged 2, Jan. 18, 1804, dau. of William and Jemima Stratton, bapt. Aug. 3, 1804.
Sarah, dau. of David and Sarah Garrison, bapt. Nov. 30, 1804.
Child of William and Jemima Stratton, bapt. April 5, 1805.
Child of Ruth Heward, widow, bapt. June 2, 1805.
Child of Henry and Elizabeth Richmond, bapt. Jan. 12, 1806.

EARLY RECORDS OF CUMBERLAND CO.

Reumah, dau. of Uriah and Reumah Davis, b. July 28, 1805, bapt. March 9, 1806.

Records of deaths kept by the Rev. Enoch Green:
William Jocelin, Sr., aged about 70 buried Aug. 25, 1771.
William Jocelin, buried Dec. 30, 1771.
Daniel Jessup, aged 23 buried Jan. 29, 1772.
Priscilla, wife of Dan Bowen, buried Feb. 6, 1772.
Benjamin Loper, buried March 9, 1772.
Joseph Davis, buried March 29, 1772.
The wife of Uriah Loper buried April 17, 1772.
Samuel Fish buried May 2, 1772.
Ichabod Sayres buried May 17, 1772.
The wife of --- Belding, buried June 2, 1772.
Abraham Leake aged 19, buried June 4, 1772.
Hannah, the wife of Ephraim Biggs, buried June 10, 1772.
Robert Dare, Sr., aged 70 buried Aug. 22, 1772.
A child of David Stratton, buried Sept. 3, 1772.
A child of Joshua Clark, buried Sept. 5, 1772.
An infant child of John Moore, buried Sept. 17, 1772.
An infant child of Joseph Bishop, buried Sept. 17, 1772.
The widow Box, buried Sept. 22, 1772.
John Applin Harris, buried Oct. 31, 1772.
A dau. of the widow, ---- Joceline, Jr., aged 14, buried Nov. 29, 1772.
Silas Hannah, aged 13 buried Dec. 2, 1772.
Priscilla, wife of --- Harris, buried Dec. 6, 1772.
Elizabeth, wife of Henry Carll, buried Jan. 13, 1773.
Ruth, wife of Michael Hoshall, buried Jan. 16, 1773.
Michael Day, buried Feb. 18, 1773.
James Hannah, buried March 4, 1773.
Widow Lydia Hannah, buried March 6, 1773.
A child of Silas Ireland, buried May 2, 1773.
John Duff, buried May 28, 1773.
A Child of Jonathan Garton, buried June 8, 1773.
The widow Thorne, buried June 22, 1773.
A child of Hannah File (Files or Filer), buried July 29, 1773.
Rufus Davis, buried July 30, 1773.
Joel Leake, buried Sept. 4, 1773.
A child of Malachi Ogden, buried Sept. 9, 1773.
An infant child of Benjamin Perry, buried Sept. 24, 1773.
Susannah White, aged 20, buried Sept. 29, 1773.

DEERFIELD PRESBYTERIAN CHURCH

The widow Elizabeth Jagger, buried Jan. 13, 1774.
Susannah Caryly buried Feb. 14, 1774.
Phebe, wife of David Garrison, buried March 12, 1774.
A child of Levi Garrison, buried April 13, 1774.
A child of Adam Horshels, buried May 7, 1774.
A child of John Ambler, buried June 29, 1774.
The widow Brooks, buried July 16, 1774.
A child of William Boyd, buried July 29, 1774.
A child of Ananias Clark, buried Aug. 11, 1774.
Elizabeth, wife of Samuel Yapp, buried Aug. 16, 1774.
William Boyd, aged 30, buried Aug. 26, 1774.
Nathaniel Bishop, buried Sept. 9, 1774.
Thomas Yapp, Jr., buried Sept. 15, 1774.
An infant child of Jonathan Foster, buried Oct. 30, 1774.
Rachel Clark, buried Nov. 6, 1774.
Mary, wife of Samuel Clark, buried Jan. 16, 1775.
Hannah, wife of Benjamin Mall, Sr., buried Jan. 17, 1775
Rachel, dau. of Constant Peck, buried Jan. 22, 1775.
A child of widow Harris buried Feb. 4, 1775.
A child of Ryneer Dare buried Feb. 7, 1775.
A dau. of John Stevens buried Feb. 17, 1775.
Abraham Garrison buried March 11, 1775.
A child of Levi Garrison buried March 20, 1775.
John Garrison buried March 20, 1775.
Mary Shute buried March 27, 1775.
Arthur Davis buried May 26, 1775.
Mrs. Elizabeth Peck buried June 24, 1775.
A child of Newcomb Thompson buried May 25, 1775.
Abigail, wife of Reuben Souder buried July 6, 1775.
A child of Isaac Johnson buried July 10, 1775.
Susannah, wife of Constant Peck buried July 20, 1775.
Esther Stratton buried Aug. 7, 1775.
A child of Uriah Mall buried Aug. 29, 1775.
A child of Thomas Burroughs buried Oct. 19, 1775.
A child of Joseph Heward (Kennard) buried Oct. 19, 1775.
Nathanial Harris, Sr. buried Nov. 2, 1775.
Nehemiah Veal buried Nov. 11, 1775.
Samuel Wells buried Nov. 11, 1775.
The wife of John Buck buried Dec. 17, 1775.
The wife of John Mall buried Dec. 31, 1775.
A child of Uriah Davis buried Jan. 6, 1776.

A child of David Jagger buried Feb. 2, 1776.
Samuel Powell buried Feb. 10, 1776.
Miriam, wife of Thomas Nichols buried Feb. 14, 1776.
William Shull buried Feb. 27, 1776.
Constant Peck buried April 10, 1776.
Samuel Clark buried April 17, 1776.
Elizabeth, wife of Lot Stratton buried April 30, 1776.
A child of Sarah Parvin buried May 19, 1776.
Sarah, wife of John Stevens buried May 24, 1776.
A child of David Garrison buried June 2, 1776.
A child of Jonas Sneathen buried June 2, 1776.
Josiah Harris buried June 18, 1776.
An infant child of David Moore buried July 11, 1776.
An infant child of Daniel Moore buried Aug. 9, 1776.
James Loper, Jr., buried Aug. 20, 1776.
A child of Jonathan Garton buried Sept. 13, 1776.
The wife of Charles Dayton buried Sept. 22, 1776.
John File (Files or Filer) buried Oct. 24, 1776.
John Leake, Jr., buried Oct. 25, 1776.
Benjamin Mall, Sr., buried Nov. 8, 1776.
Ephraim Stratton buried Nov. 11, 1776.

Records of deaths kept by Mr. Davenport:
Lydia, dau. of Broadway Davis, Jr., and Lydia, aged 1, April 17, 1794, d. Jan. 6, 1795.
Michael Hoshell, aged 55 Dec. 25, 1794, d. Feb. 16, 1795.
Ephraim and Leonard, twins children of Josiah and Rebecca Seeley died as follows: Ephraim, Feb. 14, aged 12 mo., 3 days; Leonard died. Oct. 15 aged 13 mos, 1 day. (this should be Feb. 14 and March 15, but original says Oct.)
Ruth Davis, widow aged 48 May 24, 1794, d. April 13, 1795.
Anne, wife of Ludlum Dare, aged 27 June 14, 1794, d. April 19, 1795.
Ruth, wife of David Dare aged 41, July 21, 1794, d. April 27, 1795.
Samuel, son of John and Lydia Seeley, b. Sept. 29, 1794, d. Aug. 4, 1795.
Polly, dau. of John and Sarah Lawrence, b. Oct. 13, 1794, d. Sept. 11, 1795.
Noah, son of John and Juda Brooks, b. March 24, 1795, d. Oct. 19, 1795.
Hannah Dare, aged 48, widow d. Oct. --, 1795.
Catharine, aged 6, July 24, 1795, dau. of Adam and Elizabeth Shute, d. Nov. 18, 1795.
A child of Azariah and Lydia Moore, b. Nov. 10, 1795, d. Nov. 12, 1795.

DEERFIELD PRESBYTERIAN CHURCH

Moses Moore, aged 59, b. March 10, 1795, d. Nov. 29, 1795.
Abishac Davis, aged 60 Jan. 1795, d. Nov. 29, 1795.
David Moore, aged 31, April 1795, d. Jan. 13, 1796.
Enos Harris, aged 26 April 28, 1795, d. Jan. 29, 1796.
Moses Tullis, aged 43, May 15, 1795, d. Feb. 20, 1796.
Miriam Bowen, dau. of Ephraim and Christiana Bowen, b. 1777, d. Feb. 28, 1796.
Jane Sigler, age unknown, d. March 17, 1796.
Mary, wife of Ephraim Foster, aged 36 Dec. 26, 1795, d. March 25, 1796.
John, son of Abner and Jemima Smith, b. Feb. 29, 1796, d. March 27, 1796.
Rebecca, aged 32, March 26, 1796, wife of William Stratton, d. Feb. 28, 1796.
Eleanor, aged 3, July 14, 1795, dau. of Israel and Damaris Jocelin d. Ma 2, 1796.
John Ambler aged 66, April 11, 1796, d. April 26, 1796.
Rebecca, aged 2 March 10, 1796, dau. of John and Anne Ambler d. May 2, 1796.
Joseph Hogben, aged 14, May 27, 1796, son of Joseph and Miriam Hogben, d. May 2, 1796.
Lydia, aged 27, July 20, 1795, wife of Broadway Davis, Jr., d. May 27, 1796.
Thomas Yapp, aged 81 June 4, 1796, d. July 22, 1796.
Isaac, aged 1, May 30, 1796, son of Uriah Davis, Jr., and Reumah, d. Aug. 4, 1796.
Sarah, wife of Selah Blew d. Aug. 20, 1796.
Ruth, age 2, Oct. 24, 1795, dau. of Ephraim Foster d. Sept. 22, 1796.
John, son of John and Phebe Jocelin, b. Nov. 22, 1795, d. Oct. 12, 1796.
David, son of Joel and Joanna Moore b. May 10, 1796, d. Oct. 15, 1796.
John Lawrence aged 36, April 11, 1796, d. Nov. 9, 1796.
Benjamin Keen, aged 37, Aug. 8, 1796, d. Nov. 25, 1796.
William Tullis, aged 81, June 5, 1796 (new stile), d. Dec. 9, 1796.
Abraham Carll, aged 46, April 1796, d. Jan. 2, 1797.
Isaac Elwell, aged 47, July 4, 1796, d. Jan. 4, 1797.
Jeremiah Parvin, aged 58, Oct. 16, 1796, d. Jan. 7, 1797.
Esther Foster, aged 15, March 25, 1796, d. Jan. 14, 1797.
Polly Moore, aged 48, Mar, 1796, d. Jan. 16 1797.
Job Bateman, aged 36, April 1796, d. Jan. 17, 1797.
Abigail, wife of Joseph Reeve, aged 35, May 10, 1796, d. Jan. 21, 1797.
Elizabeth Garrison, aged 18 or 16, Dec. 29, 1796, d. Jan. 21, 1797.
John Jocelin, aged 40 Aug. 14, 1796, d. Jan. 31, 1797.

Elizabeth, aged about 3, dau. of Michael and Hannah Katts, d. 1797.
Lawrence, son of Enos and Rhoda Garison, b. Jan. 13, 1797, d. Jan. 31, 1797.
Jacob Shull, aged 43, Oct. 1796, d. March 3, 1797.
Daniel Ogden, aged 79, Oct. 24, 1796, d. March 16 or 18, 1797.
Jacob Jocelin, aged 68, Oct. 28, 1796 (old stile), d. March 27, 1797.
Elizabeth, wife of Jonathan Smith, aged 37, May 9, 1776, d. April 28, 1797.
Elizabeth Davis, widow, aged 51, March 15, 1797, d. May 1797.
John Davenport Smith, son of Abner and Jemima Smith, b. March 21, 1797, d. May 10, 1797.
Statira, aged 11, Nov. 1, 1796, dau. of Abner and Jemima Smith, d. May 23, 1797.
James Glasby Berriman aged 5, Aug. 29, 1796, son of Joel and Rebecca Berriman, d. May 29, 1797.
Thomasin (or Tamson in original), wife of Benjamin Davis, aged 38, May 4, 1796, d. July 17, 1797.
Mary, dau. of Jacob and Rebecca High, b. Jan. 7, 1797, d. Aug. 1, 1797.
John Shute, aged unknown, probably 72, d. Aug. 22, 1797.
Ephraim Fithian, aged 63 Feb. 14, 1797, Oct. 31, 1797.
George Harris, son of Catharine, the wife of Johanthan Harris, Jr., aged 18, May 6, 1797, d. Nov. 18, 1797.
Ebenezer, son of Joel and Eleanor Harris, b. April 22, 1796, d. Dec. 2, 1797.
Rachel, aged 16, Jan. 11, 1797, dau. of the widow Tamsin James, d. Dec. 2, 1797.
Ruth, aged 46, Dec. 15, 1796, wife of William Garrison, d. Dec. 14, 1797.
Israel Read, aged 48 Feb. 1, 1797, d. Dec. 17, 1797.
Margaret, aged 40, Oct. 9, 1797, wife of Andrew Peck, d. Dec. 24, 1797.
Abigail, aged 23, Sept. 15, 1797, wife of Samuel Parker, d. Dec. 24, 1797.
Child of John and --- Biggs, d. Dec. 24, 1797.
Child of John and --- Biggs, d. Dec. 24, 1797.
John Biggs, aged 43, d. Feb. 2, 1798.
William, aged 15, April 2, 1797, son of Thomas and Ruth Reeve, d. April 6, 1798.
Mary, aged 35 April 27, 1797, wife of Ira Fithian, d. April 11, 1798.
Rachel, aged 52, Aug. 25, 1797, wife of John Moore, d. April 20, 1798.
Mary Garrison, widow, aged 51, March 25, 1798, d. April 25, 1798.
James Davis, aged 38, May 4, 1798, d. May 17, 1798.
Mary, dau. of Jedidiah and Mary Jocelin, b. Ap 8, 1798, d. May 21, 1798.
Hannah, aged 53, Oct. 31, 1797, wife of Daniel Davis, d. May 29, 1798.

DEERFIELD PRESBYTERIAN CHURCH

Rachel Tullis, widow d. June 16, 1798.
Susannah, aged 4 Nov. 16, 1797, dau. of Benaiah and Susannah Parvin, d. Aug. 2, 1798.
Child of John and --- Moore, d. Sept. 30, 1798.
Child of John and --- Moore, d. Oct. 4, 1798.
Child of John and --- Moore, d. Oc6 7, 1798.
David Dare d. Oct. 1798.
Stephen Moore aged 26, d. Oct. 1798.
Thomas, aged 4, July 17, 1798, son of Thomas and Ruth Reeve, d. Oct. 15, 1798.
Temperance Foy, aged 52, d. Nov. 2, 1798.
Lorana, aged 33, March 7, 1798, wife of John Jagger, d. Feb. 8, 1799.
Child of Matthias and --- Garrison, d. Feb. 10, 1799.
David, son of Preston and Sarah Stratton, b. April 6, 1799, d. April 22, 1799.
Naomi, dau. of Amos and Rachel Weeks, b. Oct. 24, 1799, d. Nov. 3, 1799.
Ruth Thompson, aged 26, May 5, 1799, d. Nov. 17, 1799.
Lydia Yapp, widow aged 87, June 22, 1799, d. Nov. 24, 1799.
Daniel Garrison, d. Dec. 9, 1799.
Nancy Bowers, aged 1 April 15, 1798, dau. of Thomas and Ruth Reeve d. Feb. 19, 1799. [The year 1800 was written then stratched out.]
Phebe, aged 36, Sept. 18, 1798, d. May 12, 1799.
Aaron, son of Joel and Rebecca Berriman, b. April 29, 1799, d. May 26, 1799.
Phebe, dau. of Uriah Davis, Jr., and Reumah, b. July 29, 1798, d. June 19, 1799.
Mary Moore, widow aged 54, Aug. 27, 1798, d. July 4, 1799.
Israel Harris, aged 28, June 22, 1799, d. July 4, 1799.
Mary, aged 6, July 15, 1799, dau. of Joel and Joanna Moore d. July 22, 1799.
Moses, aged 2, June 10, 1799, son of Joel and Joanna Moore d. July 22, 1799.
Mary, aged 1 Sept. 30, 1798, dau. of Henry and Sarah Buck d. July 28, 1799.
Amy Leake, aged 32, Nov. 7, 1798, d. Aug. 2, 1799.
Lydia, aged 74, Nov. 16, 1798, wife of James Logan, d. Aug. 14, 1799.
Robert, aged 13, April 1799, son of William and Phebe Murphy, d. Aug. 20, 1799.
Phebe, age 9, Jan. 8, 1799, dau. of William and Phebe Murphy, d. Aug. 20, 1799
Jonathan Fitz Randolph, aged 76, Oct. 22, 1798, d. Oct. 10, 1799.

EARLY RECORDS OF CUMBERLAND CO.

Zebulon, aged 3 Dec. 11, 1798, son of Zebulon and Phebe Brooks, d. Sept. 1, 1799.
Ruth, aged 2, Aug. 31, 1799, dau. of Zebulon and Phebe Brooks, d. Sept. 2, 1799.
Phebe, aged 22, Feb. 9, 1799, wife of Zebulon Brooks, d. Oct. 13, 1799.
John Moore aged 61, March 3, 1799, d. Feb. 22, 1800.
Adam, son of Adam and Elizabeth Shute, b. July 23, 1799, d. March 3, 1800.
Joseph Moore, a ruling elder. aged 59, April 12, 1800, d. April 30, 1800.
Lydia, aged 60 years wife of Col. David Moore, d. Aug. 28, 1800.
Hannah, aged 26, Aug. 16, 1800, dau. of Samuel and Jane Jocelin, d. Sept. 4, 1800.
Elizabeth Stratton, widow d. 1800.
Wife of Alexander Stewart d. Feb. 18, 1801.
Recomence Leake, a ruling elder and deacon, aged 74, Oct. 18, 1800 (new stile), d. March 5, 1801.
Zeboriah, child of Ephraim and Ruth Stewart (or Heward), b. Jan. 24, 1801, d. March 25, 1801.
John Casto, aged 24 Sept. 24, 1800, d. July 28, 1801.
Jonathan Garrison, aged 55 Sept. 8, 1801, d. Oct. 21, 1801.
Phebe, dau. of Jonathan and Phebe Jocelin, b. May 16, 1801, d. Nov. 24, 1801.
Ebenezer Lommis, a ruling elder, aged 52, May 6, 1801, d. Nov. 27, 1801.

Marriages solemnized by Rev. Enoch Green 1771:
Lewis Stom and Margaret Smith - June 17, 1771.
Richard Sayres and Esther Yapp - June 18, 1771.
Thomas Elliot Allen and Rhoda Sears - Sept. 25, 1771.
Conrad Huger and Christiana Hitchenor - Oct. 29, 1771.
Samuel Clark and Hannah Conklin - Dec. 19, 1771, 1771.
Abraham Garrison and Abigail Mall - Jan. 15, 1772.
David Page and Ruth Nixon - Jan. 15, 1772.
James Logan and Lydia Miller - Feb. 16, 1772.
Elias Whitaker and Margaret Paulding - Feb. 19, 1772.
Daniel Moore and Anne Russel - March 3, 1772.
Edward Russel and Rhoda Stevens - March 11, 1772.
Jacob Shaver and Catharine CreMarch - March 12, 1772.
Theodorus Vincent and Eva Fixen - March 24, 1772.
John Cordwall and Mary Coleman - March 24, 1772.
William Shull and Rachel Carll - March 25, 1772.
George Stites (Strites or Shutes) and Barbara Fauvern - June 4, 1772.

Jonathan Cornwall and Keturah Seely - June 16, 1772.
Barzillar Ewings and Sarah Wickward - Sept. 7, 1772.
Diament Whitaker and Rachel Keen - Sept. 10, 1772.
Philip Titus and Rhoda Biggs - Oct. 5, 1772.
Nathaniel Bishop and Damaris Moore - Oct. 7, 1772.
Noah Stratton and Rhoda Loder - Oct. 21, 1772.
William Bateman and Sarah Smith - Oct. 27, 1772.
William Johnson and Mary Garrison - Nov. 19, 1772.
John Burk and Rhoda Husted - Dec. 1, 1772.
Jonathan Davis and Esther Smith - Dec. 16, 1772.
Benjamin Perry and Esther Simkins - Dec. 23, 1772.
John Bennett and Bathsheba Miller - Dec. 24, 1772.
Abraham Sayres and Elizabeth Livingston - Dec. 29, 1772.
Lot Stratton and Elizabeth Duff - Jan. 21, 1773.
John Hardman and Mary CreaMarch - March 4, 1773.
William Stom and Sophia Halter - March 24, 1773.
Devald Zingler and Maudlin Hitchenor - April 6, 1773.
Henry Buck and Lovina Bateman - April 13, 1773.
William Filer and Hannah Owen - May 11, 1773.
Michael Hosel and Rachel Peck - May 15, 1773.
Henry Roecap and Charity CreMarch - June 29, 1773.
Garrard Garrison and Phebe Starky - July 7, 1773.
John Bragner and Susannah Eireigh - Aug. 10, 1773.
Dan Bowen and Lydia Yapp - Sept. 4, 1773.
William Richmond and Experience Read - Oct. 27, 1773.
Daniel Loder and Sarah Stratton - Nov. 17, 1773.
Nicholas Sorar and Sarah Schyner - Nov. 25, 1773.
Peter Convenover and Jemina Blackman at Egg Harbor - Dec. 3, 1773.
Jonathan Foster and Hannah Petty - Dec. 22, 1773.
Joseph Peck and Ruth Hannah - Dec. 24, 1773.
Andrew Trayer and Mary Myer - Feb. 1, 1774.
Moses Tullis and Mary Loper - March 8, 1774.
George Fisher and Elizabeth Parker - March 15, 1774.
Thomas Duff and Sarah Loper - March 15, 1774.
Noah Smith and Elizabeth Harris - March 15, 1774.
Jacob Dilshaver and Elizabeth Fulk - April 5, 1774.
Ryneer Dare and Hannah Loomis - April 6, 1774.
Abraham Robinson and Phebe Bowen - April 12, 1774.
Daniel Lupton and Prudence Cox - May 5, 1774.
Thomas Parvin and Hannah Shull - May 12, 1774.
Peter Duffel and Margaret Fisher - May 17, 1774.

Benaiah Parvin and Susannah Shull - June 14, 1774.
Jacob Shull and Lydia Hoshell - June 15, 1774.
George Taylor and Lydia Jocelin - July 20, 1774.
David Garrison and Mary Ogden - July 30, 1774.
Daniel Moore and Mary Smith - Aug. 17, 1774.
Samuel Chard and Elizabeth Blew - Aug. 17, 1774.
Reuben Loder and Abigail Stratton - Aug. 25, 1774.
Isaac Jessup and Anne Robinson - Sept. 6, 1774.
Urial Mall and Rachel Loper - Sept. 13, 1774.
Uriah Loper and Alethea Gilman - Sept. 13, 1774.
Edmond Shaw and Sarah Cornwall - Sept. 13, 1774.
Ebenezer Harris and Hannah Stathem - Nov. 23, 1774.
Arthur Davis and Mary Tullis - Nov. 23, 1774.
Isaac Atkinson and Elizabeth Davis - Dec. 20, 1774.
Dan Robinson and Rachel Bowen - Dec. 20, 1774.
George Conner and Catharine Sharer - Jan. 3, 1775.
John Stratton and Eleanor Leake - April 5, 1775.
Frederick Fries and Catharine Miller - April 19, 1775.
Caspar Hector and Mary Week - May 16, 1775.
Charles Vincent and Catharine Fixen - June 6, 1775.
Georg Haisht and Catharine Knapper - Aug. 1, 1775.
Benjamin Reynolds and Rhoda Nichols - Aug. 1, 1775.
John Turner and Elizabeth Bee - Oct. 19, 1775.
William Underwood and Mary Bee - Oct. 19, 1775.
Philip Vicars Fithian and Elizabeth Betty - Oct. 25, 1775.
Robert Harris and Mary Berriman - Jan. 2, 1776.
Henry Wheaton and Sarah Brooks - Jan. 9, 1776.
John Clemons and Eunice Hiler - Jan. 24, 1776.
Jacob Hitchenor and Christeen Sauren(?) March 12, 1776.
Moses Sutton and Rachel Garrison - April 16, 1776.
Holmes Parvin and Sarah Brasier - April 16, 1776.
Timothy Woodruff and Elizabeth Bernard - Aug. 29, 1776.
Silas Bradford and Temperance Edwards - Oct. 15, 1776.
Samuel Bennet and Rhoda Smith - Oct. 18, 1776.

Marriages solemnized by Mr. Davenport in the year 1795:
Joseph Choate and Hannah Harris, of Pittsgrove - Feb. 15, 1795.
Philip Cake and Mary McKimm, widow, of Pittsgrove - March 16, 1795.
David Leake, Deerfield and Hannah Shute, Pittsgrove - June 16, 1795.
David Conkling, Pittsgrove and Nancy Davis, Deerfield - Feb. 2, 1796.
Hoshel Shull and Hannah Peck, Deerfield, Feb. 5, 1796.

DEERFIELD PRESBYTERIAN CHURCH

Richard Caruthers and Elizabeth Jones, Pittsgrove - April 5, 1796.
Jonathan Riley, Deerfield and Sally Clark, Deerfield - June 23, 1796.
Francis Gilbert Brewster and Polly Seeley, Deerfield - Aug. 25, 1796.
Elijah Davis and Hannah Shute, Pittsgrove - Sept. 15, 1796.
David Filar and Susannah Dilshaver, Deerfield- Sept. 27, 1796.
James Garrison and Hannah Garrison, Pittsgrove - Oct. 4, 1796.
William Stratton and Jemima Davis, Deerfield - Nov. 9, 1796.
Broadway Davis, Jr., and Ruth Terril, Deerfield - Dec. 29, 1796.
John Heward and Esther Ogden, Deerfield - Jan. 24, 1797.
Henry Charles and Elizabeth Hector, Pittsgrove - Jan. 17, 1797.
John Gifford and Polly Loomis, both Maurice River - Feb. 3, 1797.
Ephraim Foster and Rebecca, Deerfield - Feb. 24, 1797.
Selah Blew and Anne Garrison, widow, Deerfield - March 8, 1797.
Jonathan Fish and Elizabeth Graham, Deerfield - April 12, 1797.
Samuel Parker and Lovina Bateman, Deerfield - July 19, 1797.
Solomon Dubois and Lydia Heward, Pittsgrove - Dec. 15, 1797.
Thomas Button and Mary Patrick, widow, Bridgeton - Feb. 5, 1798.
Richard Mulford and Rebecca Leake, Deerfield - Feb. 14, 1798.
Heman Crum and Anne Dubois, Pittsgrove - Feb. 14, 1798.
William Garrison, Esq. and Phebe Leake, Deerfield - Feb. 27, 1798.
David Garrison and Sally Davis, Deerfield - March 20, 1798.
Benjamin Davis and Ruth Reeve, Deerfield - June 13, 1798.
Daniel Davis and Susannah Leake, widow, Deerfield - Dec. 10, 1798.
Isaac Richmond, Deerfield and Rachel Sharp, Pittsgrove - Feb. 21, 1799.
Amos Weeks and Rachel Davis, Deerfield - March 6, 1799.
William Shull and Peggy Cake, Deerfield - March 12, 1799.
David Ogden, Deerfield and Rachel Murphy, Pittsgrove - April 11, 1799.
David Bennet, Fairfield and Hannah Smith, Pittsgrove - May 8, 1799.
Ephraim Magee, Fairfield and Polly Terril, Pittsgrove - June 25, 1799.
John Garrison and Rebecca Wyatt, Deerfield - Sept. 25, 1799.
Jeremiah Parvin and Sarah Read, widow, Hopewell - Feb. 8, 1800.
Recompence Whitaker, Pittsgrove and Rachel Moore, Stowe Creek, March 6, 1800.
Lewis Moore, Hopewell and Susannah Shull, Stowe Creek, - April 12, 1800.
David Buck and Deborah O'Hara, Deerfield - June 3, 1800.
Henry Buck and Keziah Newman, Deerfield - July 26, 1800.
Enoch Harris, Upper Alloway's Creek and Elizabeth Candell, Pittsgrove - Jan. 1, 1801.
Thomas Long and Bathsheba Pilgrim, widow, Stow Creek, - Jan. 27, 1801.

EARLY RECORDS OF CUMBERLAND CO.

Samuel Shull and Deborah Duffel, Stow Creek - March 14, 1801.
Cornelius Reeve and Abigail Smith, Deerfield - April 11, 1801.
John Moore, Hopewell and Phebe Moore, Stow Creek - Dec. 31, 1801.
Joseph Miller and Phebe Tullis, Deerfield - March 25, 1802.
David Mall and Polly O'Hara, Deerfield - March 31, 1802.
James Parvin and Lovisa Loomis, Deerfield - April 1, 1802.
Garret Newwkirk and Catharine Elwell, Pittsgrove - Dec. 4, 1802.
Joel Van Meter, Cape May and Sarah Alderman, Pittsgrove - Dec. 15, 1802.
Francis Robart, Maurice River and Mary Perkins, Pittsgrove - Jan. 25, 1803.
Henry Fry, Woodstown and Mary Marshall, Penns Neck - Feb. 28, 1803.
William Mayhey and Bathsheba Van Meter, Pittsgrove - March 22, 1803.
Varney Wells and Betsy Cake, Deerfield - March 23, 1803.
Daniel Davis and Abigail Crum, Deerfield - April 2, 1803.
Elkanah Powell and Lois Ritchie, Pittsgrove - April 12, 1803.
David Richmond, Pittsgrove - Elizabeth Parker, Thompson's Bridge - Sept. 20, 1803.
Richard Seeley and Betsy Moore, Deerfield - Dec. 28, 1803.
Simon Miller and Nancy Scullo, Deerfield - Feb. 11, 1804.
Enos Davis and Elizabeth Barker, widow, Deerfield - March 24, 1804.
William Dubois and Dorcas Mayhew, Pittsgrove - March 29, 1804.
Henry Cake and Dorcas Seeley, Deerfield - April 5, 1804.
Sanford Mayhew and Phila Ireland, Pittsgrove - April 16, 1804.
John Moore and Rebecca Garrison, Deerfield - May 2, 1804.
Enoch Paulding and Eunice Moore, Deerfield - May 3, 1804.
John Fithian, Hopewell and Phebe Davis, Deerfield - May 31, 1804.
John Tullis and Polly Taylor, Pittsgrove - Dec. 31, 1804.
Joel Sithen and Adah Vail, Pittsgrove - March 19, 1805.
Isaac Burdon and Sally Parvin, Pittsgrove - June 12, 1805.
Benjamin Dubos and Margaret Mead, Pittsgrove - June 13, 1805.
Moses Batton and Priscilla Richmond, Pittsgrove - June 20, 1805.
John Auld, Elsinburgh and Patty Buck, Pittsgrove - June 23, 1805.
John Howell and Rebecca Alderman, Deerfield - Feb. 9, 1806.
Levi Riley, Jr., and Hannah Brewster, Deerfield - March 1, 1806.
Broadway Davis, Jr., and Sarah Lawrence, widow, Deerfield - March 26, 1806.

GERMAN PRESBYTERIAN CHURCH COHANSEY

"This is a Record of Births & Baptisms of a Church erected in the year of 1760, by the German Settlers in Upper Hopewell Township near Cohansey formerly called New Boston in Cumberland Co., N.J. It appears by the deed was called the German Presbyterian Church, built on the lot where the old graveyard now stands, standing until the year about 1840.

"The Friesburg records says on May 28, 1836 communed with members of sister church at Cohansey by Rev. William Reynolds. Again communed with several members of sister Church, making 50 members in all. The families had their children baptized at both Churches.

"Translated in 1936 from old Teutonic German by Chas C D Baker or Danzenbaker, GGGrandson of Johann Ludwig Dantzebecher who came with Dr. Bodo Otto. in the ship Neptune arrived Philadelphia, Pa, Oct. 6, 1755."

The following is a listing of the father, mother (maiden name), child and birth or baptism:
Catherine, dau. of Larynx Knary and Anna Maria, b. Dec. 15, 1766.
Elisabeth, dau. of Catherine Duffield (Doffel), b. Sept. 17, 1766.
George, son of Johann Philip Wentzel (Wenzel) and Elisabeth, b. March 9, 1767.
Elisabeth, dau. of Peter Emmel (Emul) and Elisabeth, b. Feb. 12, 1766, 1767.
Catherine, dau. of Johann Ludwig Danzenbaker (Dantzebecher) and Catherine (Rocap), b. Sept. 9, 1767.
Elisabeth, dau. of Johann Truelender (Thuringer) and Catherine, b. Sept. 7, 1767.
Jacob, son of Jacob Miller (Muller) and Catherine (Dienger), b. Oct. 16, 1768.
Anna Maria, dau. of Peter Johnson (Janson), son of Johann and Johanna (Stoll) Janson and Barbara (Miller), b. Nov. 29, 1768.
Philip, son of Peter Souder (Sauter)and Eva Margaret (Sauter), b. Feb. 12, 1769.
Maria Anna, dau. of Adam Fox (Fix) and Elisabeth, b. Sept. 23, 1768.
Johann Jacob, son of Johann George Rocan (Rothgab) and Salome (Hichner), b. Aug. 18, 1769.

Maria Eva, dau. of Larynx Knary (Knarry) and Anna Maria, b. Nov. 9, 1768.
David, son of David Hunigal (Higuenel) and Anna Maria, b. March 6, 1769.
Jacob, son of Theobald (David) Rutter (Rotter) son of Jacob and Catherine Rotter and Maria Elisabeth, b. June 2, 1768.
Catherine, dau. of Simon Betchner (Bachtler) and Margaret, b. March 6, 1769.
Anna Margaret, dau. of Jacob Fries, Jr., and Elisabeth (Lautesbach), b. Feb. 17, 1769.
Johannes, son of Johannes George Kautz and Anna Maria, 2nd wife, b. Dec. 2, 1768.
Johannes, son of Johannes George Reibnel and Anna Catherine, b. Dec. 2, 1768
Johann Jacob, son of Catherine Thuringer (Thuringar), b. June 29, 1768.
Maria Barbara, dau. of Johannes Lutz and Anna Maria, b. July 13, 1769.
Heinrich, son of Adam Brinesholtz (Brendsholtz) and Anna Maria, b. Sept. 1, 1769.
Magdalena, dau. of Jacob Rammel (Ramael) and Magdalene, b. no date.
Johann, son of Heinrich Wolf (Woolff) and Elizabeth, b. Sept. 22, 1769.
Magdalena, dau. of Jacob Rammel and Magdalena, b. Nov. 8, 1769.
Johann Heinrich, son of Johann Ludwig Danzenbaker and Catherine (Rocap) b. Jan. 28, 1770.
Catherine, dau. of Johannes Rheiel and Maria, b. May 4, 1770.
Anna Catherine, dau. of John Martin Ott and Margaret, b. March 6, 1770.
Anna Elisabeth, dau. of Jacob Kernan (Kermann) and Anna Elisabeth, b. May 8, 1770.
Johannes, son of Freidrich Lamont (Lammond) and Catherine Elisabeth, b. Feb. 3, 1770.
Christina, dau. of Peter Souder and Eva Margaret, b. Aug. 8, 1770.
Johannes, son of Johannes Dilshaver (Dilshofer) and Maria Anna, b. Nov. 14, 1770.
Daniel, son of Johann Souder and Margaret, b. July 9, 1770.
Jonas, son of Philip Young (Jung) and Louisa, b. Aug. 28, 1770.
Susanna, dau. of Philip Souder and Christina (Shimp), b. Dec. 9, 1770.
Catherine Friedenia, dau. of Christopher Hartman and Susanna, b. Feb. 3, 1771.
Jacob, son of George Deal (Dieh) and Anna Margaret, b. March 14, 1771.
Jacob, son of Simon Souder (Sauder) and Margaret (Fries), b. June 19, 1771.

Catherine, dau. of Johann Wilhelm Souder and Catherine, b. March 10, 1771.
Johann Heinrich, son of Johann Heinrich Rheil and Susanna, b. March 26, 1771.
Christina, dau. of Bathasar Schmidt Hinne and Catherine, b. March 26, 1771.
Anna Maria, dau. of Mathis Ross and Susanna, b. June 18, 1771.
Andreas, son of Johannes Truelender (Thuringer) and Catherine, b. Feb. 22, 1772.
David, son of Peter Johnson and Barbara (Miller), b. Feb. 20 1771.
Anna Maria, dau. of Peter Emmel and Elisabeth, b. Nov. 4, 1770.
Susanna, dau. of Adam Fisher (Fisther) and Christina, b. Oct. 2, 1771.
Johann Heinrich, son of Johann Martin Ott and Margaret, b. Sept. 6, 1771.
Johann George, son of Peter Souder and Eva Margaret, Feb. 25, 1772.
Jacob, son of Bathasar Schmidt Hinner and Catherine, b. April 6, 1772.
Magdalena, dau. of Johann George Rocap (Ruthcep) and Salome (Hitcher), b. March 18, 1772.
Juliana, dau. of Simon Betchner (Bachtler) and Margaret, b. March 5, 1772.
Susanna, dau. of Zacharias Sickler (Ziglier) and Anna Maria (Miller), b. Dec. 14, 1771.
Maria Catherine, dau. of Adam Brinesholtz and Anna Maria, b. Nov. 29, 1771.
Johann Jacob, son of Johann Ludwig Danzenbaker and Cathere (Rocar), b. Nov. 8, 1772.
George, son of Peter Johnson and Barbara (Miller), b. March 11, 1773.
Margaret, dau. of Theodoras Wentzel and Eva, b. April 4, 1773.
Charles, son of Mathias Ross and Susanna, b. Sept. 25, 1772.
Johann Phillip, son of Johannes Rheil and Maria, b. Feb. 17, 1773
Johann Heinrich, son of Christopher Kunkleman and Anna Maria, b. Feb. 16, 1773.
Peter, son of Heinrich Kandle (Keadel) and Anna Maria, b. Sept. 16, 1773.
Maria, dau. of George Deal (Diel) and Anna Margaret, b. May 13, 1773.
Margaret, dau. of Heinrich Rocap (Rothgeb) and Charity (Creamer), b. Sept. 21, 1773.
Johannes, son of Johannes Souder and Margaret, b. Oct. 6, 1773,
Sarah, dau. of Freidrich Lamont (Lahmont) and Catherin Elisabeth, b. Oct. 7, 1767.
Johann Adam, son of Jacob Ott and Susanna, b. July 28, 1774.

Maria Magdalena, dau. of Urbanus Weidemeyer and Maria Magdalena, b. July 30, 1774.
Johannes, son of Jacob Dilshaver (Dillschaffer) and Elizabeth (Falk), b. Feb. 27, 1775.
Johanna Heinrich, son of Johann Martin Emmel and Rosina Catherine, b. April 4, 1775.
Barbara, dau. of Heinrich Rocap (Routhkep) and Charity (Creamer), b. Jan. 8, 1775.
Catherine, dau. of Johann Martin Ott and Margaret, b. Nov. 3, 1774.
Margaret, dau. of Heinrich Kandle and Anna Maria, b. Jan. 10, 1775.
Catherine, dau. of Wilhelm Smick (Schmick) and Anna Maria, b. April 2, 1775.
Elisabeth, dau. of Adam Fisher (Fisther) and Christina, b. March 14, 1773.
Johann George, son of Johann Ludwig Danzenbaker and Catherine (Rocap), b. July 29, 1775.
Elisabeth, dau. of Urbanus Weidemeyer and Maria Magdalene, b. April 14, 1776.
Johann Micheal, son of Philip May (Mey) and Elisabeth, b. Jan. 20, 1776.
Catherine, dau. of Johann George Kautz and Anna Maria, b. Nov. 6, 1776.
Anna Maria, dau. of Heinrich Kandle and Anna Maria, b. Oct. 30, 1776.
Margaret, dau. of Philip Souder and Christina (Shimp), b. Nov. 9, 1776.
Johannes, son of Bathasar Schmidt Hinne and Catherine, b. April 1, 1777.
Isaac, son of John George Reibnel and Margaret, b. Dec. 29, 1776.
Johanna George, son of George Moslet and Elisabeth, b. Dec. 10, 1776.
Johannes, son of Jacob Kautz and Maria, b. May 20, 1776.
Elisabeth, dau. of Jacob Fries, Jr., and Elisabeth, b. Dec. 20, 1776.
Elisabeth, dau. of Jacob Dilshaver and Elisabeth (Falk), b. June 3, 1776.
Catherine, dau. of Heinrich Rocap (Rothgeb) and Charity (Creamer), b. Jan. 9, 1776.
Magdalene, dau. of Edmond Schmidt and Elisabeth, b. March 27, 1777.
Christina, dau. of Simon Betchner and Margaret, b. April 28, 1777.
Anna Maria, dau. of Wilhelm Smick (Schmick) and Anna Maria, b. Jan. 12, 1776.
Johann Micheal, son of Johann Martin Emmel and Rosina Catherine, b. May 9, 1777.
Siballa, dau. of Daniel Morgan and Elisabeth, b. June 5, 1777.
Jacob, son of Carl (Chas) Wentzel and Catherine, b. Sept. 17, 1778.

GERMAN PRESBYTERIAN CHURCH

Johann Heinrich, son of Johann George Rocap and Salome (Hitchner), b. Oct. 2, 1777.
Elisabeth, dau. of Joseph Kandle and Margaret, b. Sept. 22, 1777.
Maria Margaret, dau. of Christopher Hartman and Susanna, b. Nov. 29, 1777.
Johann Heinrich, son of Salome Hilliard (Hilyard), b. Feb. 13, 1777.
Johannes, son of Johannes Hoffman and Anna Margaret, b. July 7, 1777.
Peter, son of Heinrich Foster (Froster) and Christina, b. July 15, 1777.
Johanna, son of Conrad Hires (Heyer) and Christina (Hitchner), b. March 3, 1777.
Peter, son of Peter Minch (Mensch) and Christina, b. Aug. 1, 1777.
Susanna, dau. of Johann Ludwig Danzenbaker and Catherine (Rocap), b. March 2, 1777.
Christina, dau. of Adam Wentzel and Sarah, b. Feb. 4, 1777.
Peter, son of Johannes Souder and Margaret, b. April 6, 1777.
Margaret, dau. of Johannas Dilshaver and Maria Anna, Aug. 9, 1778.
Mathias, son of Daniel Wentzel and Anna Maria, b. March 30, 1777.
Johannes, son of Zacharias Sickler (Zigler) and Anna Maria (Miller), b. Sept. 14, 1778.
Michael, son of Jacob Miller and Catherine, b. Sept. 10, 1778.
Philip, son of Philip Kautz and Christina, b. July 19, 1778.
Anna Maria, dau. of George Hannan (Hinnin) George and Catherine, b. June 9, 1779.
Maria, dau. of Robert Mackey (Machgay) and Acory, b. Dec. 10, 1776.
Anna Maria Barbara, dau. of George Moslet and Elisabeth, b. Feb. 27, 1778.
Susanna, dau. of Johannes Schmidt and Elisabeth, b. June 26, 1778.
Joseph, son of Joseph Schutz and Lousia, b. July 8, 1778.
Elisabeth, dau. of Johann George Kautz and Anna Maria, b. Sept. 30, 1779.
George, son of Dewaldo Theobald (David) Sickler and Magdalene (Hitchner), b. Oct. 6, 1779.
Heinrich, son of Heindrich Ernsdoff and Elisabeth, b. May 25, 1779.
Catherine Elizabeth, dau. of Johannes Frevel and Anna Margaret, b. Oct. 3, 1779.
Eva Rosina, dau. of John Micheal Wolbert (Wolpert) and Maria, 2nd wife, b. Oct. 25, 1779.
George, son of George Perry and Abbie, b. Sept. 2, 1779.
Johann Peter, son of Johann Martin and Rosina Catherine, b. Sept. 27, 1779.
Rosina, dau. of Peter Emmel and Elisabeth, b. Dec. 27, 1779.
Johann Jacob, son of Philip May and Elisabeth, b. Feb. 7, 1779.

Elisabeth, dau. of John Peter Wolbert (Wolpert) and Sophia, b. Oct. 17, 1779.
Daniel, son of Micheal Ewing (Hung) and Charolette, b. Sept. 7, 1780.
Johannes, son of Johann George Dixon and Anna Barbara, b. July 1, 1780.
Christina, dau. of Heinrich Rammel (Raemel) and Anna Maria, b. Sept. 8, 1780.
Elisabetha, dau. of Johann Ludwig Danzenbaker and Catherine (Rocap), b. Oct. 20, 1780.
Gideon, son of Urbanus Weidemeyer and Maria Magdalene, b. Feb. 12, 1781.
Christina, dau. of Henrich Hillard (Hilgert) and Salomne, b. Feb. 17, 1781.
Heinrich, son of Philip May and Elisabeth, b. Feb. 24, 1781.
Johannes, son of Johann George Kautz and Barbara, b. April 5, 1781.
Conrad, son of Conrad Hires and Christina (Hitchner), b. Nov. 1, 1781.
Micheal, son of Nathan Schwam (Schawm) and Julian, b. Sept. 1, 1782.
Catherine, dau. of Daniel Wentzel and Maria, b. April 3, 1782.
Maria, dau. of Philip Souder and Christina (Shimp), b. June 9, 1782.
Anna Margaret, dau. of Simon Souder and Elisabeth, b. Jan. 31, 1782.
Johannes, son of Freidrich Shute (Schoot) and Susanna, b. June 10, 1782.
Johann Mathias, son of John Martin Emmel (Eaemmell) and Rosina Catherine, b. April 27, 1782.
Anna Maria, dau. of Freidrich Fox (Fuchs) and Anna Maria, b. Jan. 15, 1783.
Heinrich, son of Hans George Couch (Kaucher) and Catherine, b. Aug. 4, 1783.
Maria, dau. of Carl (Chas) Wentzel and Catherine, b. Sept. 11, 1783.
Louisa, dau. of Adam Wentzel and Sara, b. Jan. 26, 1783.
Johann Jacob, son of Wilhelm Stamme and Sophia, b. Mar, 21, 1783.
Christian Ludwig, son of Johann Watson (Vatson) and Maria Anna, b. Oct. 20, 1782.
Catherine Elisabeth, dau. of Johann Schmidt and Sophia, b. March 29, 1783.
Anna Maria, dau. of Johann Cunningham and Rebecca, b. Aug. 3, 1783.
Anna Maria, dau. of Jacob Dilshaver (Dilschafer) and Susanna, b. Aug. 2, 1785.
Simon, son of Simon Souder and Elisabeth, 2nd wife, April 9, 1783.
Anna Maria, dau. of Johann George Shute (Schoot) and Elisabeth (Nollen), b. June 28, 1783.

Hannah, dau. of George Perry and Abigail, b. Jan. 6, 1784.
Anna Margaret, dau. of George Rocap and Salome (Hitchner, dau. of Jacob), b. Dec. 27, 1782.
Daniel, son of Daniel Wentzel and Anna Maria, b. Feb. 9, 1784.
Jacob, son of Philip Fries and Maria Ann, b. March 8, 1784.
Johann Philip, son of Philip May and Elisabeth, b. Mar, 5, 1784.
Maria Barbara, dau. of Joseph Schutz and Louisa, b. Sept. 30, 1784.
Johann Philip, son of Johann Stanger (Stranger) and Isabelle, b. Jan. 2, 1784.
Anna Maria, dau. of Adam Ross and Philippina, 2nd wife, b. Jan. 3, 1784.
Margaret, dau. of Simon Souder and Elisabeth, 2nd wife, b. April 11, 1785.
Elizabeth, dau. of Nathan Schwam and Julianna, b. Nov. 16, 1784.
Johann Philip, son of Heinrich Hillard (Hilgert) and Salome, b. Sept. 21, 1784.
Simon, son of Philip Souder and Christina (Shimp), b. Aug. 27, 1784.
Jacob, son of Thomas Stretch and Anna Maria, b. Nov. 22, 1784.
Micheal, son of Henrich Oxebecher (Ochsenbecker) now Potter and Christina (Micheal), b. July 18, 1784.
Caroline Catherine, dau. of Johann Martin Emmel and Rosina Catherine, Apr., 5 1785.
Samuel, son of Samuel Donelson and Susanna, b. June 4, 1784.
Philip, son of Theobald Dewaldo (David) Sickler and Magdalene (Hitchner), b. Oct. 23, 1784.
Jacob, son of Peter Paris and Susanna, b. June 17, 1785.
Johannes, son of Heinrich Bitters (a Hessian Soldier) and Elisabeth, b. Dec. 1, 1784.
Hannah, dau. of Theodoris Wentzel and Eva, b. June 11, 1784.
Philip, son of Adam Wentzel and Sara, b. Aug. 4, 1784.
Anna, dau. of Wilhelm Smick (Schmick) and Anna Maria, Dec. 23, 1784.
Susanna, dau. of Freidrich Shute (Schoot) and Susanna, b. Feb. 19, 1784.
Johann Adam, son of Heinrich Kandle and Anna Maria, b. Jan. 24, 1783.
Anna, dau. of Johann Joseph Rammel and Elisabeth, b. April 14, 1785.
Juliana, dau. of Benjamin Lee (Leig) and Elisabeth, b, July 9, 1785.
Margaret, dau. of Johann Hepner (Heappnar) and Anna Maria (Hitchner), b. Dec. 24, 1784.
Andreas, dau. of Bathasar Schmidt Hinne and Catherine, b. Jan. 1, 1785.
Jacob, son of Heinrich Hilliard (Hilgert) and Salome, b. 1788
Johannes, son of Wilhelm George Heine and Rosina, b. Feb. 6, 1796.
David, son of Johannes Wilhelm Shimp (Schimpt) and Maria Magdalene, b. Aug. 18, 1795.

Margaret, dau. of George Souder and Catherine, b. Nov. 3, 1794.
Johannes, son of Peter Hitchner (Hitzler) and Catherine, b. Feb. 21, 1795.
Peter, son of Philip Souder and Anna Maria, 2nd wife, b. Jan. 30, 1791.
Maria, dau. of Micheal Ulrich and Sarah, b. March 15, 1796.
Mathias, son of John Martin Ott and Margaret, b. Dec. 20, 1793.
George, son of Christina Laurence b. Oct. 8, 1790.
Heinrich, son of Peter Sigara (Seager) and Catherine (Danzenbaker), b. Jan. 2, 1795.
Jacob, son of Philip Souder and Anna Maria, 2nd wife, b. Feb. 10, 1796.
Margaret, dau. of John Martin Ott and Margaret, b. Jan. 15, 1796.
Betsey, dau. of Johann Hepner (Hoppner) and Anna Maria (Hitchner), b. April 2, 1798.
Johann son of George Danzenbaker and Maria (Pilgram), b. May 29, 1802.
Martin, son of George Souder and Catharine, b. May 19, 1803.
Ann, dau. of Johann George Kautz and Anna Maria, b. May 23, 1804.
Daniel, son of Micheal Johann Wolbert and Maria Catherine, b. Oct. 1, 1790.
Samuel, son of Johann Micheal Wolbert and Maria Catherine, b. June 10, 1792.
James, son of Johann Micheal Wolbert and Maria Catherine, b, Nov. 11, 1795.
John Micheal, son of Johann Micheal Wolbert and Maria Catherine, b. June 24, 1800.
Jonathan, son of Johann Micheal Wolbert and Maria Catherine, b. Feb. 26, 1802.
Wilhelm, son of Johann Hartman and Lillian, b. Nov. 14, 1798.
Margaret, dau. of Johann Hartman and Lillian, b. Aug. 1800.
Susanna, dau. of Johann Hartman and Lillian, b. Sept. 26, 1802.
Johannes, son of Johann Hartman and Lillian, b. Oct. 25, 1805.
Maria Anna, dau. of Philip Dilshaver and Margaret, b. Oct. 25, 1805.
Susanna, dau. of Heinrich Shimp (Schimpt) and Anna Maria, b. May 23, 1804.
Christina, dau. of Peter Sigars (Seggers) and Catherine (Danzenbaker), b. March 3, 1809.
Barbara, dau. of George Souder and Catherine, b. Aug. 7, 1805.
Levi, son of Maria Wentzel, b. April 24, 1808.
Clara, dau. of Peter Hartman and Estor (Emmel), b. Jan. 14, 1804.
Jane, dau. of Peter Hartman and Ester (Emmel), b. Aug. 8, 1806.
Martin, son of Peter Hartman and Ester (Emmel), b. Dec. 18, 1808.

GERMAN PRESBYTERIAN CHURCH 41

Joel, son of Peter Sigars, (Sygers) and Catherine (Danzenbaker), b. Nov. 6, 1808.
Mosey, son of George Sickler and Susanna (Danzenbaker) Casper, widow of Lorenzo Casper), b. Mar, 29. 1808.
Heinrich son of Heinrich Ott and Elisabeth (Sickler), b. Dec. 27, 1810.
Ludwig, son of John George Sigars and Margaret, b. Feb. 10, 1807.
Heinrich, son of Heinrich Ott and Elisabeth (Sickler), b. Dec. 27, 1810.
Robert, son of William Jones and Margaret, b. May 11, 1810.
Johannes, son of Heinrich Ott and Elisabeth (Sickler), b. May 1, 1812.
Martin, son of Daniel Bacon (Bakn) and Margaret, b. Nov. 10, 1811.
Johannes, son of Johann Wentzel and Susanna (Hitchner), b. Feb. 26, 1812.
Johannes, son of Johannes Sickler (Zigler) and Hannah (Fries), b. July 22, 1811.
Catherine, dau. of Peter Hartman and Ester(Emmel), b. April 20, 1811
Emuel, son of Johann Emmel and Lydia, b. June 16, 1811.
Sara Ann, dau. of Johann Emmel and Lydia, b. Oct. 3, 1813.
Isaac, son of Johann Emmel and Lydia, b. March 9, 1815.
Rudy, son of Peter Emmel and Ester, b. May 20, 1814.
Lydia, dau. of Daniel Bacon and Margaret, b. Nov. 22, 1814.
Mary, dau. of Johann Sickler and Hannah (Fries), b. May 20, 1814.

Baptisms of Children over age of 13 years

Maria Elisabeth, dau. of Michael Dilahaver (Dillschoffer) and Maria Elisabeth, b. before 1735, bapt. May 25, 1749.
Justus, son of Adam Holseit (Hollocheit) and Anna Elisabeth, b. before 1735, bapt. May 25, 1749.
Christina, dau. of Adam Holseit (Hollocheit) and Anna Elisabeth, b. before 1735, bapt. May 25, 1749.
Anna Margaret, dau. of Christian Zobell, b. before 1735, bapt. May 25, 1749.
Anna Barbara, dau. of Metrus Nicholous Hemple (Heppol) and Maria Barbara, b. before 1737, bapt. May 24, 1750.
Micheal, son of Hans Michael Miller (Muller) and Margaret, b. before 1737, bapt. June 17, 1752.
Heinrich, son of Hans Jacob Hitchner (Utzner) (Utz) and Anna Maria, b. before 1739, bapt. July 1, 1753.
Jacob, son of Jacob Rigger b. before 1739, bapt. July 1, 1753.

Anna Barbara, dau. of Hans Micheal Miller and Margaret, b. before 1740, bapt. July 20, 1756.
John George, son of Hans Micheal Miller and Margaret, b. before 1740, bapt. July 20, 1756.
Jan. Stoll, dau. of Johannes Johnson (Janson) and Johanna (Stoll), b. before 1740, bapt. July 20, 1756.
Hans, son of Johannes Johnson (Janson) and Johanna (Stoll), b. before 1740, bapt. July 20, 1756.
Philip, son of Johannes Johnson (Janson) and Johanna (Stoll), b. before 1740, bapt. July 20, 1756.
Anna Catherine, dau. of Johannes Johnson (Janson) and Johanna (Stoll), b. before 1740, bapt. July 20, 1756.
Peter (Petrus), Johannes Johnson (Janson) and Johanna (Stoll), b. Oct. 2, 1732, bapt. July 20, 1756.
Johannes, dau. of Freidrich Deneslbeck (Tondelspach) and Anna Margaret, b. before 1740, bapt. July 20, 1756.
Johanna Micheal, son of Adam Holseit and Anna Elisabeth, b. before 1740, bapt. July 20, 1756.
Anna Louisa, dau. of Adam Holseit and Anna Elisabeth, b. before 1740, bapt. June 9, 1758.
Jacob, son of Jacob Fries and Anna Margaret (Herkin), b. Oct. 14, 1741, bapt. June 9, 1758.
Margaret, dau. of Jacob Fries and Anna Margaret (Herkin), b. Feb. 5, 1744, bapt. June 9, 1758.
Eva Maria, dau. of George Kaucher and Maria, b. before 1743, bapt. June 9, 1758.
Anna, dau. of Johann Thuringor and Barbara, b. before 1743, bapt. June 9, 1758.
Johannes, son of Jacob Fries and Anna Margaret (Herkin), b. March 26, 1746,
Freidrich Christopher, son of Colonel Dr. Bodo Otto and Dorthea Catherine, b. 1743, 17 years old, bapt. July 24, 1756.
Dr. Ott was a Colonel 1st Battalion, under George Washington, 1777 .d. Jan. 20, 1782. Came to America in ship *Neptune* with Johann Ludwig Danzenbaker, and others. Arrived at Philadelphia, PA, Oct. 7, 1755. Settled near Friesburg, NJ. Catherine, wife of Bodo Otto, d. Aug. 11, 1765.
George, son of Micheal Horn and Anna, b. before 1745, bapt. June 9, 1762.
Christina, dau. of Micheal Horn and Anna, b. before 1745, bapt. June 9, 1762.

GERMAN PRESBYTERIAN CHURCH 43

Simon, son of Micheal Dilshaver and Maria Elisabeth, b. 1745, 17 years old, bapt. Oct. 30, 1765.

Johann George, son of Johann Micheal Wolbert (Wilpert) and Maria Catherine, b. 1745, 17 years old, bapt. Oct. 30, 1765.

No name, child of Theobald Gross and Elisabeth Margaret, b. 1741, 19 years old, bapt. Oct. 30, 1765.

Anna Maria Catherine, dau. of Theobald Gross and Elisabeth Margaret, b. 1745, 17 year old, bapt. Oct. 30, 1765.

No name, child of Johann Casper Ulrich and Augutha Catherine, b. 1744, 18 years old., bapt. Oct. 30, 1765.

Charity, dau. of Mathias Cramer (Kreamnor) and Anna Margaret, b. 1750, 15 years old, bapt. Jan. 28, 1768.

Salome, dau. of Mathias Cramer (Kreamnor) and Anna Margaret, b. 1746, 19 years old, bapt. Jan. 28, 1768.

Catherine, dau. of Jacob Hitcher (Utzner), Jr., and Maria Magdalene, b. 1747, 18 years old, bapt. Jan. 28, 1768.

Johannes, son of Micheal Dilshaver and Maria Elisabeth, b. 1746, 22 years old, bapt. Jan. 28, 1768.

Johann Micheal, son of Johann Micheal Wolbert and Maria Catherine, b. 1749, 19 years old, bapt. Jan. 28, 1768.

Frantz, son of -- Pilgram and Anna Maria, b. 1750, 19 years old, bapt. Jan. 28, 1768.

Caroline, dau. of Johann Micheal Dilshaver and Maria Catherine, b. 1754, 14 years old, bapt. Jan. 28, 1768.

Christina, dau. of Jacob Hitchner, Jr., and Maria Magdalene, b. 1752, 16 years old, bapt. Jan. 28, 1768.

Anna Maria, son of George Fisher (Fischer) and Margaret, b. 1752, 16 years old, bapt. Jan. 28, 1768.

Johanna, son of -- Pilgram and Anna Maria, b. 1751, 16 years old, bapt. Jan. 28, 1768.

Catherine, dau. of Adam Fox (Fuchs) and Elisabeth, b. 1764, 14 years old, bapt. Jan. 28, 1768.

Eva Maria, dau. of Adam Fox (Fuchs) and Elisabeth, b. 1752, 16 years old, bapt. Jan. 28, 1768.

Elisabeth, dau. of Adam Falck and --, b. 1751, 17 years old, bapt. Jan. 28, 1768.

Johanna George Halter (Kolter), Servant of Jacob Fries, b. 1755, 16 years old, bapt. April 28, 1771.

Johanna Peter, son of Johann Micheal Wolbert and Catherine, b. 1754, 17 years old, bapt. April 28, 1771.

Magdalene, dau. of Jacob Hitchner, Jr., and Maria Madalena, b. 1754, 17 years old, bapt. April 28, 1771.

Maria Barbara, dau. of Jacob Hitchner, Jr., and Maria Madalena, b. Jan. 6, 1756, 15 years old, bapt. April 28, 1771.

Anna Maria, dau. of Mathias Cramer and Anna Margaret, b. 1753, 18 years old, bapt. April 28, 1771.

Anna Maria, dau. of Nichols Hahn and Margaret, b. 1751, 20 years old, bapt. April 28, 1771.

Johannes, son of Johannes Shimp (Schimpt) and Elisabeth, b. 1761, 18 years old, bapt. Sept. 1, 1779.

Johannes, son of Paul Johnson and Elisabeth, b. 1759, 20 years old, bapt. Sept. 1, 1779.

Charolette, dau. of Adam Fox and Elisabeth, b. 1764, 14 years old, bapt. Sept. 1, 1779. Married John Shimp.

Anna, dau. of Micheal Null (Noll) and --, b. 1760, 19 years old, bapt. Sept. 1, 1779.

Elisabeth, dau. of Nichols Hemple (Heppel) and Maria Barbara, b. 1760, 19 years old, bapt. 1779.

BURIALS IN OLD COHANSY GERMAN PRESBYTERIAN GRAVEYARD AT COHANSEY

Catherine Sigars, wife of Peter, d. April 30, 1834, age 66 years 7 mo., 2 das. Peter Sigars buried at Clarksboro, NJ.
John Martin Ott, b. May 28, 1745, d. Oct. 25, 1811.
Margaret Ott, wife of Martin, d. Jan. 1, 1835, age 87 years.
Henry Ott, son of Martin, b. Sept. 9, 1771, d. Dec. 29, 1833.
Elizabeth (Sickler) Ott, wife of Henry, d. July 14, 1831, age 56 y, 6 mo., 24 da.
Philip Souder, d. May 10, 1843, age 80 years.
Simon Souder, son of Johannes, d. Dec. 11, 1790, age 47 years.
Margaret (Fries) Souder, 1st wife of Simon, d. April 27, 1778, age 34 years, 2 mo.
Elisabeth Souder, 2nd wife of Simon, d. April 11, 1828, age 76 years.
Mary M. Souder, dau. of Simon, d. Nov. 1, 1853, age 69 years.
Catherine Souder, wife of George, d. Aug. 31, 1834, age 59 years, 9 mo., 27 das.
John Emmel, d. 10th mo., 16th da., 1848, aged 74 years.
Lydia Emmel, wife of John, 8th mo., 12th da., 1841.
Isaac Emmel, son of John, d. 7th mo., 4th da., 1845, aged 28 years 5 das.
Adam Hannan, d. Nov. 11, 1837, age 79 years 5 mo., 5 das.
Susanna (Miller) Hannan, wife of Adam, d. June 28, 1833, aged 70 years.
John Shiner, d. Oct. 19, 1835, age 36 years.
Phebe (Casper) Shiner, wife of John, d. Jan. 22, 1851, aged 68 years, dau. of Lawrence Casper.
Catherine Shiner, dau. of John, d. July 20, 1817, aged 10 years.
Lawrence Casper, d. Mar, 1810 aged 90 years, son of Johannes, who had a farm with a German graveyard on it near the church town on the Delaware river in 1714. Johannes's father, Thomas Kaiser arrived at Philadelphia, Aug. 20, 1683 on the ship *American*, lived until 1710.
Margaret Casper, dau. of Lawrence, b. March 30, 1746, d. Nov. 30, 1806.
Lawrence Casper, son of Lawrence, Jr., and Eliza (Wentzel), d. Jan. 1, 1825, 3 years, 7 mo., 27 days.
Chas (Carl) Wentzel, b. Sept. 8, 1750, d. April 3, 1842.
Catherine (Falk) Wentzel, wife of Chas, b. Jun, 1754, d. Sept. 4, 1842.
Johann Wilhelm Wentzel.
Anna Maria Catherine Wentzel, called Maria, wife of Wilhelm.
Johann Wentzel.

Daniel Wentzel, b. Nov. 4, 1748, d. Rev. soldier, son of Wilhelm.
Balthasar Smith, d. Feb. 7, 1786, aged 43 years.
Catherine Smith, wife of Balthasar, d. Dec. 9, 1827 aged 79 years.
Heinrich Danzenbaker, b. June 28, 1770, d. Oct. 27, 1833 aged 69 years 8 mo., 30 days.
Catherine (Randel) Danzenbaker, wife of Henry, b. June 3, 1770, d. Sept. 20, 1796.
Anna (Filer) Danzenbaker, 2nd wife of Henry, b. Dec. 7, 1781, d. Oct. 8, 1811.
Maria Ann Dilshaver, 3rd wife of Henry, b. Oct. 21, 1780, d. Oct. 15, 1814.
Johann Ludwig Danzenbaker, b. in German 1736, d. July 9, 1809.
Catherine (Rocap), wife of J. Ludwig Danzenbaker, b. Jan. 19, 1738, d. March 6, 1803.
Lorenzo Capser, d. Jan. 8, 1800, age 28 years.
Susan (Danzenbaker) Sickler, widow of Lorenzo Casper, wife of George Sickler, b. March 29, 1778, d. June 10, 1836.
Hosie Sickler, b. March 27, 1808, d. June 28, 1860, son of George and Susan Sickler.
John Geo Stuts, b. Oct. 28, 1776, d. July 6, 1832, son of George and Barbara Stuts.
Elizabeth (Danzenbaker) Stuts, wife of George, b. Oct. 28, 1776, d. June 3, 1818.

IMMIGRANTS LIVING AT COHANSEY

Names of some immigrants, time of arrival at Philadelphia, PA, name of ship. These immigrants from Germany settled in Old Greenwich twp.

Albright (Albrocht), Johannes, Nov. 3, 1750, ship, Capt. John Thomson.
Albright, Henrich, Sept. 13, 1749, ship *Christian*, Capt. Thomas Brady.
Bauer (Baur), Johann Micheal, Aug. 27, 1739, ship *Samuel*, Capt. Hugh Percy.
Bauer, Conrad, Sept. 19, 1764, ship *Polly*, Capt. Robert Porter.
Bender Hans George, Sept. 14, 1751, ship *Duke of Bedford*, Capt. Richard Jeferys.
Bitter, John Jacob, Sept. 16, 1751, ship *Edinburgh*, Capt. James Russel,
Brinesholtz, John Adam, Aug. 13, 1750, ship *Bennet*, Capt. John Wadham.
Conrad, George, Nov. 25, 1740, ship *Loyal Judith*, Capt. Paynter.
Couch (Kooch) John George, April 17, 1731, ship *Samuel*, Capt. Hugh Percy.
Couch, Micheal, Sept. 24, 1742, ship *Robert and Alice*, Capt. Marly Cussack.
Creamer (Kramer) Johan George, Dec. 3, 1740, ship *Robert and Alice*, Capt. Walter Goodman
Creamer (Kramer), Mathias, Sept. 5, 1748, ship *Robert and Alice*, Capt. Marly Cussack.
Croneberger, John Peter, Oct. 31, 1774, ship *Sally*, Capt. John Osmond.
Crumrine (Krumrein) Geo Lenhart, Sept. 5, 1748, ship *Edinburgh*, Capt. James Russel.
Danzenbaker (Dantzebecher), Johann Ludwig, Oct. 7, 1755, ship *Neptune*, Capt. Geo Smith.
Denelsbeck (Tendeslspach) Freidrich, Sept. 23, 1732, ship *Adventurer*, Capt. Rob Corson
Fisher (Fiecher), Hans Geo, Oct. 7, 1749, ship *Lesbie*, Capt. J. Balledium.
Evans, Lott, left Liverpool Feb. 18, 1698, died at sea. Family settled in Glouster Co.
Fox (Fuche), Johan Adam, Sept. 2, 1743, ship *Loyal Judith*, Capt. James Cowie.
Mahn, Micheal, Aug. 27, 1739, ship *Samuel*, Capt. Hugh Percy.
Mahn, Johannes, Aug. 27, 1739, ship *Samuel*, Capt. Hugh Percy.
Halter, Hans Martin, Sept. 9, 1738, ship *Two Sisters*, Capt. James Marahall.

Hartman, Johann, Sept. 25, 1754, ship *Adventurer*, Capt. Joseph Jackson.
Hartman, Heinrich, Sept. 19, 1749, ship *Patience*, Capt. Hugh Steel.
Heinrich, Peter, Sept. 14, 1749, ship *Two Brothers*, Capt. Thomas Arnot.
Hemple (Hippel), Johan Nicklaus, Dec. 3, 1740, ship *Robert and Alice*, Capt. Walt Goodman.
Hepner (Happener), Johannes, Sept. 28, 1753, ship *Halifax*, Capt. Thomas Coatam.
Hires (Heier), Conrad (Kunrad) Oct. 5, 1767, ship *Salley*, Capt. John Osman
Mitchner (Utz)(Utzner), Hans Jacob, Sept. 28, 1733, ship *Richmond and Eliz*, Chris Clymer.
Mitchner (Utz)(Utzner), Hans George, Sept. 28, 1733, ship *Richmond and Eliz*, Chris Clymer.
Mitchner (Utz)(Utzner), Martin, Nov. 9, 1738, ship *Charming Nancy*, Capt. Chas Stedman.
Mitchner, (Utz)(Hitschner), Peter, Sept. 17, 1753, ship *Richard and Mary*, Capt. John Moore.
Holseit (Hohenschilt), John Adam, Sept. 1, 1736, ship *Marle*, Capt. Ralph Marle.
Hoover, Jacob, Sept. 16, 1731, ship *Edinburgh*, Capt, James Russel.
Horn, Johannes, Sept. 23, 1741, ship *Marlborugh*, Capt. Thomas Bell.
Ganger, Johan Conrad, Sept. 16, 1736, ship *Princess Augusta*, Capt. Samuel Merchant.
Gross, Theobald, Nov. 20, 1741, ship *Europa*.
Kautz, Hans George, Nov. 8, 1752, ship *Louisa*, Capt. John Pittcarne.
Lang, Joat, Sept. 27, 1740, ship *Lydia*, Capt. James Allen.
Loudenslacker (Lautenschlager) Hans Micheal, Nov. 19, 1771, ship *Tyger*, Capt. Johnson.
Martin, Johannes, Aug. 27, 1739, ship *Betsy*, Capt. Richard Buden.
Meyers, Jacob, Sept. 16, 1736, ship *Princess Augustus*, Capt. Sam Merchant.
Meyers, George, Sept. 16, 1736, ship *Princess Augustus*, Capt. Sam Merchant.
Miller (Muller) Hans Micheal, Sept. 23, 1732, ship *Adventurer*, Capt. Robert Carson.
Miller, Jacob, Sept. 25, 1732, ship *Loyal Judith*, Capt, Robert Turpin.
Minch (Mensch), Adam, Aug. 24, 1750, ship *Brothers*, Capt. Muir.
Mowers (Mauer), Johann Adam, Oct. 7, 1749, ship *Lesbie*, Capt. J. Balledium.

IMMIGRANTS LIVING AT COHANSEY 49

Null (Noll), Hans George, Sept. 25, 1732, ship *Loyal Judith*, Capt. Robert Turpin.
Oxenbecher (Ochssenbecher), Heinrich, Sept. 20, 1764, ship *Sarah*, Capt. Francis Stanfield
Ott, Johann Martin, Sept. 26, 1764, ship *Brittania*, Capt. Thomas Arnot.
Otto, Dr. Bodo, Oct. 7, 1753, ship *Neptune*, Capt. Geo Smith,
Rammel, Hans Jacob, Sept. 26, 1743, ship *Rosannah*, Capt. James Reason.
Rammel, (Reimmel) Hans George, Sept. 10, 1737, ship *Molly*, Capt. John Howell
Reibnel (Reibell), Johann George, Oct. 29, 1733, ship *Pink Mary*, Capt. James Benn.
Reiss, Christian, Oct. 18, 1766, ship *Polly*, Capt. Robert Porter.
Rocap (Rokop) Heinrich, Feb. 7, 1739, ship *Jamaica*, Capt. Robert Harrison.
Sheidner (Schneider) Hans George, Sept. 23, 1740, ship *Friendship*, Capt. Wm Vittery.
Shaffer, Johannes, Oct. 26, 1768, ship *Crawford*, Capt. Chas Smith.
Shaffer, Conrad, Nov. 3, 1752, ship *Queen of Denmark*, Capt. Geo Parish.
Shaffer, Jacob, Oct. 31, 1771, ship *Recovery*, Capt. Bull.
Shimp (Schinmpff), Mathias, Sept. 25, 1751, ship *Phoenix*, Capt. John Spurrier.
Sickler (Ziegler) Hans George, Sept. 21, 1727, ship *William and Sarah*, Capt. Wm Hill.
Sickler (Ziegler), George, Oct. 20, 1752, ship *Duke of Wirtenberg*, Capt. Dan Montpelier.
Sigars (Seger), Johann Peter, Aug. 4, 1750, ship *Brothers*, Capt. Muir.
Sigars (Seger), Johann George, Oct. 5, 1737, ship *Townshead*, Capt. Thomas Thompson.
Stangar (Stenger), Johan Adam, Sen Oct. 16, 1768, ship *Betsy*, Capt. S Hawk.
Stanger (Stenger), Solomon, Oct. 16, 1768, ship *Betsy*, Capt. S Hawk.
Stanger (Stenger), Christian, Oct. 16, 1768, ship *Betsy*, Capt. S Hawk.
Stutz, Johannes, Oct. 3, 1764, ship *King of Prussia*, Capt, James Robinson.
Weeks (Wecks), Johann Nickel, Nov. 10, 1764, ship *Boston*, Capt. Matthew.
Waikel, Jost, Oct. 1, 1773 ship *Hope*, Capt. George Johnston.
Weidemeyer (Weydenmoyer) Johan George, Oct. 27, 1764, ship *Hero*, Capt. Ralph Forster.

Wentzel, John Carl, Sept. 18, 1773, ship *Brittania*, Capt. James Peter.
Wentzel, Johann Wilhelm, Sept. 9, 1738, ship *Two Sisters*, Capt. Peter Marshall.
Wentzel, Johann George, Sept. 18, 1773, ship *Brittania*, Capt. James Peter.
Young (Jung) Johan Philippus, Sept. 26, 1749, ship *Ranier*, Capt. Henry Browning
Zimmerman, Hans Adam, Oct. 7, 1743, ship *St. Andrew*, Capt. Robert Brown.

REGISTERY RECORDS OF THE METHODIST EPISCOPAL CHURCH OF PORT ELIZABETH, NJ

From the records of Rev. Paul Pedrick, trustees Lewis Fitzgerald, Jr., Herbert Reeves, and Herbert Vanaman.

Baptisms At Morris River:
Elizabeth Vaneman, dau. of Luke Vaneman and Elizabeth, his wife, b. May 16, 1798, bapt. Aug. 28, 1798, by Jacob Egbert.
Rachel Vaneman, dau. of Thomas Vaneman and Rebeckah, his wife, b. Jan. 22, 1792, bapt. Aug. 28, 1798, by Jacob Egbert.
Isaac Vaneman, son of Thomas Vaneman and Rebeckah, his wife, b. June 16, 1798, bapt. by Jacob Egbert.
Mary Vaneman, 14 years old the 30th da., of last Mar, bapt. Aug. 28, 1798, by Jacob Egbert.
Deborah Vanhook, bapt. Aug. 28, 1798.
DeLucy Camburn, bapt. Aug. 28, 1798.
Hannah Camborn, dau. of John Camburn and DeLucy, his wife, b. Aug. 10, 1791, bapt. Aug. 28, 1798, by Jacob Egbert.
Margaret Camburn, dau. of John Camburn and DeLucy, his wife, b.March 22, 1795, bapt. Aug. 28, 1798, by Jacob Egbert.
Nancy Camburn, dau. of John Camburn and DeLucy, his wife, b. May 27, 1797, bapt. Aug. 28, 1798, by Jacob Egbert.
Anne Bordon, bapt. Aug. 28, 1798, by Jacob Egbert.
Daniel Hieffer, son of George Hiefer and Lydia, his wife, b. Sept. 17, 1797, bapt. Nov. 11, 1798, by Jacob Egbert.
Margaret Collett, dau. of Silas Collett and Hester, his wife, b. May 6, 1798, bapt. Nov. 11, 1798, by Jacob Egbert.
Mary Egbert, dau. of Jacob Egbert and Lotitia, his wife, b. Nov. 13, 1800, bapt. May 10, 1801.

MARRIAGES PERFORMED BY METHODIST MINISTERS
OF THE SALEM CIRCUIT
(one or both parties from Cumberland Co.)

Constant Cobb and Rachel Bailey, md. April 1, 1797 by James Campbell, minister. Witnesses: Edward Shipshire and Mary Sutton.
William Machaney of Salem Co. and Elenor Parson of Cumberland md. April 9, 1797 by James Campbell, minister. Witnesses: Eli Budd and John Cope.
James Campbell and Elizabeth Wooston md. Sept. 7, 1797 by William Silver, minister. Witnesses: Eli Budd and Anne Budd.
Fithian Stratton and Sarah Gray, both of the township of Morris River, Cumberland Co. m. Nov. 28, 1798 by Jacob Egbert, minister.
John Donnelly and Rachel Crandle, both of the Twp. of Morris River, Cumberland Co. md Jan. 28, 1799 by Jacob Egbert, minister. Witnesses: George Donnelly and Elisha Smith.
William Hawkins and Rhoda Daniel, both of the Twp. of Hopewell, Cumberland Co. md. Feb. 13, 1799 by Jacob Egbert, minister. Witnesses: Eli Daniels and Benamin Mills.
Thomas Henderson and Mary Spencer, both of the Twp. of Maurice River, Cumberland Co., md March 29, 1799.
Andrew Stillman of the Twp. of Maurice River, Cumberland Co. and Z... Swain of Weymouth, Gloucester Co. md. July 24, 1799 by Richard Swain, minister.
Stephen Stephenson and Sarah Corson, both of the Twp. of Weymouth, Gloucester Co. md. Oct. 15, 1799 by Richard Swain, minister.
James Buchalod of the Twp. of Maurice River and Mica Morgan of the same place, Cumberland Co. md. Dec. 24, 1799 by Wesley Budd, minister. Witnesses: Thomas Ewing and Anna Morgan.
Thomas Lacy of Pilesgrove, Salem Co. and Phebe Jeffers of the Twp. of Fairfield, Cumberland Co. md. Oct. 1, 1799 by Michael Swing, min.
Jacob Egbert and Lotitia Huler, both of the Twp. of Maurice River, Cumberland Co. md. May 9, 1799 by Benjamin Fisher, minister. Witnesses: William Silver and Eli Budd.
Levin Robns and Judith Black, people of Greenwich, Cumberland Co., md. Feb. 25, 1800 by Richard Swain, minister.
William Cripsing and Lidia Goff, both of the Twp. of Maurice River, Cumberland Co. md. Jan. 26, 1800 by Richard Swain, minister.
Patrick Hay and Catharine Morgan, both of the Twp. of Maurice River, Cumberland Co. md. Oct. 20, 1800.

MAURICE MONTHLY MEETING BIRTHS AND DEATHS

Samuel Townsend, son of Richard and Millicent Townsend, b. 10th mo., 12th da., 1728, d. 1st mo., 25th da., 1819, was an elder.
Rebeccah Corson, dau. of Peter Corson, b. 5th mo., 11th da., 1735.
Lydia Townsend, dau. of Isaac Townsend, b. 1st mo., 23rd da., 1748, d. 1825, was an elder.
Children of Elisha and Lydia Baner: Jacob, b. 12th mo., 26th da., 1775; Hannah, b. 11th mo., 8th da., 1780; Lydia, b. 11th mo., 10th da., 1782.
Mark Baner, son of Elisha and Lydia Baner, b. 1776.
Rachel Townsend, dau. of Daniel and Rebecca Townsend, b. 12th mo., 2nd da., 1760.
Rachel Graveston, dau. of Job and Millicent Graveston, b. 4th mo., 24th da., 1795.
Hannah Dole, dau. of Isaac and Rachel Dole, b. 3rd mo., 3rd da., 17??.
Elizabeth Townsend, dau. of Jacob Clements, b. 9th mo., 20th da., 1757.
Children of Mark and Elizabeth Townsend: Mark, b. 4th mo., 9th da., 1783; Elizabeth, b. 11th mo., 13th da., 1786; Rebeccah, b. 5th mo., 18th da., 1789; Lydia, b. 9th mo., 27th da., 1794; Sarah, b. 8th mo., 27th da., 1797; Ruth, b. 2nd mo., 12th da., 1800; Rachel, b. no date.
Children of Aaron and Rachel Shaw: Amos, b. 12th mo., 19th da., 1790; Peter, b. 7th mo., 20th da., 1792; Elie, b. 2nd mo., 25th da., 1795; Joshua, b. 11th mo., 12th da., 1798; Aaron, b. 10th mo., 1st da., 1800; John, b. 9th mo., 8th da., 1803, d. 8th mo., 16th da., 1805.
Children of Isaac and Cassandra Baner: Nathan b. 11th mo., 22nd da., 1783; Ruth, b. 9th mo., 26th da., 1785; Isaac, b. 8th mo., 26th da., 1788; Hannah, b. 4th mo., 27th da., 1789.
Millicent Townsend, dau. of Samuel and Rebecca Townsend, b. 1st mo., 11th da., 1772.
Job Graveston, son of Samuel Graveston, b. no date.
Children of Job and Millicent Graveston: Rebecca, b. 10th mo., 22nd da., 1793; Lucinda, b. no date; Elizabeth, b. 11th mo., 10th da., 1798; Townsend, b. 10th mo., 1st da., 1800; Reuben, b. 10th mo., 8th da., 1803.
Children of Mark and Rachel Baner: dau.(?), b. 9th mo., 2nd da., 1802; Eliza, b. 4th mo., 11th da., 1804.
Children of Isaac and Rachel Dole: Rachel, b. 4th mo., 9th da., 1791; Hannah, b. no date.
Martha Corson, wife of Jesse Corson, b. 8th mo., 20th da., 1767.

Children of Jesse and Martha Corson: Jesse, b. 2nd mo., 16th da., 1781;
Edith, b. 2nd mo., 26th da., 1786; James, b. 2nd mo., 9th da., 1789;
Aaron, b. 10th mo., 3rd da., 1792; Rem, b. 4th mo., 15th da., 1797.
Vincent Leeds, son of John and Sarah Leeds, b. 7th mo., 30th da., 1756.
Catharine Leeds, dau. of Noah and Judith Leeds, b. 11th mo., 13th da., 1754.
Children of Vincent and Catharine Leeds: Noah, b. 8th mo., 17th da., 1788; Warren, b. 2nd mo., 21st da., 1791; Catherine, b. 10th mo., 12th da., 1794.
Mary Langstaff b. 11th mo., 9th da., 1736.
Children of Mary Langstaff: James, b. 7th mo., 22nd da., 1762; Samuel, b. 4th mo., 30th da., 1764.
Elizabeth Langstaff, wife of James, b. 2nd mo., 1776.
Hannah Langstaff, wife of Samuel Langstaff, b. 9th mo., 6th da., 1778.
Children of Samuel and Amy Langstaff: Deborough, b. 4th mo., 8th da., 1787; William, b. 5th mo., 6th da., 1790; George, b. 3rd mo., 30th da., 1792; Samuel, b. 4th mo., 9th da., 1804.
Thomas Langstaff, son of Samuel and Mary Langstaff, b. 10th mo., 26th da., 1772.
Rhoda Langstaff, wife of Thomas Langstaff, b. 4th mo., 1771.
Mallachi Langstaff, son of Mary Langstaff, b. 12th mo., 30th da., 1769.
Children of James and Keziah Jess: Henry, b. 2nd mo., 6th da., 1785; Maurice, b. 2nd mo., 6th da., 1787; Zula, b. 3rd mo., 3rd da., 1789.
Amos Stratton, b. 1st mo., 3rd da., 1743.
Rachel Stratton, wife of Amos Stratton, b. 9th mo., 14th da., 1745.
Children of Amos and Rachel Stratton: Hannah, b. 2nd mo., 10th da., 1777; Rachel, b. 11th mo., 5th da., 1787.
Rebeccah Dollis, b. 5th mo., 4th da., 1738.
Ann Clark, dau. of Rebecca Dollis, b. 5th mo., 20th da., 1764.
Nathaniel Buzby, son of Isaac Buzby, b. 12th mo., 5th da., 1772.
Melicent Buzby, wife of Nathaniel Buzby and dau. of Rebecca Dollas b. 6th mo., 14th da., 1768.
Children of Nathaniel and Melicent Buzby: Martha, b. 10th mo., 2nd da., 1794; Rebecca, b. 2nd mo., 30th da., 1777; Sarah, b. 3rd mo., 2nd da., 1799; Isaac, b. 3rd mo., 10th da., 1801; William, b. 5th mo., 6th da., 1803.
Eli Stratton, b. 12th mo., 20th da., 1772.
Eunice Stratton, wife of Eli Stratton and dau. of Rebecca Dollas b. 10th mo., 7th da., 1771.
Children of Eli and Eunice Stratton: Sarah, b. 5th mo., 24th da., 1801; Jonathan, b. 11th mo., 8th da., 1804.

MAURICE MONTHLY MEETING BIRTHS & DEATHS 55

Children of Isaac and Naomy Buzby: Martha, b. 6th mo., 9th da., 1786; Joseph, b. 12th mo., 8th da., 1788; Rachel, b. 8th mo., 25th da., 1791; Sarah, b. 8th mo., 7th da., 1795.

Sarah Buzby, dau. of Isaac and Sarah Buzby, b. 5th mo., 2nd da., 1803.

Steven Murphey, b. 12th mo., 14th da., 1776.

Prudence Murphey, wife of Stephen Murphey and dau. of Isaac Buzby, b. 2nd mo., 19th da., 1779.

Children of Stephen and Prudence Murphey: Isaac, b. 9th mo., 14th da., 1798; Richard, b. no date; Mary, b. 4th mo., 15th da., 1802; Hudson, b. 4th mo., 25th da., 1804.

John Dole, son of Isaac and Rachel Dole, b. 8th mo., 22nd da., 1762.

Mary Dole, wife of John Dole and dau. of Joshua Stratton, b. 12th mo., 21st da., 1772.

Children of John and Mary Dole: Mary, b. 9th mo., 25th da., 1802; Sarah, b. 3rd mo., 28th da., 1804.

Daniel Buzby, b. 10th mo., 1747.

Beulah Chitten, b. 5th mo., 10th da., 1762.

Owen Jones, son of Jonathan and Mary Jones, b. 2nd mo., 4th da., 1787.

Children of Joseph and Tabitha Whittecar: Joseph, b. 10th mo., 1st da., 1783; Azabund, b. 6th mo., 24th da., 1791; Ruth, b. 6th mo., 30th da., 1793.

Ruth Kimble, b. 11th mo., 5th da., 1755.

Isaac Lavery, b. 10th mo., 20th da., 1776.

Margaret Lavery, wife of Isaac Lavery, b. 12th da., 5th mo., 1778.

John S. Lavery, son of Isaac and Marget Lavery, b. 3rd mo., 1st da., 1804.

Hannah Brick, wife of Joshua Brick and dau. of Jeremiah and Mary Ebert, b. 10th mo., 6th da., 1779.

Joshua Owen, son of Joshua Owen, b. 4th mo., 13th da., 1784.

Joseph Whittecare, b. 3rd mo., 6th da., 1755.

FAIRTON PRESBYTERIAN CHURCH
FAIRTON, CUMBERLAND CO.
(later called Fairfield Presbyterian Church)

Some of the following information was taken from records abstracted by Frank H. Stewart as published in the Vineland Historical Magazine.

Rev. William Ramsey, an elder brother of the celebrated historian and stateman David Ramsey of Charleston, SC was called after the death of Daniel Elmer as pastor of the Fairfield Presbyterian Church in 1756.

On March 22, 1756, Mr. William Ramsey was called to the pastoral care of the church paying him £80 per annum. The following signing in agreement:

Thomas Bateman	Moses Heusted
Thomas Ogden	James Ray
Thomas Whiteccar	Benjamin Stratton
Ephraim Buck	Joseph Westcoe
John Powell	Thomas Joslane
Nathaniel Diament	Zadok Thomppson
Henry Peirson	William Nichson
Jonathan Lorance	John Ogden
Robert Low	Jonathan Stratton
Jeremiah Buck	Ephraim Harris
David Ogden	Daniel Westcote
Israel Petty	Joseph Seeley
Edward Loomis	Amos Ireland
Abraham Sayre	Jonathan Diament
David Husted	David Fithian
Joseph Ogden	Jeremiah Nichson
David Wescote	Henry Sparks
James Diament	Daniel Bateman

Copied from a written article in the book of the minutes of the session of 1813-1846 Fairfield Presbyterian Church.

The Rev. Wm. Ramsey, pastor died Nov. 4, 1771, at which time Rev. Wm. Greenman became pastor.

FAIRTON PRESBYTERIAN CHURCH

Members of Fairfield Presbyterian Church - as recorded Oct. 23, 1759:

Minister - Wm. Ramsey
Ruling Elders - Henry Peirson
Nathaniel Diament
Moeses Hustead
David Westcote
Thomas Ogden
Henry Westcote
Joseph Ogden

Persons in full communion:
David Ogden and his wife.
Jeremiah Buck, Esq.
Daniel Elmer
Mathew Parvin
Capt. Thomas Harris.
Benjamin Thompson, Sr.
Ebenezor Bower
Joseph Daten

Joseph Westcote and his wife.
Wife of Henry Peirson
Wife of Nathaniel Diament
Susannah, wife of David Westcote
Sarah, wife of Thomas Ogden
Johnathan Diament
James Diament and his wife.
Seaborn Troy, wife of Jeremiah Nixon.
Jeremiah Nixon, Jr.
Richard Powel
Priscilla, relict of John Powell, dec.
Bathsheba, relict of Maj. Johnson
Benjamin Chand and his wife
William Nixon
Johnathan Smith

In 1790 elders were appointed: Eleaser Smith, Jeremiah Nixon, Ephraim Harris, John Bower, Levi Stratton, John T. Hampton, Amos Westcott, Jedediah Ogden, Jeremiah Harris.

EARLY RECORDS OF CUMBERLAND CO.

Sexton Record

Burials at the Old Stone Presbyterian church, 1775-1800:
John Bateman was the first sexton of the Old Stone Church, Fairton, NY, then called Fairfield until 1789 when he died. His son, John Bateman, 2nd was sexton until 1813, when he died. Thomas Bateman, grandson of John Bateman, the first was sexton from 1813 until 1857.

Thomas Bateman married Lydia Westcott, dau. of Samuel and Mary (Brick) Westcott, sister of Hannah (Westcott) Seeley, the great-grandmother of William Bradford Taylor. William Bradford Taylor copied the records in 1936 from the original records.

Accounts of graves dug 1785
Joseph Sfyn, two children's graves.
Thomas Earls
John Hennery
Baes Newcomb (he had a son John, died Sept. 28, 1785).
Nechaney
Lues Wescot
Urben Dixon
Zebniah Husted
John Ogden
Daniel Soper
Mrs. Husted
Buress buried one person.
Joseph Syen
Thomas Earls
John Skinner
Joseph Daniels
Bucks Brucks (Brooks)
Lues Wescott
Samuel Ogden, 3 graves
Daniel Benet
Daniel Newcomb 2 graves
Noer Lumis
Lewis Statten
Nosten Laurence

John Oden (Ogden)
Joe Bateman
Ggeddedials Sele, 2 graves
Theodores Elman
Ephrin Lubian, a grave for his wife
Plany Ward

1784
Claford Dorman
John Blizzard
John Steddams
Priscilla Janson
Beniamen Ogden
Hannah Dixon
Ephiam Fithen
Joseph Sele
Amos Bateman

1791
Joseph Westcott
Aaron Petteson
Jeremiah Harris
Joseph Ogden
Rachel Whittecar
Martha Sele
Dalton Newcom

FAIRTON PRESBYTERIAN CHURCH

Rachel Husted
Ebenezer Sele
Liddah Husted
John Westcott
Naome Jammison
William Stephans
Noar Burr
David Garton
Jonathan Banst
Base Newcomb
Nanse Broulas
Nethaniel Whitiam
John Burt
Frenchman
Hennery Shaw
Richard Burt

1792
Jonathan Bennett
Burgin Bateman
Levi Stratton
Frenchman's wife
Thomas Muchelroy (McAvay)
Samuel Westcott
Jalin Harris
Peason Harris
Hannah Nickols
Ebenezer Bawen
John Garrison
Reuben Bateman
Richard Perce
Icabud Bichess
Urbin Dixon
Daniel Elmore
Rubin Powell
Thomas Reaves
Rubon Bateman
Aamus Westcott
Enos Boen
Webster Newcomb

1793
Allen Whittecar
Mical Swing
Thomas Mosse
Elizabeth Bateman
Amariah Harris
Daniel Fichian
Adam Mine
Jedidiah Ogden
Jedediah John
John Powell
Samuel Westcott
Thomas Reeves
William Bateman
Nathaniel Gande
Harris Ogden
Lemone Sears
Burgin Bateman
Joseph Ogden
Jeremiah Miles
Isaac Bennett
Josiah Dimon
Herre Case
John Harris
Abigal Shaw
James Clark
Titus Davis
Nathian Eare
Samuel Westcott
Norton Larrence
Jeffia Parvin
Daniel Soper
Isabel Bishop
James Bradford

1794
Susa Bateman
Jesphus Burt
John Ogden
Rodah Powell
Nathaniel Whittecar

John Fellas (Fellows)
Ame Stephens
Rodah Parvin
Daniel Hand
James Ogden
David Ogden
Andrew Perce
David Newcomb
David Newcomb
Ebenezer Sales
John Trensher
Bets Trensher
Lenord Shaw
Sarah Long
Uriah Long
Joseph Ogden
Doctor Hampton
Ephraim Newcomb
Azrial Person
Ambos Clark
Anree Sheppard
Charles Westcott
Urbin Dixon
Ansee Sheppard
Richard Whittecar
Ephraim Harris
Jonathan Bennett
Thomas Erl
John Stevens
Abigail Stevens
Silas Whittecar
Jane Holl

December 8, 1794
Amus Westcoatt
Jeremiah Nixon
Julia Bateman
Antone, the female
Christen Whittecar
Ephrain Daton

January 1, 1795
Oliver Rusel
Celah Simpkins
Mary Pady
Masse Hampton
Bets Mince
Mical Swing

October 3, 1795
Norton Larence
Jeams Bradford
Isaac Jarrel
Joseph Luise

February 20, 1795
John Rulong
Jeffard Parvin
Elmer Ogden
Joseph Swen
John Linsey, two graves
Jeffard Parvin
Jeffard Parvin
Beniamen Ogden
Levy Westcott
Mason Boen
John Whittecar
Jeremiah Harris
Hannah Michel
Jonathan Elmore
Jeffard Parvin
Johnathan Maris
Jeremiah Sears

July 5, 1795
Ellenailian Whittecar
Joseph Bennett
Thomas Mickel
John Blizzard

August 1795
Daniel Mickel

FAIRTON PRESBYTERIAN CHURCH 61

Ellener Barton
Richard Shaw
Jeremiah Sears
Ephraim Newcomb

September 1795
Urbin Dixon
Mordici Barton
Jonathan Elmore
Jeams Mecray
Betz Misse

October 1795
Jonathan Garton
Thomas Mullica
James Megrine
William Cobb
James Clark
Aabrin Sears

November 1795
Ruth Dimon
Widdow Fellers
Lat Fahen
Gabriel Cocks (Cook)
Daniel Burt
Nathan Gande

January 1796
John Demaries
Samson Whittecar
Urbin Dixon, two graves
William Gifford
Giffard's wife
George Ogden
John Burton
John Whittecar
James Whow (Hood)
Jeremiah Ogden
Joll Husted
Thomas York

Nathaniel Ogden
Beniaman Ogden
Mary Megumery
Norton Larrance
Ruth Blackman
Joseph Anderson
Anna Rusee
Allen Whitecar
Ruth Nickelson
Sarah Buck
Marcy Parven
Abigal Bateman
Nathan Gande
Elazer Smide
Jonathan Bennett
Ruth Wescott

January 6, 1797
Eli Bowers
Charles Holl (Howell)
Enaus Parvin
Judah Furman
Lois Joslin
Ephraim Haten
Isac Baken
Allen Whittecar
Rodha Harris
Ezekel Westcoat
Aaron Parvin
William Mickelson
Ephraim Smith
Nathaniel Gande
James Ogden
Beniman Larsan
Isabel Linze
Silas Smith
David Person
William Hand
John Elmore
Samuel Westcott
Phillip Westcott

Uriah Soper
David Newcom
William Joslin
Beminiam Tomson
Henry Wetcott

January 14, 1798
John Hilman (Hillman)
Ebinzar Bowers
Pashience Ogden
France Olben

Jeams Shaw
Alle Williams
Rachel Westcott
Robert Megummery
Aaron Husted
James Bennet
Hennery Westcott
John Burt

CUMBERLAND COUNTY MARRIAGES 1795-1800

Charles Stratton to Hannah Garrison - April 23, 1795.
Frederick Taylor to Prudence Lupton - Sept. 16, 1795.
Preison [Peirson*] Shaw to Polly Bishop - March 17, 1795.
Jacob Emmon to Ruth Coney - April 7, 1795.
Benjamin Champneys to Sally Potter - Aug. 18, 1795.
Jeremiah Nixon to Ruth Garrison - May 19, 1795.
Daniel Mickle to Polly Ryley - July 1, 1795.
Jeremiah Harris to Rhoda Fithian - July 15, 1795.
William Joslin to Lois Bennett - Sept. 23, 1795.
Samuel Kemble to Susanna Blizard - Oct. 15, 1795.
Joseph [John*] Mickell to Rachel Harris - Sept. 1, 1795.
Jonathan Harden to Mary Maines - Nov. 3, 1795.
Stephen Davis to Lydia Golden - March 31, 1795.
James Harris of Salem Co. to Elizabeth Thompson of Salem Co. - April 7, 1795.
David Cook to Mary Bacon - July 2, 1795.
John Dalton to Mary Fismire - July 17, 1795.
Samuel Leeds to Ann Walton - July 21, 1795.
Isaac Allen of Salem Co. to Ruth Reeves of Salem Co. - Aug. 11, 1795.
John Blackwood of Salem Co. to Sarah Smith of Salem Co. - Aug. 19, 1795.
Joshua Crowell of Cape May Co. to Rachel Bacon - Sept. 8, 1795.
Jason Pavey to Martha Barker - Oct. 8, 1795.
David Mills to Mary Carle - Dec. 8, 1795.
George Cremer to Elizabeth Karns - Dec. 24, 1795.
William Brackney to Anne Bowen - Dec. 28, 1795.
David Royal of Salem Co. of Salem Co. to Ruth Bowen - Dec. 28, 1795.
Ephraim Padgett to Tamzen Dare - Dec. 29, 1795.
Bastion Shimp to Catharine Couts - May 23, 1795.
Stephen Ayars to Elizabeth Bacon - June 2, 1795.
John Dare to Elizabeth Stedham - July 5, 1795.
Enoch Brooks to Yocomintine Elwell - Sept. 3, 1795.
David Wilson to Martha Filer - Sept. 30, 1795.
David Garton to Elizabeth Ryley - Nov. 17, 1795.
David Johnson to Sarah Stackhouse - Nov. 19, 1795.
John Lloyd to Kesiah Ayars - Nov. 25, 1795.
Carle Shaw to Violet Barrat - Dec. 29, 1795.
David Edwards to Almeda Nichols - Oct. 17, 1795.

Jacob Joslin to Mary Barrett - Nov. 12, 1795.
David Conklin of Pittsgrove to Nancy Davis - Feb. 2, 1796.
Hopwell Shull to Hannah Peck - Feb. 5, 1796.
John Timnal to Jane Richman - May 12, 1795.
Enoch Moore to Amy Lummis - Sept. 17, 1795.
John Clark to Rebecca Richman - Dec. 3, 1795.
Daniel Dixon to Polly Nixon - Dec. 24, 1795.
Josiah Parvin to Polly Scullards - Dec. 20, 1795.
John Blew to Elizabeth Minty - Jan. 1, 1796.
James Westcott to Amy Hampton - Jan. 1, 1796.
Charles Howell to Patty Sheppard - Jan. 12, 1796.
Jacob Fulse to Betsey Page - Feb. 11, 1796.
Ishmael Perry to Sarah Murray - Feb. 17, 1796.
Joseph Hannah to Ruma Gould - Feb. 12, 1796.
William Ballanger to Abagail Newcomb - Feb. 29, 1796.
George P. Williams to Polly Mickle - March 1, 1796.
Amos Westcott to Mercy Hampton - March 16, 1796.
John Elmer to Ruth Preston - March 29, 1796.
John Yates to Betsey Fithian - April 4, 1796.
Daton Newcomb to Sally Wescott - May 4, 1796.
Richard Caruthers to Elizabeth Jones of Pittsgrove - April 5, 1796.
Jonathan Ryley to Sally Clark of Pittsgrove - June 23, 1796.
Amos Bradford to Anne Cambell - Aug. 9, 1796.
William Welch to Elizabeth Cobb - Feb. 19, 1796.
Ichabod Love to Anne Love - March 1, 1796.
John Miller to Hannah Hall - March 7, 1796.
Mathias Taylor to Sarey Cheasman - March 7, 1796.
Sillet Sheppard to Unes Long - March 16, 1796.
Isaac Love to Marey Walker - March 8, 1796.
John Tullis to Sarah Cambell - April 12, 1796.
William Pepper to Elizabeth Camp - April 6, 1796.
John Linn of Salem Co. to Mary Underwood of Salem Co., Dec. 31, 1795.
John Harland to Hannah Sheppard - Dec. 31, 1795.
Ephraim Garten to Lydia Stratton - Jan. 12, 1795.
Samuel Curtis of Salem Co. to Sarah Barrett of Salem Co. - Jan. 26, 1796.
Josiah Hix to Elizabeth Pearce - Feb. 10, 1796.
David Reeves to Ann Williams - Feb. 16, 1796.
John Stom to Abigail Davis - Feb. 17, 1796.
David Evans of Salem Co. to Mary Stretch of Salem Co. - March 2, 1796.
Isaac Elwell to Sarah Wood - March 16, 1796.

CUMBERLAND COUNTY MARRIAGES 65

Henry Ott to Elizabeth Sickler - March 22, 1796.
Ephraim Dunham to Ruth Hall - March 24, 1796.
William Houseman to Sarah Wood - March 29, 1796.
Reeves Matcliff to Mary Bacon - April 6, 1796.
Zappaniah Marts to Letitia Husted - April 7, 1796.
Lemuel Whitecar to Ruth Barker - April 12, 1791.
Jaid Thompson of Salem Co. to Mary Finley of Salem Co. - April 19, 1796.
Jonathan Butcher of Salem Co. to Sarah Dole of Salem Co. - April 19, 1796.
David Duffile to Hannah Wood - April 20, 1796.
Noah Bowen to Phebe Parey - April 20, 1796.
Ephraim Lummis to Mary Westcott - April 28, 1796.
William Sears of Salem Co. to Mary Evans of Salem Co. - May 3, 1796.
John Sullivan to Rachel Wheaton Noblit - May 5, 1796.
Enoch Parvin of Salem to Ruth Davis of Salem - May 18, 1796.
Aarmathea Wethman to Susanna Eldredge - May 20, 1796.
Jonathan Sheppard to Sarah Mills - June 1, 1796.
Samuel Wood to Priscilla Ludlam - June 1, 1796.
James McLong of Salem to Lydia Peirson of Salem - June 1, 1796.
Aaron Husted to Mary Sheppard - June 21, 1796.
John Pedrick of Salem to Temperance Sims of Salem - June 29, 1796.
Daniel Simpkins to Rachel Ayars - June 31, 1796.
Jacob Hemington to Mary Rupell - July 7, 1796.
Edward Hamilton to Ann Adoesson - July 20, 1796.
Philip Dilshaver to Margaret Taver - July 26, 1796.
Henry Brenistholby to Phebe Shenshore - July 26, 1796.
Dr. Francis Gilbert Brewster to Polly Seely - Aug. 25, 1796.
Elijah Davis to Hannah Shute - Sept. 15, 1796.
David Filar to Susannah Dilshaver - Sept. 26, 1796.
Thomas Sutton to Dolla Musentine - July 7, 1796.
Joseph Garrison to Dorcas Nugen - July 7, 1796.
James Garrison to Hannah Garrison - Oct. 4, 1796.
Archibald Stewart to Susanna Lee - June 13, 1795.
Jaid Bowers to Mary Peirson - June 22, 1795.
Andrew King to Jerisha Weldin - July 11, 1795.
Thomas Fowler to Sarah Laton - Jan. 13, 1796.
David Peacock to Millicent Lee - Aug. 20, 1796.
William Stratton to Jemina Davis - Nov. 9, 1796.
Job Sheppard to Sarah Kelsay - April 26, 1796.
Joseph Credis to Silvia Barrett - May 7, 1796.

Thomas Williamson to Dina Sayre - May 28, 1796.
John Kimsey to Joanna Wilkins Davis - June 2, 1796.
Abraham Garrison to Rebecca Holeton - Sept. 13, 1796.
Enos Bacon to Rachel Harris - Oct. 4, 1796.
Joseph Miller to Hannah Filer - Oct. 11, 1796.
Daniel Ingersunn to Drusilla Hoffman - March 14, 1797.
John Leeds of Gloucester Co. to Margaret Garrison of Gloucester Co. - Jan. 5, 1797.
Enos Johnson to Ruth Symkins - May 31, 1796.
Isaac Hunter to Katharine Rowcap - June 21, 1796.
Christopher Gumin to Freelove Bennett - June 23, 1796.
David Ogden to Sally Earls - July 6, 1796.
Ephraim Preston to Peggy Shaw - July 18, 1796.
Reeves Robinson to Lavicy Clark - July 19, 1796.
Ogden Daniels to Betsey Peirson - July 21, 1796.
Jonathan Jaggers to Patty Hillman - Aug. 2, 1796.
Zechariah Jerril to Judith Causon - Nov. 15, 1796.
William Covenhoven to Barbara Rowcap - Dec. 31, 1796.
David Harris to Rhoda Semy (Terry) - Jan. 4, 1797.
Elijah Thompson to Rebecca Ryley - Jan. 12, 1797.
Silas Whitecar to Peggy Williams - Jan. 12, 1796.
Sheppard Gandy to Phebe Garrison - Jan. 16, 1797.
Richard Matthews to Kezia Murry - March 2, 1796.
Levi Preston to Hannah Bauer - March 7, 1796.
John Peirson to Lydia Shaw - March 22, 1797.
Williams Williams to Mary Law - March 22, 1796.
Silas Robinson to Rachel Read - Nov. 6, 1796.
Anamias Wescott to Nancy Newcomb - Dec. 12, 1796.
Joel Clark to Anee Dollass - Oct. 24, 1796.
Edward Davis to Ruth Pepper - Nov. 8, 1796.
Joab Chard to Temperance Robinson - May 3, 1797.
John Garrison to Dorkies Simkins - May 8, 1797.
Patrick Leanerd to Lydia Mukentine - May 19, 1797.
Job Glaspey to Hannah Mayhew - May 21, 1797.
Broadway Davis, Jr., to Ruth Teml - Dec. 29, 1796.
John Henard to Ester Ogden - Jan. 4, 1797.
Henry Charles to Elizabeth Hector - Jan. 17, 1797.
John Griffard to Polly Loomis - Feb. 3, 1797.
Ephraim Foster to Rebecca Watson - Feb. 24, 1797.
Selah Blew to Ann Garrison (widow) - March 8, 1797.
Jonathan Fish to Elizabeth Graham - April 12, 1797.

Samuel Parker to Levina Bateman (widow) July 19, 1797.
John Mathes to Easter (a black woman) - Sept. 21, 1797.
William Stewart to Margery Brown - July 19, 1797.
John Emberson to Elizabeth Bowers - Sept. 20, 1797.
Benjamin Baker to Tabitha Clifton - Sept. 20, 1797.
William Miller to Rebecca Gall - Nov. 15, 1797.
Ephraim Nixon to Sally Thompson - May 9, 1797.
Jacob Hunter to Rachel Irvin - June 6, 1797.
Theopilia Hughes to Lydia Westcott - July 16, 1797.
Daniel Read to Bathsheba Harris - Aug. 3, 1797.
William Smith to Betsey Westcott - Aug. 8, 1797.
Charles Riley to Charlotte Demaris - Aug. 16, 1797.
Jeremiah Harris to Susannah Bateman - Aug. 30, 1797.
John Garrison to Rebecca Mills - Dec. 11, 1794.
Festus (negro) to Phillis (negro) - Jan. 1, 1795.
David Shaw to Margaret Filer - Jan. 8, 1795.
Joseph Joslin to Sarah Austin - Jan. 26, 1795.
Jonathan Fithian to Rhoda Lupton - Jan. 27, 1795.
David Woodruff, Jr., to Hannah Padgett - March 17, 1795.
George Baracliff to Mrs. Mary McKee - April 2, 1795.
Samuel M. Shute to Sarah Elmer - April 2, 1795.
Rev. Samuel Laycock to Miss Harris - April 11, 1795.
Nicholas McKnight to Rhoda Codington - Sept. 9, 1795.
Jaid Hyat to Peggy Parvin - Nov. 21, 1795.
Jeremiah Sears to Phebe Bishop - June 6, 1796.
William Gardner (negro) to Polly Glascom (negro) - Aug. 11, 1796.
Henry Rusted to Rebecca Bannett - Sept. 12, 1796.
Moses Parker (negro) to Jude Meredith (negro) - Sept. 16, 1796.
Burton Jacobs (negro) to Mary Clark (negro) - Nov. 26, 1796.
Felix Cocke to Mrs. Bowles - Jan. 20, 1797.
Joshua Reeves to Rachel Parvin - Jan. 20, 1797.
Seeley Fithian to E. Hunt - Feb. 4, 1797.
David Bowen to Ruth Fithian - Feb. 16, 1797.
Jno. Beesley to Elizabeth Dare - Feb. 20, 1797.
Abner Ewing to Elizabeth Smith - March 6, 1797.
Jeremy Bishop to Anna Sears - March 9, 1797.
David Davis to Mably Bennett - March 9, 1797.
Abraham Van Vincle to Dorcas Bennett - May 18, 1797.
Harry Brown (negro) to Miller Stuphen (negro) June 3, 1797.
Amos Woodruff to Seabury Woodruff - June 27, 1797.
Glover Fithian to Prudy Hosman - Sept. 3, 1797.

Samuel Smith to Sally Reid - Sept. 18, 1797.
George Rocap to Anna Gunnell - March 14, 1797.
Harvey Sheppard to Hannah Smith - March 21, 1797.
William Mickleson to Elizabeth Sheppard - June 15, 1797.
Enoch Ayars to Anna Davis - July 17, 1797.
Reuben Jarman to Hannah High - July 18, 1797.
Alexander Graydon to Priscilla Corson - July 19, 1797.
John Jaggers to Lorana Jessup - Sept. 26, 1797.
Samuel Holmes to Abigail Brooks - Feb. 24, 1798.
John Carl to Ann Woodruff - Oct. 27, 1795.
James Hood to Lurina Buck - March 14, 1796.
John Brookfields to Ann Wheaton - Aug. 19, 1796.
John Filer to Margaret Shuster - Aug. 19, 1796.
William Wetherby to Jude Terry - Dec. 6, 1796.
Enos Seeley to Hope Riley - Nov. 15, 1796.
John Shoemaker to Hannah Dalton - Feb. 14, 1797.
Wanak Pervis to Mary Murray - Feb. 15, 1797.
Seth Bowen to Mary Barker - Feb. 18, 1797.
Zachariah Lawrence to Elizabeth Campbell - June 15, 1797.
Jesse Pervie to Catherine Stoms - Aug. 24, 1797.
George Madon to Catherine Van Horne - Aug. 24, 1797.
Charles Mitchell to Sarah Taylor - Oct. 28, 1797.
George Souder to Lydia Corson - Oct. 28, 1797.
William Standley to Mary Davis - Oct. 31, 1797.
Elias Seeley to Mary Middleton - Sept. 15, 1797.
William Casto to Martha Grant - Dec. 11, 1797.
Abijah Walling to Hannah Blanja - Feb. 3, 1798.
John Goff to Juda Corson - Feb. 14, 1798.
Michael Aarons to Naomi Gentry - Oct. 16, 1797.
Andrew Hichner to Rhoda Bowen - Dec. 27, 1797.
William Vanmeter of Salem to Sarah Nichols - Sept. 19, 1797.
John Plumbley to Mary Filer - Nov. 27, 1797.
David Dare to Rachel Seeley - Feb. 7, 1798.
Silas Robinson to Ann Weaton - Nov. 1, 1797.
Abraham Vandeford to Mary Blizzard - April 11, 1798.
John Campbell to Ruema Roberson - May 12, 1798.
Stephen Murphen to Prudence Bushby - Sept. 15, 1797.
Robert Quigly to Mary Brown - Dec. 25, 1797.
Joseph Oliver to Barbery Corson - Feb. 24, 1798.
Aaron Carrow to Tabitha Blizard - April 24, 1798.
Charles Smart to Catarina Fight - May 26, 1798.

CUMBERLAND COUNTY MARRIAGES

Isaac Carrell to Prudence Lupton - May 18, 1798.
Phineas Lupton to Rhoda Westcoat - Ma 18, 1798.
Joal Chard to Temperance Roberson - May 3, 1797.
John Garrison to Dorkis Simkins - May 8, 1797.
Andrew Garrison to Lydia Steenson - June 25, 1797.
Amos Pepper to Jude Wetherbee - July 23, 1797.
John Errickson to Levisa Hoffman - Aug. 17, 1797.
Jacob Hoover to Rachel Whitecar - Dec. 7, 1797.
Daniel Ellass to Elizabeth Garrison - Dec. 8, 1798.
Job Ellass to Eve Fleetwood - Jan. 5, 1798.
Isal Mayhew to Gate Booen - May 13, 1798.
Ishael Nicholls to Rachel Harris - May 3, 1798.
John Barker, Jr., to Margaret Low - Feb. 13, 1798.
Preston Stratton to Sarah Bateman - June 2, 1798.
Daniel Forsman to Nancy Garton - June 6, 1798.
John Camble to Ruhanna Roberson - May 12, 1798.
Jesse Pepper to Elizabeth Townsend- July 17, 1798.
Solomon Du Bois to Lydia Howard - Dec. 15, 1797.
Thomas Button to Mary Patrick (widow) - Feb. 5, 1798.
Richard Mulford to Rebecca Leake - Feb. 14, 1798.
Henry Crum to Anne Du Bois - Feb. 14, 1798.
William Garrison to Phebe Leake - Feb. 27, 1798.
David Garrison to Sally Davis - March 20, 1798.
Benjamin Davis to Ruth Reeve - June 13, 1798.
David Clark to Mary Potter - May 1, 1798.
Theophilus Parvin to Bathsheba Clark - Dec. 6, 1797.
Smith Bowen to Mrs. Jane Bowen - Feb. 21, 1798.
James Page to Ruhanne Ogden - Nov. 23, 1798.
Joseph Waterson to Phebe Simpkins - July 10, 1798.
Robert Low to Mary Walling - May 6, 1798.
Ebenezer Hall to Mary Thompson - Jan. 1, 1799.
Joseph Harris to Hannah Sheppard - Dec. 6, 1798.
Urban Dixon to Eleanor Ray - Jan. 1, 1798.
Jonathan Sheppard to Lydia Harris - Jan. 16, 1798.
William Joslin to Sally Irwin - March 6, 1798.
William Connor to Ruth Burt - April 4, 1798.
John Stratton to Phebe Bateman - April 10, 1798.
Ethniel Johnson to Polly Williams - May 16, 1798.
Jonathan Shaw to Sally Taylor - Aug. 14, 1798.
William Chard to Rebecca Campbell - Aug. 14, 1798.
Lawrence Westcott to Susanna Daniels - Aug. 22, 1798.

Jonathan Elmer to Amelia Walters - Sept. 4, 1798.
Aaron Smith to Caty Harris - Dec. 6, 1798.
Ishamel Perry to Hope Thomas Dec. 7, 1798.
Timothy Burch to Silvia Burke - Dec. 20, 1798.
John Harris to Lovice Sheppard - Dec. 20, 1798.
James Smith to Pleasant Stites - Jan. 16, 1799.
Andrew Jones to Judith Shaw - Jan. 17, 1799.
Curtis Trenchard to Ruth Westcott - Jan. 22, 1799.
Josiah Ogden to Judith Garrison - Jan. 31, 1799.
Ephraim Westcott to Abigail Ogden - Feb. 20, 1799.
Henry Westcott to Priscilla Whitaker - Feb. 26, 1799.
Jonathan Sockwell to Urania Whitakar - March 5, 1799.
Thomas Bateman to Lydia Westcott - March 11, 1799.
Vayer Husbands to Mary Brooks - March 6, 1798.
William West to Mary Ayars - March 19, 1798.
Samuel Bacon to Elizabeth Harris - March 20, 1798.
John Sibly to Sarah Brooks - March 26, 12798.
Mark Bowen to Sarah Harris - April 3, 1798.
Samuel Stockton to Mary Tucker - April 10, 1798.
Jonathan Hann to Elizabeth Duffield - May 1, 1798.
Joseph High to Sarah Barrett - May 1, 1798.
Daniel Bowen to Phebe Ireland - June 30, 1798.
Enoch Mulford to Temperance Mathews - Aug. 13, 1798.
Isaac Miller to Mary Webster - Sept. 25, 1798.
Joseph Bowen to Nancy Corrant - Nov. 20, 1798.
Ira Brooks to Esther Sayrs - Dec. 4, 1798.
Mark Westcott to Amy Perry - May 17, 1798.
Davis Ireland to Jane Worthington - Dec. 29, 1798.
Daniel Bacon to Nancy Shits - Feb. 27, 1799.
Ambrose Ladow to Phebe Heaton - Dec. 9, 1798.
John Mussentine to Rebecca Gardner - Feb. 21, 1799.
Hosea Rankins to Sarah Hoffman - April 22, 1799.
Isaac Murphy to Fanny Hand - May 1, 1799.
Jeremiah Carter to Lydia Foster - May 8, 1799.
Ambrose Walker to Mary Yungs of Salem - April 24, 1799.
James Smith of Gloucester to Deborah Ogden - April 30, 1799.
Jonathan Parvin to Amey Bateman - Dec. 17, 1798.
Thomas Hampton to Ruth Diament - Dec. 18, 1798.
Daniel Blizard to Mary Gandy - Jan. 1, 1799.
John Morgan to Prudence Peirson - Sept. 19, 1799.
Daniel Davis to Susannah Leake - Dec. 10, 1798.

Isaac Richmond to Rachel Sharp - Feb. 21, 1799.
Ames Weeks to Rachel Davis - March 6, 1799.
William Shull to Peggy Cake - March 12, 1799.
Isaac Painter to Mary Parvin - March 20, 1799.
David Ogden to Rachel Murphy - April 11, 1799.
David Bennett to Hannah Smith - May 8, 1799.
Ephraim Magee to Polly Terrill - June 26, 1799.
James McGilliard to Lodema Keen - April 4, 1799.
Jacob Davis to Martha Youngs - Aug. 22, 1799.
Daniel Johnson to Beuler Beckler - April 11, 1797.
George Johnson to Nancy Steelman - Oct. 21, 1797.
Adam Wentzell to Barbary Brinesthold - Oct. 20, 1798.
Silas Reynolds to Christiana Dilshaver - Jan. 8, 1799.
David Halter to Christiana Souder - May 4, 1799.
John Dare to Elizabeth Kirnsey - April 18, 1799.
Jonathan Garrison to Hannah Reeves - April 23, 1799.
John Harden to Elizabeth Husted - May 14, 1799.
Zebadiah Davis to Sarah Ayars - June 25, 1799.
Elijah Sap to Mary McPherson - July 30, 1799.
Anthony Welldone to Anna Riley - Aug. 26, 1799.
David Weastcoat to Mary Harris - Sept. 30, 1799.
Delamore Harris to Letitia Acton - Oct. 15, 1799.
David Sheppard to Miriam Smith - Oct. 17, 1799.
Peter Groom to Tabita Lore - Oct. 22, 1799.
John Sheppard to Elizabeth Smith - Oct. 30, 1799.
Ephraim Garrison to Mary Bowen - Nov. 31, 1798.
Nathan Solly to Sarah Hackett - Sept. 28, 1798.
Albina Wood to Susanna Humphreys - Aug. 17, 1799.
Clinton Mepiz to Letitia Mills - Sept. 10, 1800.
Jesse Bacon to Hannah Whitacar - Oct. 1, 1799.
George Westcott, Jr., to Marthew Sheppard - March 22, 1799.
Lewis Abrahams to Sally Montgomery - March 19, 1799.
David Stiters to Hannah Shaw - March 21, 1799.
Ephraim Fithian to Victoria Johnson - April 2, 1799.
Reuben Buck to Abagail Brown - April 9, 1799.
Enoch Bowen to Betsey Heaton - April 10, 1799.
John Bateman to Anna Steddems - July 16, 1799.
James Simpson to Miriam Barton - Oct. 8, 1799.
Jonathan Westcott to Abigail Bateman - Dec. 27, 1799.
Elick McDonal to Mary Harmer - July 27, 1799.
Thomas Cheesman to Elizabeth Wesk - Jan. 1, 1800.

Ephram Joslen to Susannah Garison - Dec. 3, 1799.
Philop Cornwell to Dalia Blackwood - Oct. 8, 1799.
Joseph Conklyn to Rachel Riley - Oct. 22, 1799.
William Fithian to Hannah Yapp - Dec. 24, 1799.
Abijah Harris to Hannah Harris - Oct. 17, 1799.
Samuel Thompson to Ruth Foster - May 17, 1800.
George Meal to Sarah Jones - Jan. 13, 1800.
Philip Stathem to Clementia Remington - Jan. 16, 1800.
Thomas Tribet to Mary Busy - Jan. 28, 1800.
Forazor Glan to Mary Ladow - April 6, 1800.
Josiah White to Abegail Brick - Jan. 26, 1799.
Edward Moore to Mary Glasbey - July 14, 1799.
Jessey Dragston to Anney Henderson - Sept. 15, 1799.
John Shoemaker to Susanna White - May 3, 1800.
John Garrison to Rebecca Wyatt - Sept. 25, 1799.
Jeremiah Parvin to Sarah Reed - Feb. 8, 1800.
Recompence Whitacaar to Rachel Moore - March 6, 1800.
Lewis Moore to Susannah Shulll - April 12, 1800.
David Buck to Debby O'Ward - June 3, 1800.
Joseph Reeves to Elizabeth Fithian - March 6, 1798.
Caleb Ayars to Hannah Pettil - March 20, 1798.
Jabez Smith to Sarah Dare - March 23, 1798.
Abigiah Maskill to Polly Wood - April 11, 1798.
Jonathan Holmes to Lydia Ludley - May 8, 1798.
David Woodruff to Widow Lupton - May 22, 1798.
Daniel Miller to Lydia Moore - June 19, 1798.
Joseph Finnaman to Hannah Dare - July 13, 1798.
Thomas Brown, Jr., to Polly Kelsey - Oct. 4, 1798.
William Fithian to Polly Clark - Oct. 27, 1798.
John Brown to Polly Wood - Nov. 5, 1798.
Ephraim Riley to Temperance Wood - Nov. 5, 1798
David Sheppard to Esther Fithian - Dec. 7, 1798.
Abraham Miller to Anna Brown - Dec. 24, 1798.
John Reeves, Jr., to Patty Reeves - Dec. 25, 1798.
Enoch Burgin to Elizabeth Souders - Jan. 17, 1799.
Ephraim Padgett to Hannah Dare - Jan. 15, 1799.
Joshua Barrett to Rachel Swinney - March 25, 1799.
Gabriel Dare to Sally Wood - Aug. 20, 1799.
John Reeves to Penninnat Sullivan - Dec. 1, 1799.
Henry Rittenhouse to Sally Coke - Dec. 15, 1799.
John Ireland to Molly Davis - March 12, 1800.

Thomas Reeves, Sr. to Widow Randolph April 12, 1800.
Mark Remmington to Sally Miller - May 14, 1800.
David Woodruff, Sr. to Elizabeth Woodruff May 27, 1800.
Dr. Lewis Garrison to Rachel Sheppard - June 7, 1800.
Samuel Davis to Sarah Sheppard - Dec. 5, 1799.
Josiah Sheppard to Lydia Ewing - Dec. 24, 1799.
Daniel Maul to Mary Allen - Dec. 25, 1799.
David Bateman to Ruth Sheppard - Dec. 31, 1799.
Dickeson Sheppard to Margaret Davis - Jan. 8, 1800.
Robert Medelbeeks to Mary Rocap - Jan. 21, 1800.
David Coburn to Margaret Stathems - Feb. 19, 1800.
Job Johnson to Sarah Woodroe - March 27, 1800.
Richard Jerman to Lydia Neal - July 23, 1800.
Joseph Couch to Sarah Smith - June 24, 1800.
Jonathan Meriott to Sarah Jerell - March 27, 1800.
Jacob Randolph to Margaret Ayars - July 28, 1800.
Reuben Pepper to Mary Moore - March 6, 1800.
Peter Ladow to Mary Jenkins - April 11, 1800.
David Stites to Ann Sheppard - April 16, 1800.
Joshua Garrison to Ann Morris - May 3, 1800.
Joseph Page to Sarah Ingerson - May 2, 1800.
John B. Polhemus to Hannah Howard - July 30, 1800.
Josiah Newcomb to Hannah Missey - May 21, 1800.
William Backley to Abigail Nucomb - June 9, 1800.
Jeremiah Stratton to Seviriah Bateman - Nov. 8, 1800.
Daniel Loder, Jr., to Keziah Lupton - Dec. 15, 1800.
Isaac Lanning to H. McLong - Aug. 16, 1800.
Joseph Brown to Phebe Woodruff - Oct. 15, 1800.
Capt. D. Seeley to N. Seeley - Nov. 15, 1800.
Noah Woodruff to A. Reeves - Nov. 15, 1800.
Jonathan Taylor to Elizabeth Chard - Dec. 25, 1800.
Henry Buck, Jr., to Kezia Newman - July 26, 1800.
Henry Husted to Abigail Bishop - Dec. 17, 1799.
William Smith to Esther Bateman - Jan. 7, 1800.
Asa Fish to Sally Machesny - Feb. 4, 1800.
Nathan Bennett to Betsey Bennett - March 6, 1800.
John Elmer to Abigail Howel - March 5, 1800.
Curtis Edwards to Polly Newcomb - July 10, 1800.
Jonathan Bateman to Sally Ogden - Sept. 10, 1800.
John Earls to Theodosia Elmer - Dec. 16, 1800.
Peter Demaris to Polly Shaw - Dec. 25, 1800.

Daniel G. Fillman to Ruth Cook - Sept. 18, 1800.
John Mikener to Rachel Walling - Aug. 30, 1800.
Thomas Casto to Nancy Heritage - Nov. 11, 1800.
Elisha Smith to Mary Wetcott - Nov. 22, 1800.
William Compton to Sarah Shrophsir - July 27, 1800.
Daniel Brown to Tasse Kemble - Sept. 28, 1800.
Joseph Scott to Marey Henry - Oct. 26, 1800.
Joshia Ayars to Sarah Winckester - Sept. 30, 1800.

COMBINED REGISTER OF THE MORAVIAN MISSIONARIES IN WEST NEW JERSEY, 1742-1762

"About 1743, two acres of land were purchased, most probably from John Hoffman, a short distance above Spring Garden Ferry, and a Swedish church was erected for the use of the Brethen and dedicated to the worship of God by (the Revds.) Abraham Reincke, Owen Rice, Matthew Reutz, and Pastor Lawrence T. Nyberg, on December 18, 1746. ...The only stones left standing in the yard were those to mark the graves of Hezekiah Lore and his wife Elizabeth. The one died June 19, 1770 (ae. 73 yrs.) and the other January 2, 1761(ae. 60 yrs.). These stones were removed in 1881 to the M.E. Churchyard (at Port Elizabeth)." (From F.W. Bowmen, *History of Port Elizabeth, Cumberland County, N. J.*, 1885; repr. 1936; pp. 9-10).

In 1937-8, The N. J. Swedish-Finnish Tercentenary Commission sought without success to have this river-eroded churchyard preserved as public property. These Moravian missionaries officiated also in the Swedish Lutheran congregations in Penn's Neck and in Racoon as well as in their own church on Oldman's Creek. The following register is compiled from three contemporary records, viz:

[1] The register of the Swedish-Moravian Church of Maurice River, 1748-1798, the first seven leaves of which are missing, published in *History of Port Elizabeth, Cumberland, Co., N. J.*, by F.W. Bowen (1885), p. 84; reprinted 1936. Some of the missing items are supplied by [3].

[2] The Rev. Abraham Reincke's "Private Record of official acts performed among his countrymen and others in New Jersey, on Delaware, during his occasional ministry in the Brethen's mission of that Province" 1744-1752, published as an appendix by the editor in the English edition of Acrelius' *History of New Sweden* (1874). The Rev. Mr. Reincke died April 7, 1760, at Bethlehem, Pa. Dates in are in new style.

[3] Moravian Register of Births, Baptisms, Marriages and Deaths in West New Jersey, 1742-1794, the original of which is in the Archives at Bethlehem, Pa. Dates are in old style.

Baptisms

Catherine Izard, dau. of Gabriel and Martha Izard, of Morris River, b. May 23 1742, bapt. by the Rev. Paul Daniel Byrcelius. [3]

John Wiseman, son of John Wiseman, of Cohansy, b. Dec, bapt. Aug 3, 1743, by Leonard Schnell.[3]

Christina Petersen, dau. of Luke and Christina Petersen, of Morris River, b. June 6, 1743.[3]
Isaac Guest, son of William and Christina Guest, of Raccoon, b. Dec 6, 1743, bapt. by Rev. Paul Daniel Byrcelius.[3]
Catherine Hoffman, dau. of Peter and Mary Hoffman, of Morris River, b. Feb 10, 1744, bapt. 20th of same mo. by Rev Paul Daniel Byrcelius.[3]
Samuel Cobb, son of Samuel and Catherine Cobb, of Morris River, b. June 6, 1744, bapt. by Rev. Paul D. Byrcelius.[3]
Peter Lock, son of John and Rebecca Lock, of Raccoon, b. Sept 22, 1744, bapt. 25th of same mo. by Rev P.D. Byrcelius.[3]
Magdalene Gill, dau. of Matthew and Magdalen Gill, b. Nov. 6, 1744, was bapt. by Rev. Paul D. Byrcelius.[3]
Eric, infant son of Eric and Catherine Kyn (Keen) of Morris River, b. Dec. 25, 1744, bapt. April 7, 1745, by Rev. Abraham Reinke at Goeran Kyn's house.[2 & 3]
Deborah Hoffman, dau. of Laurance (Lorens) and Mary Hoffman, of Raccoon, b. ---, bapt. May 4, 1745 (Apr. 23, o.s.?) by Rev. Abraham Reinke.[2 & 3]
Seth Samuel Ward, son of Samuel and Sarah Ward, bapt May 4, 1748 in Lorenz Hopman's house in Raccoon by Rev. Abraham Reinke.[2]
Priscilla Lock, dau. of John and Rebecca Lock, b.---, bapt. June 9, (May 7, o.s.) 1745, by Rev. Abraham Reinke in the parents house in Raccoon. Priscilla Lock d. in Aug. 1748.[2 & 3]
Elizabeth Philpot, dau. of Nicholas and --- Philpot of Penn's Neck, b.---, bapt. June 20, (9, o.s.) 1745, by Rev. Abraham Reinke in the church in Penn's Neck.[2 & 3]
Mary Keen, dau. of John and Rachel Keen, of Raccoon, b.---, bapt. June 21, (10, o.s.), by Rev. Abr. Reinke in the parsonage of Raccoon.[2 & 3]
Margaret Rawlins (Raol), dau. of John and Margaret Rawlings (Raol), of Pilesgrove, b. ---, bapt. June 22, (11, o.s.), 1745, by Rev. A. Reinke, in William Graceberry's house in Pilesgrove. The father a Swede, the mother Irish.[2 & 3]
Jeremiah Petersen, son of Lawrence and Susannah Petersen, b. ---, bapt. June 27, 1745, by Rev. A. Reinke, in the new church on Maurice River, at the close of the first sermon preach within its walls...[2 & 3]
Sarah Lynmeyer, dau. of Christopher and Ann Lynmeyer, of Penn's Neck, b. June 19, 1745, bapt. July 7, 1746, by Rev. John C. Pyrlaeus.[3]
Jonah Jones, son of Joseph and Margaret Jones, of Morris River, b. Aug. 1, 1745, bapt. July 6, 1746, by Rev. J. C. Pyrlaeus.[3]
Catherine Gill, dau. of Matthew and Magdalene Gill, b. Jan. 2, 1746, bapt. Jan. 12, 1746, by Rev. Matthew Gottshalk.[3]

Samuel Hoffman, son of John and Elizabeth Hoffman, b. Jan. 18, 1746, bapt. July 6, 1746, by Rev. J. C. Pyrlaeus.[3].

Mary Hoffman, dau. of Peter and Ann Hoffman, of Morris River, b. June 1, 1746, bapt. July 6, 1746, by Rev. J. C. Pyrlaeus.[3]

Zachariah Petersen, son of Zachariah and Magdalene Petersen, of Raccoon, b. 30 June 1746, bapt. June (July?) 7, (1746?) by Rev. J. C. Pyrlaeus.[3]

Christopher Lynmeyer, son of Christopher and Ann Lynmeyer, of Penn's Neck, b. July 5, 1746, bapt. July 7, 1746, by Rev. J. C. Pyrlaeus. [3]

Nathaniel Guest, son of William and Christina Guest, b. Oct. 3, 1746, bapt. Oct. 13, 1746, by Rev. J. C. Pyrlaeus.[3]

Rebecca Jones, dau. of Abraham and Gunla Jones of Morris River, b. Dec. 5, 1746, bapt. Dec. 7, (18 n.s.), 1746, by Rev. Abr. Reinke, "in the church immediately after its dedication to the worship of God." [2 & 3]

Elizabeth Maslander, dau. of William and Elizabeth Maslander, of Morris River, b. ---, bapt. Dec. 7, (18 n.s.) 1746, by Rev. Abr. Reinke, (as above). [2 & 3]

William Cobb, son of Samuel and Catherine (Caroline ?) Cobb, of Morris River, b. ---, bapt. Dec 7, (18 n.s.), 1746, by Rev. Abr. Reinke, (as above).[3]

John and Abraham Keen, twin sons, of Eric and Catherine Keen of Morris River, b. May 10, 1747 and bapt. ---, by Rev. M. Gottshalk. [3]

John Mulicka, son of Eric and Catherine Mulicka of Morris River, b. Dec. 17, 1747, bapt. ---; by Rev. Lawrence Nyberg.[3]

Isaac Vanneman, son of John and Mary Vanneman, of Pilesgrove, b. Dec. 19, 1747, bapt. by Rev. Lawrence Nyberg.[3]

Joseph Guest, son of William and Christina Guest, of Raccoon, b. Dec. 25, 1747, bapt. by Rev. John Wade.[3]

Deborah Gill, dau. of Matthew and Magdene Gill, of Raccoon, b. Jan. 1, 1748, bapt. by Rev. John Wade.[3]

Christina Lynmeyer, dau. of Christopher and Ann Lynmeyer, of Penn's Neck, b. Mar. 26, (27?), 1748, in Piles Grove, bapt. Oct. 23, 1748, by Rev. A. Reinke, in the new church on Oldman's Creek on the 20th Sunday after Trinity. Garret Van Inmen and William Guest and their wives, sponsors. [2 & 3]

Abraham Peterson, son of Laurence and Susanna Peterson, b. May 30, 1748, bapt. by Rev. John Wade.[1]

Rebecca Lock, dau. of John and Rebecca Lock, of Raccoon, b. Oct. 31, bapt. Nov. 24, 1748, by Rev. Abraham Reinke "in the father's house, in the presence of Garret Van Inmen, John Jones, old Stephen Jones, Eric Mullica, and ten other witnesses." [2 & 3]

Mary Holstine, dau. of Lawrence (Lorenze) and Mary Holstine (Holstein) of Pilesgrove, b. Nov 11, bapt. Nov. 27, 1748, by Rev. A. Reinke, in Yerred Van Emmen's house. Note. Mary Holstine, the mother d. on the 19th of Nov, eight days after the birth of the child, Mary and was buried near the new church on Oldman's Creek. She was the first interment there after the erection of the church. [2 & 3]

Frederick Hopman (Hoffman), son of Frederick and Catherine Hopman (Hoffman), of Morris (Maurice) River, b. Aug. 1, 1748, bapt. Nov. 30, 1748, by Rev. Abraham Reinke in the Church on Maurice River, at the close of the Swedish sermon.[1, 2, 3]

Joseph Jones, b. May 7, 1749.[1]

Andrew Kemp, son of Paul and Jane Kemp of Morris River, b. Mar. 31, 1749, bapt. by Rev. John Wade.[1,3]

Ann Gracebury, dau. of William and Mary Gracebury, of Penn's Neck, b. June 28, bapt. July 3, 1749, by Rev. John Wade.[3]

William Avise, son of George and Jane Avise, of Oldman's Creek, b. Aug. 17, 1749, bapt. by Rev. Lawrence Nyberg.[3]

Thomas Keen, son of Eric and Catherine Keen, of Morris River, b. Dec. 3, 1749, bapt. Dec 7, 1749, by Rev. Lawrence Nyberg. (By John Wade, per 3).[1,3]

Lawrence Peterson, son of Lawrence and Susanna Peterson, b. Feb. 28, (1749 ?), bapt. by Rev. Abraham Reinke.[1]

Nicholas Lynmeyer, son of Christopher and Ann Lynmeyer, of Penn's Neck, b. Feb. 24, 1750, bapt. by Rev. Lawrence Nyberg.[3]

Mary Gill, dau. of Matthew and Magdalene Gill, b. Mar. 16, 1750, bapt. April 21, 1750, by Rev. Abr. Reinke.[3]

David Hopman, son of John and Elizabeth Hopman, b. July 17, 1750, bapt. by Mr. Eric. Onander.[1]

Abigail Peterson, dau. of Thomas and Abigail Peterson, b. Dec. 22, 1750, bapt. by Gabriel Noesman. Abigail, the elder was dau. of John Purple.[1]

Abraham Hopman (Hoffman), son of Frederick and Catherine Hopman, b. Dec. 10, 1750, bapt. by Rev. Abraham Reinke, in the father's house at Marantico.[1,2,3]

Sarah Jones, dau. of Joseph and Margaret Jones, of Morris River, b. Oct. 30, 1750, at Menomuskin, bapt. Jan. 21, 1751, by the Rev. Abr. Reinke in the church on Morris River.[1,2,3]

Mary Jones, dau. of Abraham and Jane Jones, b. Oct. 7, 1751, bapt. by Rev. Abraham Lidenius.[1]

Catherine Guest, dau. of William and Christina Guest, of Racoon, b. Nov. 18, 1750, bapt. Jan. 22, 1751, by Rev. Abraham Reinke in our church on Oldman's Creek.[2 & 3]

Mary Gill, dau. of Matthew and Mary Gill, of Raccoon, b. Mar. 16, 1751 in Raccoon, bapt. Apr. 21, 1751, in her father's house.[2]
James Avise, son of George and Jane Avise, of Oldman's Creek, b. Dec. 2, 1750, bapt. Aug. 16, 1751, by Rev. A. Reinke, in the church on Oldman's Creek.[2 & 3]
Charity Lloyd, dau. of Obadiah and Rebecca Lloyd, of Pilesgrove, b. Mar. 12, 1752, bapt. Apr. 12, 1752, by Rev. A. Reinke, in our church on Oldman's Creek.[2 & 3]
Rebekah Peterson, dau. of Samuel and Susanna Peterson, b. May 10, 1752, bapt. by Mathew Reitz.[1]
Lydia Peterson, dau. of Samuel and Mary Peterson, b. ---, 1752, bapt. by Mathew Reitz.[1]
William Vanaman, son of Jonah and Lydia Vanaman b. and bapt. Aug. 9, 1752 by Mathew Reitz.[1]
Catharine Hopman, dau. of John and Elizabeth Hopman, b. Aug. 9, 1752, bapt. by Mathew Reitz.[1]
Christiana Gill, dau. of Matthew and Magdalene Gill, b. Mar. 16, 1752, bapt. by Rev. Matthew Reutz.[3]
Mary Guest, dau of William and Christiana Guest, b. Oct 8, 1752, bapt. by Rev. Matthew Reutz.[3]
Lydia Peterson, dau. of Samuel and Mary Peterson, b. --- and bapt. 1752 by Matthew Ruetz.[1]
Catherine Hoffman, dau of John and Catherine Hoffman of Morris River, b. Jan 21, bapt. Jan 28, 1753 by Rev. Matthew Reutz.[3]
John Holstine, son of Lawrence and Margaret Holstine of Pilesgrove, b. Nov. 10, 1752, bapt. Nov. 16, 1752, by Rev. Matthew Reutz.[3]
Catharine Hopman, dau. of John and Elizabeth Hopman, b. Aug. 9, bapt. 1752 or 1753 by Matthew Reutz.[3]
Peter Lauterbach, son of Conrad and Elizabeth Lauterbach of Piles Grove, b. Feb. 3, bapt. Feb. 5, 1753, by Rev. M. Reutz.[3]
Lydia Peterson, dau. of Thomas and Abigail Peterson, b. March 20, 1753.[1]
Elizabeth Vanaman, dau. of David and Metachabel Vanaman b. Sept. 28, 1753, bapt. by Mathew Reitz.[1]
Peter Vaneman, son of Peter and Catherine Vaneman of Penn's Neck, b. Dec. 9, bapt. Dec. 16, 1753, by Rev. Matthew Reutz.[3]
Lydia Peterson, dau. of Samuel and Mary Peterson, b. and bapt. Aug. 9, 1753, by Mathew Reitz.[1]
Susanna Holstein, dau. of Lawrence and Margaret Holstein of Pilesgrove, b. Dec. 19, 1753, bapt. Jan. 6, 1754, by Rev. Matthew Reutz.[3]

Anna Peterson, dau. of John and Christiana Peterson, b. May 10, 1753 or 1754, bapt. same year by Mr. Bryselius.[1]
Ann Lynmeyer, dau. of Christopher and Ann Lynmeyer of Penn's Neck, b. Jan. 6, bapt. by Rev. M. Reutz. (1754).[3]
Abraham Jones, son of Joseph and Margaret Jones, b. Nov. ---, 1753, bapt. Feb. 1, 1754, by Mathew Reitz.[1]
Elizabeth Jones, dau. of Abraham and Jane Jones, b. May 30, 1754, bapt. by Paul Bryselius 1754.[1]
Zaccheus Avise, son of George and Jane Avise, of Oldman's Creek, b. Jan. 28, 1754, bapt. Jan. 30, 1754, by Rev. Matthew Reutz.[3]
Rebecca Lloyd, dau. of Beekman and Lydia Lloyd of Piles Grove, b. Nov. 11, 1754, bapt. Mar. 21, 1755, by Rev. Ernest Gambold.[3]
Adam and Mathias Lauterbach, twin sons of Conrad and Elizabeth Lauterbach, b. Nov. 28, 1754, bapt. Mar. 30, 1755, by Rev. Ernest Gambold.[3]
Elizabeth Hoffman, dau. of John and Elizabeth Hoffman of Morris River, b. Jan. 3, bapt. Apr. 6, 1755, by Rev. Ernest Gambold.[1 & 3]
Matthew Gill, son of Matthew and Elizabeth Gill of Raccoon Creek, b. Feb. 7, bapt. Mar. 20, 1755, by Rev. Ernest Gambold.[3]
Michael Kats, son of Jacob and Barbara Kats, of Penn's Neck, b. Mar. 14, bapt. Apr. 9, 1755, by Rev. Ernest Gambold.[3]
George Shute, son of William and Ann Shute of Olman's creek, b. Apr. 18, bapt. May 18, 1755, by Rev. John Bradbiller.[3]
Rebecca Lloyd, wife of Obadiah Lloyd, b. July 4, 1731, bapt. Mar. 20, 1755, by Rev. A. Reinke.[3]
Benjamin Lloyd, son of William and Christiana Lloyd, of Raccoon Creek, b. July 10, bapt. Aug. 7, 1755, by Rev. E. Gambold.[3]
Mary Adams, dau. of Abraham and Bridger Adams of Raccoon Creek, b. Jan. 13, bapt. May 9, 1756, by Rev. Ernest Gambold.[3]
Ann Gambold, dau. of Ernest and Eleanor Gambold, b. at Oldman's Creek, Feb. 9, bapt. Feb. 19, 1756, by Rev. Thomas Yarnell.[3]
Rosine Kats, dau. of Michael and Mary Kats of Penns Neck, b. Apr. 1, bapt. May 5, 1756, by Rev. E. Gambold.[3]
Joseph Avise, son of George and Jane Avise, b. Mar. 31, bapt. May 27, 1756, by Rev. E. Gambold.[3]
William Holstine, son of Lawrence and Margaret Holstine of Pilesgrove, b. Mar. 19, bapt. May 16, 1756, by Rev. E. Gambold.[3]
Daniel Vanneman, son of Peter and Catherine Vanneman of Penns Neck, b. May 29, bapt. June 2, 1756, by Rev. E. Gambold.[3]
Bateman Lloyd, son of Bateman and Lydia Lloyd of Piles Grove, b. Aug. 28, bapt. Oct. 24, 1756, by Rev. E. Gambold.[3]

Samuel Lloyd, son of Odediah and Rebecca Lloyd of Piles Grove, b. Oct. 25, bapt. Nov. 18, 1756, by Rev. E. Gambold.[3]
William Schute, son of William and Anne Schute of Oldman's Creek, b. Apr. 6, bapt. May 15, 1757, by Rev. E. Gambold.[3]
Martin Kats, son of Jacob and Barbara Kats, of Penns Neck, b. May 16, bapt. June 8, 1757 by Rev. E. Gambold.[3]
Conrad Lautenbach, son of Conrad and Elizabeth Lautenbach, son of Conrad and Elizabeth Lautenbach, b. May 16, bapt. June 22, 1757, by Rev. E. Gambold.[3]
Samuel Vanneman, son of Samuel and Sarah Vanneman, b. Mar. 20, 1756, bapt. July 7, 1757, by Rev. E. Gambold.[1,3]
Mary Hoffman, dau. of Frederick and Catherine Hoffman of Morris River, b. Jan 11, 1755, bapt. Dec. 5, 1757, by Rev. E. Gambold. [1,3]
Margaret Vanneman, dau. of David and Mehitabel Vanneman, of Morris River, b. Oct. 10, (5?), 1755, bapt. Dec. 3, 1757, by Rev. E. Gambold. [1,3]
Samuel Jones, son of Joseph and Margaret Jones of Morris River, b. April 19, 1756, bapt. Dec. 3, 1757, by Rev. E. Gambold.[1,3]
Rebecca Steelman, dau. of Charles and Anne Steelman, of Morris River, b. Jan. 7, 1756, bapt. Dec. 3, 1757, by Rev. E. Gambold.[1,3]
Margaret Hoffman, dau. of John and Elizabeth Hoffman of Morris River, b. May 20, 1756, bapt. Dec. 3, 1757, by Rev. E. Gambold.[1,3]
Jane Jones, dau. of Abraham and Jane Jones of Morris River, b. July 7, 1756, bapt. Dec. 3, 1757, by Rev. E. Gambold.[1,3]
Andrew Holstein, son of Lawrence Holstein of Piles Grove, b. Oct. 16, 1756, bapt. Jan. 1, 1757, by Rev. E. Gambold.[3]
Priscilla Adams, dau. of Abraham and Bridget Adams of Raccoon Creek, b. Sept. 10, 1756, bapt. Mar. 18, 1757, by Rev. E. Gambold.[3]
Hannah Avise, dau. of George and Jane Avise of Oldman's Creek, b. April 26, bapt. July 2, 1758, by Rev. Jasper Payne.[3]
Joseph Shute, son of William Jr., and Ann Shute, of Oldman's Creek, b. Sept. 21, 1758 and bapt. by Rev. C. Otto Krogstrup. Sponsors: Obediah Lloyd, Magdalene Gill, William Shute, Ann Shute.[3]
Sarah Guest, dau of William and Christiana Guest of Racoon Creek, b. Oct 9, 1758, bapt. by Rev. C. O. Krogstrup. Sponsors: Obediah Lloyd, Magdalene Gill, William Shute, Ann Shute.[3]
Daniel Lloyd, son of Obadiah and Rebecca Lloyd of Piles Grove, b. Oct. 31, 1758, bapt. by Rev. C. O. Krogstrup.[3]
Josiah Gill, son of Matthew and Magdalene Gill of Raccoon Creek, b. Aug. 21, 1759, bapt. Aug. 6, 1760, by Rev. P. D. Bryzelius.[3]
Rebecca Hoffman, dau. of Lawrence and Sarah Hoffman of Piles Grove, b. 14 Feb. and bapt. 5 Aug. 1760, by Rev. P. D. Bryzelius.[3]

Sarah Holstin, dau. of Lawrence and Margaret Holstin of Piles Grove b. 17 Jan. 1760, bapt. by Rev. P. D. Bryzelius.[3]

Marianna Kats, dau. of Martin and Anna Kats, b. Jan. 30, 1759, bapt. by Rev. P. D. Bryzelius.[3]

Jacob Kats, son of Jacob and Barbara Kats of Penn's Neck, b. --- and bapt. --- by Rev. P. D. Bryzelius.[3]

Elizabeth Jones, dau. of Jacob and Ann Jones of Raccoon Creek, b. --- and bapt. ---, by Rev. Paul Daniel Bryzelius.[3]

Mary Jones, dau. of Andrew and Mary Jones of Raccoon Creek, b. May 18, 1760, bapt. by Rev. P. D. Bryzelius.[3]

Martin Kats, son of Martin and Anna Kats of Penn's Neck, b. Aug. 17, bapt. Sept. 17, 1760, by Rev. P. D. Bryzelius.[3]

Jaconias Lloyd, son of Obediah and Rebecca Lloyd of Piles Grove, b. Feb. 25 and bapt. Mar. 8, 1761, by Rev. C. O. Krogstrup. Sponsors: William and Christiana Guest, Ann Lynmeyer, Jaconias Wood.[3]

Diana Shute, dau. of William and Ann Shute of Oldman's Creek b. Nov. 6, 1760, bapt. Mar. 4, 1761, by Rev. Christian O. Krogstrup. Sponsors: William and Christiana Guest, George and Ann Avise.[3]

Rachel Avise, dau. of George and Ann Avise of Oldman's Creek, b. Jan. 13, bapt. Mar. 4, 1761, by Rev. C. O. Krogstrup. Witnesses: William and Christian Guest, William and Ann Shute.[3]

Jacob Lloyd, son of Bateman and Lydia Lloyd of Piles Grove, b. Dec. 10, 1761, bapt. Oct. 28, 1762, by Rev. George Neisser.[3]

Benjamin Hoffman, son of Lawrence and Sarah Hoffman of Piles Grove, b. Nov. 25, 1761, bapt. Oct. 29, 1762, by Rev. George Neisser. Sponsors: Jackoniah Wood and Theodore Neisser.[3]

Margaret Holstein, dau. of Lawrence and Margaret Holstein, Pilesgrove, b. Oct. 8, bapt. Nov. 1, 1762, by Rev. George Neisser. Sponsors: William and Christiana Guest, Obediah and Rebecca Lloyd.[3]

Dorthea Kats, dau. of Martin and Anna Dorthea Kats of Penn's Neck b. Jan. 29, 1762, bapt. at Philadelphia July 6, 1762, by Rev. George Neisser. Sponsors: Grandparents and Anna Parsons.[3]

Marriage

June 8, 1745; George Kyn, widower, aged 64, to Margaret Justis, widow, age 53, in the groom's house on Maurice River, in the presence of the entire Swedish congregation of said neighborhood, after the banns had been thrice published, -- first at Raccoon, next at Penn's Neck, and for the last time, in Maurice River. [3 & 3]

Burial Records
from the register of [1] the Church on Maurice River

1748 - John Hopman departed this life in the beginning of --- and was buried in the churchyard.

1748- Catharine Hopman, the wife of the above John Hopman, departed this life 12 days after her husband, and was buried in the churchyard.[1,3]

1748 - Peter Streng departed from this life Nov. 2, and was buried in the churchyard.

1748 - William Rosen (Rawson) departed this life in January and was buried in the churchyard.

1749 - Lydia Vanaman, dau. of Samuel Vanaman, departed this life in April, and was buried in the churchyard.

1749 - Samuel Iszard departed this life in April, and was buried in the churchyard.

1749 - John Garrison departed from this life in May, and was buried in the churchyard.

1749 - Gabriel Glann departed this life in June, and was buried in the churchyard.

1749 - Martha Vanaman, dau. of Gabriel Vanaman departed this life, about ---- years old, and was buried in the churchyard.

1750 - Mary Vanaman, wife of Samuel Vanaman, departed this life, March 1, and was buried in the churchyard.

1750 - Priscilla Jones, the daughter of Abraham Jones, about six years old, departed this life, 2nd day of April, and was buried in the churchyard.

1750 - Lydia Jones, the dau of Abraham Jones, about a year old, departed this life Oct 27, and was buried in the churchyard.

NEW ENGLAND TOWN BURYING GROUND
Fairton, Fairfield Township
Compiled by Frank D. Andrews

Rohada Sparks, wife of Henry Sparks died 28 Dec 1760, age 25 years.
Preston Stratten, d. 18 Nov 1759 age 18 years.
Benjamin Stratton, d. 20 Jul 1750 (1751) age 50 years.
Benjamin Stratton, son of Benjamin and Sarah Stratton, d. 2 Oct 1750, age 17 years.
Thomas Walling, d. 10 May 1765 age 29 years.
Elizabeth Westcot, wife of Joseph Wescot, d. 14 Oct 1770 age 57 years.
Ezekiel Wescote, d. 20 Mar 1763 age 19 years.
Rachel Westcote, d. 3 May 1751 age 38 years.
David Westcote, d. 16 Jul 1778 age 37 years.
William Ramsey, M.A., d. 5 Nov 1771 age 39 years. Pastor of the Presbyterian Church for 16 years.
David Sayre, Esq., d. 11 Apr 1767 age 47 years.
Ephraim Seeley, Esq. d. 22 Jun 1774 age 62 years.
Sarah Smith, wife of Revd. William Ramsey and Revd. Dr. Robert Smith of Pequia, d. 9 Aug 1801 aged 63 years.
Violetta Ogden, wife of Thomas Ogden, d. 19 Nov 1760 age 24 years.
Zephanian Ogden, d. 24 Mar --- age 52 years.
Ruth Page, wife of Capt. David Page, d. 30 Mar 1777 age 29 years.
Benjamin Parvin, d. 28 Mar 1755 age 31 years.
Thomas Parvin, d. 28 Aug 1743 age 80 years, 1 mo, 3 days.
Israel Petty, Jr., d. 11 Oct 1763 age 34 years.
David Powell, d. 24 Apr 24 1772 age 38 years.
Richard Powell, d. 9 Sep 1764 age 36 years.
Levi Preston, d. 17 Jan 1752 age 91 years.
Ephraim Ramsey, son of Revd William Ramsey and Sarah, his wife, d. 28 Jan 1765 age 9 months.
Abigal Nixon, wife of Reuben Nixon, d. 25 Dec 1770 age 21 years.
Reuben Nixon, d. 29 Oct 1773 age 27 years.
Jonathan Orange, d. 19 Feb 1764 age 41 years.
Abdon Ogden, d. 3 Mar 1773 age 23 years.
David Ogden, Esq., d. 1 Dec 1760 age 53 years.
Hannah Ogden, wife of David Ogden, d. 29 Apr 1742 age 36 years.
John Ogden, Esq., d. 22 Dec 1745 age 75 years.
John Ogden, Jr., Esq., d. 10 Mary 1759 age 52 years.
Joseph Ogden, Esq., d. 21 Jul 1772 age 48 years.

NEW ENGLAND TOWN BURYING GROUND 85

Sarah Ogden, wife of Thomas Ogden, d. 23 Mar 1760 age 38 years.
Thomas Ogden,, d. 10 Jan 1768 age 25 years.
David Fithian, d. 23 Feb 1754 age 45 years.
Hannah Harris, d. 14 Nov 1784 age 64 years 8 months.
Isaac Harris, d. 17 Oct ?75 (Stone broken, inscription partly gone.)
Jeremiah Harris, d. 22 Feb 1755 age 35 years.
Susannah Harris, wife of Capt. Thomas Harris, d. 2 Apr 1774 age 62 year.
Susanna Harris, d. 14 Nov 1784 age 64 years 8 months.
T H, d. 15 Feb 1759 age 5 years.
Thomas Harris, Jr., d. 6 Feb 1759 age 29 years.
Capt. Thomas Harris, d. 7 Apr 1783 age 72 years 5 months.
V. H. did. 25 Feb 1759 age 3 years.
Jonathan Loranco, d. 19 Feb 1774 age 41 years.
W M, d. 30 Aug 1769 age 9 months.
W M, d. 27 Aug 1770 age 2 years.
William Meek, d. 23 Dec 1773 age 48 years.
Thoephilus Elmer, Esq., d. 1 Aug 1783 age 54 years.
Theodotia Elmer, wife of Theophilus Elmer, d. 18 Feb 1765 age 34 years.
Mrs. Elmer, d. 10 Aug 1775.
Hannah Elmer, widow of Theophilus Elmer, Esq., d. 27 Sep 1783 age 53 years.
Timothy Elmer, Esq., d. 16 May 1780 age 32 years.
William Ramsey Elmer, son of the Honorable J. Elmer and Mary, his wife, d. 6 Nov 1784 age 4 years, 7 months. By his side lie 4 more of their children who all died in early infancy.
Abigail Daten, d. 20 Oct 1774 age 2 years.
Infant dau of David and Ann Daten,, d. 3 Apr 1760.
Eli Daten, d. 9 May 1775 age 23 years.
Joseph Dayten, d. 28 Nov 1770 age 56 years.
Prudence Daton, d. 21 Jul 1779 age 50 years.
Lois Diament, Sr., d. 21 Apr 1770 age 67 years.
Nathaniel Diament, Sr., d. 4 Apr 1767 age 72 years.
Abigail Elmer, relict of Daniel Elmer, dec'd, d. 2 Jul 1770 age 54 years.
Rev. Mr. Daniel Elmer, late Pastor of Christs Church, d. 14 Jan 1775 age 65 years.
Daniel Elmer, Esq., d. 2 May 1761 age 46 years.
Daniel Elmer, Esq., d. 30 Jun 1775 age 33 years.
James Boyd, d. 23 Dec 1775 age 40 years.
Mary Boyd, widow of James Boyd, d. 19 Sep 1812 age 80 years.
James Boyd, of Philadelphia, a merchant, d. 14 May 1795 age 28 years.
Judith Buck, wife of Ephraim Buck, d. 9 Mar 1769 age 33 years.

Sarah Burch, wife of James Burch, d. 2 Nov 1787 age 22 years.
Theophilus Burch, son of James and Sarah Burch, d. 11 Jan 1788 age 2 months 11 days.
John Clark, d. 1 Apr 1789 age 26 years.
Mariah Clun, dau of Charles and Rachel Clun, d. 20 Oct 1778 age 1 year.

BAPTIST CHURCH AT DIVIDING CREEK

About 1749 several families came from Cohansey and settled at Dividing Creek. In May, 1761 Church of the Dividing Creek was constituted and recognized as a Baptist Church. Rev. Samuel Heaton, from Cape May formed a committee consisting of: Rev. Samuel Heston, Jonadab Shepherd, David Shepherd, William Paulin, Thomas Shepherd, William Dollis, Seth Lore, Jonathan Lore, John Terry and Jeremiah Goff.

This committee along with Eve Sockwell, Patience Paulin, Sarah Terry, Nancy Shepherd and Temperance Shepherd signed the church covenant.

The names of the church members in 1761
Samuel Heaton, Minister
Jonadab Shepherd
David Shepherd, Deacon
William Dolles, Deacon
William Paulin
John Terry
Thomas Shepherd
Joseph Jones
John Garrison
John Robbins
William Pepper
William Newcomb
Eve Sockwell
Patience Paullin
Sarah Terry
Temperance Shepherd
Nance Shepherd
Margaret Jones
Rebecca Garrison
Sarah Robinson
Mary Robins
Abigal Bedent
Sarah Pepper
Rachel Garrison

Benjamin Blizzard
David Pague
Jonadab Shepherd
William Robinson
William Garrison
David Casto
Abbia Gandy
Esekiah Lore
Gideon Heaton
William Golden
Jacob Garrison
Isaac Scull
Joseph Enganfull
Mary Bragg
Naomy Blizzard
Prissilla Shepherd
Sarah Shepherd
Sarah Jones
Ruth Terry
Ann House
Mariah Sissen
Phebe Casto
Catherin Garrison
Mary Goldin
Tabitha Scull
Jane Enganfull.

Baptized in the year 1765
Jonathan Lore
John Bragg

EARLY RECORDS OF CUMBERLAND CO.

The following contributed to the fund to buy the parsonage in 1761:

Rev. Samuel Heaton	William Dolles	Silas Church
Jonadab Shepherd	Seth Lore	Jonadab Sockwell
David Shepherd	Jonathan Lore	Dickason
William Paullin	John Terry	Shepherd
Thomas Shepherd	Jeremiah Goff	
	Joseph Page	
Owan Ugnay	Daniel Lore	William Hewet
John Shaw	John Robins	John Holiday
William Newcomb	Garrett Garrison	Gideon Heaton
Isaac Reeves	Henry Wood	Isaac Garrison
Aron Gandy	Abel Sissen	Silas Bradford
John Bragg	James Anderson	Isaiah Reed

The Church at Cohansie

Enoch Shepherd	Eve Sockwell
Richard Lore	Ann Lore
Jacob Garrison	Cibel Robins
Joseph Whitaker	Aran Peterson
Cornelius Garrison	Randal Daniels
George Shaw	John Richardson
William Pepper	Daniel Taylor
Stephan Kinney	William Robinson
Gabriel Glann	William Robinson, Jr.
John Bedent	Nathaniel Hewet

The following paid to the building of the meeting house at Dividing Creeks 1772

Samuel Heaton, Minister	Thomas Shepherd
David Shepherd, Deacon	Abiah Gandy
William Dollis, Deacon	John Terry, Jr.
William Newcomb, Deacon	John Garrison
William Paulin	Stephen Clark, Esq.
Gideon Heaton, Clerk	Silas Newcomb
Jonathan Lore	Hosea Shepperd
John Terry	William Lore, Est.
John Robins	Dan Lore
Jonadab Shepherd	Richard Lore

BAPTIST CHURCH AT DIVIDING CREEK

John Terry
David Terry
William Auls
David Lore
David Page
Eligah Huet
Jonathan Wood
Silas Roberson
David Garrison
William Woodlard
David Gandy
William Mason
John Garrison
Levy Blisard
Daniel Reed
Moses Reves
William Persons
Gabril Glan
William Bright
Thomas Sheppard
Samuel Mils
William More
William Huet
Silas Bradfoot
Enock Boen
John Terry
William Garrison
Joseph Goff
Jeremiah Goff

William Madkiff
David Peterson
Cornelis Garrison
Jacob Garrison
John Rogers
Elbonar Sheppard
Jonathan Ryley
David Smith
Forster Wessket
John Blisard
Rachel Shaw
Benjamin Whittaker
John Robins
John Daniels
Captin Scull
Nathaniel Lore
Ephraim Sheppard
Daniel Lore
Philadelphia Church
Allaways Crick
Piscatanay
Scotch Plains
Coansey
Cape May Church
Jeremiah Leaman
Jonathan Hand
Wido Spicelor
Church Hopewell
South Hampton

The Church members 1793 - Rev. Garner Hunt, Pastor
Jonadab Sheppard
Daniel Tullis
William Pepper, Jr.
David Page
Hosea Sheppard
Patrich Burne
David Garrison
Abraham Garrison
Captain Price

Nathan Newcomb
William Mason
Silveneous Tubman
Jonathan Stites, dead
Reuben Cheeseman
Jonathan Terry
William Pepper (dec'd Dec 9)
Nathaniel Lore
Richardson Stevenson

John Tullis
Jacob Garrison
Jacob Jay
John Robinson
Amos Bradford
Deamon Whittiker
John Souders
Constant Long
Ambros Ledeu
Thomas Campble
Daniel Loper
John Hambleton
Temperance Lore
Mary Westcot
Elizabeth Sheppard
Rachel Tulis
Hannah Sheppard
Sarah Riley
Grace Page
Ruth Garrison
Phebe Heaton
Rachel Lore
Elizabeth Burns
Rachel Camel
Sarah Daniels
Mary Jinkins
Sary Kelsey
Pleasant Yates
Elizabeth Camel
Mrs. Price
Temperance Bradford (dec'd Dec 20)
Sarah Pepper
Temperance Robins
Prudence Newcomb
Mary Dollis
Prudence Stites
Mary Sydden
Mary Garrison
Rachel Whittiker
Elizabeth Jay

Ruth Lore
Rachel Syddens
Juda Mason
Elizabeth Lore
Phebe Bradford
Sarah Barrot
Cattren Brandford
Lydda Taler
Eunice Long
Dorcas Roberson
Sary Smith
Mary Campble
Elizabeth Chard
Omy Garrison
Elizabeth Lopper
John Tullis
Rachel Tullis
Elener Garrison
Sarah Daniels

Names of members Sep 10, 1810
Peter Campbell
Abram Garrison
Nathan Newcomb
Prudance Newcomb
Elizabeth Sheppard
Rachel Pepper
John Robbins
Temperance Robbins
Lyddea Mason
Martha Hand
Ruth Lore
Mary Garrison
Silvanus Tubman
Jeremiah Garrison
John Lore
John Sowder
Rebeca Laws
Jacob Jay
Elizabeth Jay

BAPTIST CHURCH AT DIVIDING CREEK 91

John Tullis
Sarah Tullis
Rachel Lore
Phebe Ladow
Elanor Garrison
Mary Garrison
Sarah Daniels
Sarah Smith
Sussannah Dollis
Silas Bradford
Hanah Sheppard
Dorcas Robeson
Neoma Garrison
Richard Heverson
Ezebel Heverson
Cathrine Bradford
Sarah Young
Elias Bradford
Hope Shaw
Daniel Loper

Mary Moor
Amos Bradford
Anna Bradford
William Pepper
Abiah Blizzard
John Orr
Elizabeth Blizzard
Hary Bradford
Joshua Garrison
Butler Newcomb
Annah Newcomb
Tabitha Conner
Mary Main
James Orr
Peggy Orr
Sopiah Orr
David Mason
Phebe Mason
Sarah Mason
Mary Bradford

GREENWICH PRESBYTERIAN CHURCH RECORDS

John Woodruff and Phebe Stratton m. 16 Aug 1757 and their children: a son, b. 7 Jan 1758, d. 9 Feb 1758; John Woodruff, 11 Mar 1759; Phebe Woodruff, b. 26 Dec 1761, d. 25 Apr 1762; Stratten Woodruff, b. 6 Aug 1763; Silas Woodruff, b. 7 Apr 1766.

Thomas Waithman and Elizabeth Carle m. 8 Apr 1756 and their children: Clemens Waithman, b. 29 Mar 1757; Thomas Waithman, b. 22 Feb 1769 (but suppose it means. 1759, C. E. S); Mary Waithman, b. 21 Jan 1762; Philathea Waithman, b. 1 April 1764; Elisabeth Waithman, b. 2 Dec 1766.

David Woodruff and his wife, Pheba, 20 Jun 1784 had their children: David, James, Noah and Ame baptized by Mr. Faitoute.

William Fithian and Deliverance Caruthers m. 8 May 1754 and their children: Hope Fithian, b. 9 Mar 1755; William Fithian, b. 22 Nov 1757; Deliverance Fithian, b. 8 Jun 1759; George Fithian, b. 24 1761 (March has been added in Dr. Fithian's handwriting, C. E. S.); Priscilla Fithian, b. 5 Jan 1763, d. 7 June 1764; James Fithian, b. 25 November 1766; Jeremiah was b. 18 June 1772; Esther Fithian, b. Nov. 26, 1774; Hannah Fithian, b. Feb. 29, 1776, m. to Isaac Coffee of Salem; Mathias, b. Oct. 21, 1776, d. Sept, 3, 1781.

William Fithian d. Nov. 25, 1788. Deliverance, wife William Fithian, d. Jan, 29, 1786.

James Fithian, 3rd son of William and Deliverance Fithian m. Mary, dau. of Jonathan and Mellicent Wood, May 31, 1787. Mary Fithian, wife of James Fithian d. Nov. 30, 1787.

James Fithian and Karenhappuch ..., his 2nd wife, m. March 18, 1789 and their children were: William Fithian. b. 18 Feb 1791; Job Fithian, b. 3 Feb 1793. Kerenhappuch Fithian, 2nd wife of James Fithian, d. 21 Dec 1794.

James Fithian m. Sarah Mills, his 3rd wife, 18 Jan 1797: Hope Fithian, b. Feb. 16, 1798 and James Carothers Fithian, b, Feb. 28, 1802.

James Fithian m. Elizabeth Ritchie, (widow of George Ritchie, his 4th wife, 7 Dec 1803: George R. Fithian, b. Sept 26, 1804; Isaac Fithian, b. March 10, 1806, Rhoda Fithian, b. Jul 2, 1809; Gervas Reeves Fithian, b. April 18, 1813, Deliverance Fithian, b. Feb. 23, 1819 (d. in 1821.).

James Fithian, the 3rd son of William and Deliverance Fithian, d. 28 Apr 1828, aged 61 years 5 months and 1 day.

William Fithian b. 21 Jan 1733, and was the son of Matthias and Martha (Hughes) Fithian. His wife Deliverance Carothers was b. Sept. 24, 1935.

Thomas Ewing, son of Thomas and Mary Ewing, was b. 6 Oct 1722 and Phebe Sayre, dau of Ananias and Martha Sayre, b. 23 Nov 1725 m. 24 of Nov 1743 and their children: Joel Ewing, b. 14 Feb 1744/5, d. 8 Jun 1745.

Phebe wife of Thomas Ewing, d. 23 Feb 1744/5.
Rachel, wife of Thomas Ewing, d. 29 Dec 1749.

Rachel Dixon, dau of James and Rebecca Dixon, b. 12 Dec 1726, m. Thomas Ewing 13 Aug 1745 and their children: Rebeca Ewing, b. 4 Aug 1746, d. 6 Oct 174; a son b. 26 Jun 1748, unbaptized; Dixon Ewing, b. Nov 21, 1749.
Sarah Vickers, dau of Philip and Hope Vickers, b. 8 Nov 1731 m. Thomas Ewing 20 Jun 1751 and their children: Rachel Ewing, b. 4 May 1752,O.S.; George Ewing, b. 18 Mar, 1754, N.S.; dau still born, b. 12 Feb, 1756; Hope Ewing, b. 28 Mar, 1757; Joel Ewing, b. 17 Mar, 1760; Phebe Ewing, b. 5 Nov, 1762; Hannah Ewing, b. 17 Jun 1765; Hope Ewing, b. 21 Oct 1767; Thomas Ewing, b. Apr 18, 1768, bapt 15 May, 1768, d. 25 May 1768.
Sarah, dau of Thomas and Sarah Ewing, b. 9 May 1769, bapt 11 Jun, 1769.

Thomas Ewing, d. 29 May 1771.

George Ewing, son of Thomas and Sarah Ewing, b. 18 Mar, 1754, n.s. and Rachel Harris, dau of Nathaniel and Abigail Harris, b. 2 Sep 1750, m. 10 Aug 1778 and their children: George Ewing, b. 11 Mar, 1779, bapt by the Rev Nehemiah Greenman; Abigail Ewing, b. 1 Feb, 1781.
John Reeves, b. 30 Jan, 1726 and Mabel Johnson, b. 3 Jun 1732, m 12 Sept 1750 and their children: Jonson, b. 11 Aug 1751; Elijah Reeves, b. 14 Mar 1753, d. 5 Oct 1755; Lemuel Reeves, b. 19 of Mar, 1755; Joseph Reeves, b. 25 Jun 1757; Mabel Reeves, b. 26 Nov 1759; Sarah Reeves, b. 13 of Jan 1752, d. the next day; Abraham Reeves, b. 30 Jul 1763; Unas (Eunice) Reeves, b. 6 Mar 1767; Stephen Reeves, b. 11 Feb 1769; Nancy Reeves, b. 6 Nov 1771.

Rev. Geo Faitoute and Euphemia, his wife and their children: Lidya Faitoute, bapt Dec 1, 1782 by Rev. Daniel McCalls; James Faitoute, bapt 5 Sep 1784.

Maskell Ewing, eldest son of Thomas and Mary Ewing, b. 31 Mar 1721 and Mary Padgett, eldest dau of Thomas and Dorothy Padgett, b. 15 May 1725, m. 31 Mar 1743 and their children: Abigail Ewing, b. 4 Feb 1744, bapt 20 May following; Phebe Ewing, b. 13 May 1746, bapt 19 Jun; Thomas Ewing, b. 13 Sep 1748, bapt 17 Oct following; Ame Ewing, b. 20 Jan 1751, bapt 28 Feb following; Mary Ewing, b. 26 Apr 1753, bapt 31 May following; Sarah Ewing, b. 19 Apr 1756, bapt 29 May following; Maskell Ewing, b. 30 Jan 1758, bapt 13 Mar following; Rachel Ewing, b. 25 Dec 1759, bapt 6 Feb following; David Ewing, b. 18 Mar 1752, bapt 21 Apr following; Susanna Ewing, b. 27 May, 1764, bapt 24 Jun following.

Thomas Ewing, son of Thomas and Mary Ewing m. Sarah Fithian, dau of Samuel and Abigail Fithian May 30, 1770.

Isaac Watson m. Abigail Ewing, dau of Maskell and Mary Ewing Feb 28, 1771.

Maskell Ewing, d. 6 Apr 1796, Mary Ewing, his wife d. 30 Oct 1798. Sarah Mulford, d. 1 Apr 1806.

Thomas Ewing, son of Maskell and Mary Ewing, b. 13 Sep 1748, d. 7 Oct 1782 m. May 30, 1770 Sarah Fithian, dau of Samuel and Abigail Fithian, b. 16 Feb 1752, bapt 24 Nov 1771 and their children: Samuel Fithian Ewing, b. 27 Sep 1771, bapt 24 Nov 1771, d. 21 Oct 1772 at noon; William Belford Ewing, b. 12 Dec 1776, bapt 8 Jun 1777.

William Mulford and Sarah Ewing m. 5 Apr 1787 and their children: Thomas Ewing Mulford, b. 25 Jun 1788; James Woodburn Mulford, b. 25 Jun 1791.

John Peck, b. 15 Feb 1743.

William Belford Ewing m. Harriet Seeley, dau of Joseph Seeley and Rebecca, of Deerfield 16 Jun 1808 and their children: James Josiah Ewing, b. 4 Jun 1809; Harriet Seeley Ewing, b. 8 Jan 1812, d. 6 Sep 1812, aged 8 months. Harriet Ewing, wife of William Belford Ewing, d. 13 Jan 1812.

John Bently, b. 30 Oct 1738 and Hannah Caruthers, b. 28 Nov 1738 m. 23 Oct 1752 and their children: Elizabeth Bently, b. 19 Sep 1763; Gardner Bently, b. 9 Feb 1765; Lydia Bently, b. 7 Feb 1767.

David Reed and his wife, Rachel had two children, Sarah and James Reed bapt. 22 Jun 1783; Rachel Reed bapt 7 May 1784.

Benjamin Peck, b. 24 Dec 1745.
Richard Caruthers, b. 28 Dec 1740 and Philenah Mills, b. 25 Feb 1749, m. 24 Sep 1766 and their children: Obediah Caruthers, b. 4 Mar 1769, d. 21 Sep 1786; Rebecca Caruthers, b. 2 Apr 1771.

Philenah Caruthers, wife of Richard Caruthers, d. 30 Apr 1777.

Richard Caruthers m. Mary Ewing, dau of Maskell and Mary Ewing Dec 19, 1780 and their child: Richard Ewing Caruthers, b. 6 Nov 1781, bapt Jun 1781, d. 9 Feb, 1790.
William Carle, b. 28 Feb 1730 and Issable Dixon, b. 27 Aug 1732 m. 28 Mar 1753 and their children: Rebecca Carle, b. 12 Apr 1754; Pamela Carle, b. 8 Jan 1756; Issable Carle, b. 25 Oct 1759; Burton Carle, b. 7 Nov 1761; Jeremiah Carle, b. 7 May 1765; Lusinda Carle, b. 19 Feb 1768.
Francis Brewster m. Mary Crawford 23 Jul 1730 and their children: Daniel Brewster, b. 16 Aug, 1734; Ebenezar Brewster, b. 26 Apr 1741; Benjamin Brewster, b. 24 Mar 1743; Hannah, b. 9 Aug, 1753.
Francis Brewster m. Rebecca Peck, 10 Jan 1758 and their children: Ruth Brewster, b. 18 Nov 1758; Anna Brewster, b. 10 Aug 1760; Samuel Brewster, b. 17 Jul 1763; Joseph Brewster, b. 20 Oct 1765; Francis Gilbert Brewster, b. 19 Oct 1768, bapt. 11 Dec 1768.

Francis Brewster d. 25 Nov 1768.

Ladis Walling and Ruth Brewster m. 25 Sep 1775 and their children: Jonathan Walling, b. 5 Nov 1777; Ladis Walling, b. 18 Oct 1779; Mary Walling, b. 18 Jul 1781; George Walling, b. 21 Mar 1785.
John Gibbon m. Ester Seeley 30 Mar 1761 and their children: Nicholas Gibbon, b. 29 Nov 1761; Hannah Gibbon, b. 23 Apr 23, 1763; Ephriam Gibbon, b. 8 Nov 1764; Leonard Gibbon, b. 17 Nov 1766.
Phineas Carel, b. 22 Jul 1739 and Rachel Mills, b. 8 Sep 1744 m. 16 Sep 1760 and their children: Elizabeth Carel, b. 16 Oct 1761, bapt 1762; Ephraim Carel, b. 1765, bapt the same year.
Maskell Mills Carll bapt 25 Jan 1783.
Thomas Parks and his wife, Sarah and their children: Rachel Parks, b. 4 May 1757, bapt 10 Oct 1781; Rebecca Parks, b. 12 Dec 1762, bapt 10 Oct 1781; James Dixon Parks, b. 5 Apr 1765, bapt. 12 May 1782.
William Shute, b. 11 Apr 1728, bapt 20 May 1728 and Hope Moor, b. 19 Nov 1738, bapt 10 Jan 1737, m. 28 Jan 1756 and their children: Margaret Shute, b. 9 Oct 1757, bapt 15 Aug 1759; Sarah Shute, b. 18

Feb 1761, bapt 22 Apr 1761; Samuel Shute, b. 28 Feb 1763, bapt 22 Apr 1763; Enoch Shute, b. 6 Mar 1765, bapt 10 May 1765; Mary Shute, b. 29 Jul 1767, bapt 18 Sep 1767.
Joel Fithian and his wife, Elizabeth and their child: Charles Beatty Fithian, bapt. 24 Aug 1783 by Rev. George Faitoute.
William Mulford and his wife, Prudence, m. 24 Feb 1762 and their children: Abigail Mulford, b. 25 Jan 1763; Jacob Mulford, b. 3 Mar 1766, bapt. in May 1766; Hope Mulford, b. 5 Jan 1768; William Mulford, Jr., b. 11 Dec 1778; Maskell Mulford, b. 6 Sep 1781.

William Mulford, d. 19 Apr 1801 aged 62 years 7 mo and 6 days.

James Solley, son of Timothy and Margaret Solley, b. 22 May 1787, bapt. Dec 1792 by Rev. Ethan Osborn.
John Miller, b. 11 Jan 1711 and Rachel Reed, b. 11 Dec 1722 m. 2 Nov 1740 and their children: Samuel Miller, b. 22 Sep 1741, d. 4 Aug 1754; Keziah Miller, b. 13 Mar 1744, d. 28 Sep 1748; Mary Miller, b. 19 Mar 1748; Eunice Miller, b. 1 Oct 1747. {These two dates are as here copied, but probable Mary's birth date should be 1746.]; Ephraim Miller, b. 6 Apr 1750; William Miller, b. 12 Dec 1751; Rachel Miller, b. 2 Sep 1755, d. 6 Sep 1762; Rebecca Miller, b. 11 Apr 1760, d. 16 Aug 1762; John Miller, b. 2 Oct 1762; Rachel Miller, b. 16 Jul 1766.

Jacob Mulford, b. 12 Mar 1714 and Jean, his wife, b. 20 Dec 1713 and their children: William Mulford, b. 13 Sep 1738, d. 19 Apr 1801; John Mulford, b. 2 Mar 1741; Jacob Mulford, b. 11 Apr 1743; Lovesoe Mulford, (dau), b. 3 Mar 1745; Jonathan Mulford, b. 29 Jul 1747; Jean Mulford, b. 29 Jul 1753.

Benjamin Lupton, b. 1719, Ame, his wife, b. 1734.
Esther Lupton, b. 1743.
Benjamin Parvin, b. 1753.
David Parvin, b. 1755.
Rachel Mills, b. 1762.
Jerymiah Bishop, b. 1745 and Anne Garison, b. 1742 m. 25 Feb 1767.

David Mills, b. 7 Mar 1736 and Abigal Garison, b. 24 Dec 1731 m. 25 Oct 1756 and their children: Sarah Mills, b. 24 Apr 1758; Rachel Mills, b. 13 Dec 1762; Daniel Mills, b. 9 Jun 1766.

Abigal Mills, wife of David Mills, d. 10 Jun 1766.

David Mills and his 2nd wife, Ann Garison, b. 12 Oct 1742 m. 17 Mar 1767.
Thomas Ewing from Londonderry in Ireland m. Mary Maskell 27 Mar 1720 and their children: Maskell Ewing, b. 31 Mar 1721; Thomas Ewing, b. 6 Oct 1722; Mary Ewing, b. 25 or 27 Feb 1726/7 o.s.; John Ewing, b. 7 Jun 1732; Joshua Ewing, b. 8 or 7 Nov 1736; Samuel Ewing, b. 23 Apr 1739; James Ewing, b. 12 Jul 1744.
Thomas Ware m. Margaret Reed 14 Jan 1750 and their children: Priscilla Ware, b. 29 Mar 1750 or 1751; Jacob Ware, b. 13 Feb 1752; Amy Ware, b. 22 Sep 1755; Thomas Ware, b. 15 Dec 1757; Hannah Ware, b. 20 Sep 1760; Isaac Ware, b. 13 Apr 1764; Lydia Ware, b. 21 Oct 1767; Enoch Ware, b. 6 Mar 1769.

Thomas Ware, d. 3 May 1769.

Daniel Bishop, b. 9 Oct 1739 and Rodah Platts, b. 24 Feb 1745 m. 11 Feb 1762 and their children: Daniel Bishop, b. 8 Nov 1762; Phebe Bishop, b. 27 Aug 1765; Ephraim Bishop, b. 17 May 1767.
James Ewing, youngest son of Thomas Ewing and Mary Maskall, b. in Greenwich twp 12 Jul 1744 and Martha Boyd, eldest dau of James and Mary Boyd, late of Belleaston, Antrim County, Ireland, b. in that place 1755 m. at Bridgeton, Cumberland County, in Fairfield Congregation 15 Oct 1776 by Rev. William Hollingshead and their child: Charles Ewing, b. at Queensborough, Burlington County, N.J 8 Jul 1780, bapt 1 Jul 1781 at Fairfield by Rev. William Hollingshead.
Jerymiah Bennett m. Sarah Beriman 22 Nov 1757 and their children: Lovise Bennett, b. 20 Jul 1760; Leonard Bennett, b. 12 Aug 1762; Jerymiah Bennett, b. 7 Aug 1764; Sarah Bennett, b. 27 Jun 1766.

Joseph Fithian m. Hannah Vickers, 31 Jul 1746 and their children Philip Fithian, b. 29 Dec 1747, d. in New York 9 Sep 1776; Enoch Fithian, b. 11 Apr 1750; Josiah Fithian, b. 8 Oct 1752; Rebecca Fithian, b. 19 Apr 1755; Jonathan Fithian, b. 18 Oct 1757; Amos Fithian, b. 11 Oct 1759; Thomas Fithian, b. 27 Jan 1767.
John Finlew m. Sarah 12 Sep 1759 and his children: Elizabeth Finlew, b. 24 Dec 1760; Finlaw Finlew, b. 13 Jan 1762; Elenor Finlew, b. 16 Jan 1763.
Philip Stathans m. Hannah Mills, 25 Apr 1753 and their children: Thomas Stathans, b. 29 Mar 1754; Sarah Stathans, b. 1 Oct 1757; Deliverance Stathans, b. 5 Jun 1760; Rebecca Stathans, b. 10 Mar

1762; Dorcas Stathans, b. 21 Nov 1764; Naomi Stathans, b. 28 Mar 1766.
Thomas Reeves, b. 28 Feb 1727/8 and his wife, Thankful m. 12 Jun 1756 and their children: John Reeves, b. 23 Mar 1755; Josiah Reeves, b. 5 Sep 1757; Hannah Reeves, b. 25 Apr 1759; Thomas Reeves, b. 18 Dec 1760; Mary Reeves, b. 23 Dec 1762; Sarah Reeves, b. 16 Dec 1764; Abigal Reeves, b. 4 Jan 1767; Ame Reeves, b. 4 Jan 1769; Anna Reeves, b. 10 Mar 1772.
Joseph Fithian, b. 12 Aug 1724, d. 8 Feb 1772 and Hannah, wife of Joseph, d. 2 Feb 1772.
Samuel Fithian, son of William and Margaret Fithian of East Hampton, on Long Island, d. 1700, 1701 or 1702.
Josiah Fithian, son of Samuel and Priscilla Fithian, d. 3 Apr 1741 and his wife, Sarah and their children: John Fithian, d. 24 Mar 1732; Jeremiah Fithian, d. no date; Samuel Fithian, d. 2 Nov 1777; Hannah Fithian, d. 29 Nov 1799; Esther Fithian, d. no date; Joseph Fithian, d. 7 Feb 1772; Sarah Fithian, d. no date; Josiah Fithian, d. 24 Nov 1766.
Samuel Fithian, 3rd son of Josiah and Sarah Fithian d. 2 Nov 1 1777; Phebe Fithian, wife of Samuel Fithian, d. 12 Mar 1764.
Ephraim Fithian, b. 9 Feb 1739 and his wife, Temperance, b. 24 Oct 1740 m. 4 Feb 1761 and their children: Mathias Fithian, b. 20 Dec 1761; Ira Fithian, b. 23 Jul 1766.

William Fithian, d. at East Hampton, Long Island, 1678 and his wife, Margaret and their children: Enoch Fithian, Samuel Fithian, Sarah Fithian, Hannah Fithian and Martha Fithian. No birth dates given.

Samuel Fithian, son of William and Margaret Fithian, of East Hampton m. Priscilla Burnett of South Hampton, 6 Mar 1679 and their children: John Fithian, b. 1 Sep 1681; Josiah Fithian, b. 6 May 1685; Samuel Fithian, b. 17 Apr 1688; Esther Fithian, b. 6 Mar 1691/2; Mathias Fithian, b. 3 Feb 1694; William Fithian, b. 23 Mar 1698.
Josiah Fithian son of Samuel Fithian and his wife, Priscilla m. Sarah Dennis of Cumberland County, NJ 7 Nov 1706 and their children: John Fithian, b. 5 May 1709; Jeremiah Fithian, b. 5 Apr 1713; Samuel Fithian, b. 12 Oct 1715; Hannah Fithian, b. 5 Nov 1718; Esther Fithian, b. 12 Apr 1721; Joseph Fithian, b. 12 Aug 1724; Sarah Fithian, b. no date; Josiah Fithian, b. 20 Sep 1728.
Samuel Fithian, 3rd son of Josiah and Sarah Fithian m. Phebe Seeley, dau of Ephraim Seeley, 3 Sep 1741 and their children were: Hannah Fithian, b. 4 Aug 1742; Rachel Fithian, b. 7 Jul 1744; Amy Fithian, b.

Jul 16, 1745; Joel Fithian, b. 29 Sep 1748; Elizabeth Fithian, b. 13 Dec 1750; Mary Fithian, b. 1 Apr 1752; Sarah Fithian, b. 3 Mar 1754; Ruth Fithian, b. 25 May 1756; Seeley Fithian, b. 15 Oct 1758; Samuel Fithian, b. 23 Jul 1761.

Joel Fithian, eldest son of Samuel and Phebe Fithian and Rachel, youngest dau of Jonathan and Anne Holmes and Anne m. 3 Sep 1771 and their children: Josiah Fithian, b. 30 Sep 1776.

Rachel Fithian, wife of Joel Fithian, d. 12 Sep 1779.

Joel Fithian m. 2nd to Elizabeth, dau of Rev. Charles Beatty and Ann (Reading) 4 Mar 1780 and their children: Charles B. Fithian, b. 18 Dec 1782; Samuel Fithian, b. 26 Feb 1785, d. 28 Sept 1806; Philip Fithian, b. 24 Jan 1787; Erkurius B. Fithian, b. 10 May 1792.

Jonathan Holmes and his wife, Anna m. 7 Jul 1729 and their children: Eunice Holmes, b. 9 May 1736; Phebe Holmes, b. 14 Feb 1738; Anna Holmes, b. 23 Oct 1739; Abijah Holmes, b. 3 Apr 1741; Rachel Holmes, b. 14 Jan 1751.

In Dr. Fithian's handwriting: Eunice Holmes m. --- Brewster; Phebe Holmes m. Dr. Samuel Ward; Anna Holmes m. Daniel Clark; Abijah Holmes m. Rachel Seeley; Rachel Holmes m. Joel Fithian, d. 12 Feb 1779.

Abijah Holmes m. Rachel Seeley 18 May 1767 and their children: Sarah Holmes, b. 1 May 1771; Mary Holmes, b. 29 Mar 1774; Jonathan Holmes, b. 10 Sep 1776; John Holmes, b. 3 Aug 1778; Ephraim Holmes, 13 Jul 1780.

Enos Reeves b. 4 Feb 1753.

John McGillard m. Hannah Reves 28 Aug 1758 and their children: John McGillard, b. 3 Jul 1759; James McGillard, b. 11 Dec 1761; Hannah McGillard, b. 5 Apr 1766, d. 16 Oct 1767.

John McGillard, d. 1 Nov 1767.

Alexander Moore, b. Sep 1706 m. Sarah Reves, Oct 1747 and their children: Sarah Moore, b. 21 Aug 1748, m. 12 Feb 1767; Ann Moore, b. 8 Sep 1753; Alexander Moore, b. 30 Aug 1754.

John More, son of Jacob and Abigil More, b. 3 Mar 1738 and their children: Azariah More, b. 23 Jul 1739; Joseph More, b. 12 Apr 1742;

Ruth More, b. 1 Jul 1744; Mary More, b. 12 Mar 1746; Martha More, b. 13 Dec 1747; Bathsheba More, b. 1 Mar 1750.

Abigail More, relict of Jacob More, d. 23 Jul 1794 aged 83 years.

Isaac Mills and Rebecca, his wife m. Mar 1762 and their children: Charles Mills, b. 3 Nov 1763, bapt May following; Lois Mills, b. 16 Aug 1766, bapt Sept following.

James Booth Hunt, eldest son of Batholomew and Margaret Hunt, b. 28 Oct 1753 m. Sarah Ewing, dau of Maskell Ewing, Esq. & Mary, his wife, b. 19 Apr 1756 m. 12 May 1782 and their children: Thomas Ewing Hunt, 2 Mar 1783; Reuben Hunt, b. 9 Feb 1785; Sarah Hunt, b. 30 Mar 1787, d. 11 Aug 1789; James B. Hunt, b. 2 Mar 1790, d. 28 Aug 1791; William Ferguson Hunt, b. 31 Dec 1792.

Jean Campbell and her children: James; Elizabeth; Charles; Rebecca; Sarah; Nicholas. All baptized in infancy (no date given).

William Ferguson Hunt and Susan Ewing, dau of Maskell Ewing, Esq. m. 2 Apr 1789 and their child: Mary, b. 18 Oct 1791, bapt. May 1792.

John Burgin and Zeruriah Beriman m. 7 Jul 1757 and their child: Gilbert Burgin, b. 14 Apr 1758.

Zeruiah wife of John Burgin, d. 15 Sep 1759.

John Burgin m. 2nd wife Elizabeth Abel 12 Mar 1761 and their children: Hannah Burgin, b. 31 Mar 1762; Reuben Burgin, b. 27 Sep 1763; George Burgin, b. 15 Jul 1765; Ruth Burgin, b. 18 Aug 1767.

Constant Smith b. 11 Oct 1742 m. Rebeca McNight b. 7 Jan 1744 or 1745 and their child: Hannah Smith, b. 17 Dec 1767.

Daniel Brewster m. Eunice Holmes 26 May 1756 and their children: Mary Brewster, b. 21 Oct 1757; Abijah Brewster, b. 22 Jun 1759; Amee Brewster, b. 15 Mar 1762; Jonathan Brewster, b. 29 Mar 1764; Francis Brewster, b. 4 Nov 1766, d. 27 Dec 1766.

Nathan Lupton, b. 1 Feb 1707 and his wife, Susannah, b. 16 Oct 1716 m. 25 Dec 1734 and their children: Phebe Lupton, b. 25 Aug 1737; Amee Lupton, b. 17 Oct 1739; Jeams Lupton, b. 1 Feb 1743; John Lupton, b. 11 Jan 1748; Rachel Lupton, b. 1 May 1750; Hannah Lupton, b. 15 Sep 1752; Rumah Lupton, b. 15 Sep 1754; Nathan Lupton, b. 3 Jul 1757.

James Ward m. Parthenia Beriman 17 Sept 1751 and their children: Lovisa, b. 18 Feb 1756; Oliver, b. 14 Aug 1764; Mary, b. 8 Mar 1767.

Stephen Lupton and wife and their son: Stephen Lupton, bapt. 17 Aug 1783.

Richard Wood b. Jun 5, 1745; Mary Wood b. 14 Nov 1747.

GREENWICH PRESBYTERIAN CHURCH 101

Bartholomew Hunt and his wife, Margaret m. 29 Apr 1749 and their children: James Booth Hunt, b. 28 Oct 1753; John Hunt, b. 28 Apr 1756; Elizabeth Hunt, b. 28 Aug 1758; William Hunt, b. 14 Jan 1761; Reuben Hunt, b. 24 Mar 1763; Esther Hunt, b. 29 Jul 1765.
John Hunt, son of Bartholomew m. Anna Brewster, dau of Francis and Rebecca Brewster 1 Jun 1778 and their children: Richard Hunt, b. 26 Apr 1779; Elizabeth Hunt, b. 10 May 1782.

John Hunt, d. 8 Oct 1787; Reuben Hunt, d. 18 Aug 1789.

Preston Bishop, b. 17 Jun 1739 and Esther Woodruff, his wife, b. 1 Jul 1740 m. 22 May 1761 and their child: Rachel Bishop, b. 4 Mar 1762, d. 1771.
Samuel Miller and Experience Read m. 9 Sep 1735 and their children: Noah Miller, b. 23 Nov 1736; Israel Miller, b. 19 Jun 1744; Joel Miller, b. 22 Sep 1747; Lovice Miller, b. 16 Nov 1752.
Noah Miller, son of Samuel and Experience Miller m. Mary Mills Oct 1752 and their children: Oliver Miller, b. Sept 1763; Ephraim Miller, b. Oct 1765; Samuel Miller, b. Nov 1767.
William Tullis and his wife, Elinor Denton and their children: Ann Tullis, b. 13 Sep 1739; William Tullis, b. 22 Aug 1742; John Tullis, b. 18 Feb 1745; Daniel Tullis, b. 3 Sep 1747.
William Tullis m his 2nd wife, Mary Platts and their children: Moses Tullis, b. 13 May 1752; Mary Tullis, b. 23 Aug 1756; Ellinor Tullis, b. 1 Jan 1759; Eli Tullis, b. 19 Aug 1761; Ruth Tullis, b. 8 Oct 8, 1763; Annah Tullis, b. 2 Aug 1765.
Silas Parvin and Lidia Jones m. 11 Jun 1736 and their children: Silas Parvin, b. 4 Jun 1737; Lovisa Parvin, b. 23 Dec 1739; Ann Parvin, b. 18 Aug 1742; Lydia Parvin, b. 4 Jun 1745; Clarance Parvin, b. 21 Jul 1750; Lydia Parvin, b. 2 Jul 1753.
Thomas Harris and his wife Pamely and their child: Rebeccah bapt 1 Dec 1782.
Richard Sayre b. 4 Sept 1748.
Children of Moses Platts: Rachel Platts, b. 27 Nov 1725; Mary Platts, b. 25 Apr 1728; Elezebeth Platts, b. 1 Dec 1731; Phebe Platts, b. 28 Jan 1733; Sarah Platts, b. 17 Oct 1738; David Platts, b. 24 Mar 1739; Judah (Judith) Platts, b. 9 Aug 1741; Rodah Platts, b. 17 Feb 1744; Moses Platts, b. 25 Mar 1759.
Sabra Woodruff, dau of Enos Woodruff and Sarah, his wife bapt 9 Nov 1782 by Rev. Geo. Faitoute.

Unis (Eunice) Bennett, dau of James Bennett and Dorcas, his wife bapt 9 Nov 1782 by Rev. Geo. Faitoute.

Peter Soulard m. Mary Piate 20 Oct 1738 and their children: John Soulard, b. no date; Mary Soulard, b. 21 Apr 1740.

John Soulard, son of Peter and Mary Soulard m. Hannah Mulford, b. 5 Jun 1762 and their children: Rachel Soulard, b. 16 Nov 1762, bapt Oct following; John Soulard, b. 28 Nov 1764, bapt 5 Apr 1768.

Jacob Mulford, b. 11 Apr 1743 m. Sarah Peek, b. 16 Jul 1738 m. 3 Jul 1766.

William Mulford, son of W. & Prudence Mulford b. 17 Dec 1778 and Elizabeth Bacon, dau of Davis and Sarah Bacon, b. 28 Feb 1787, m. 23 Feb 1804. Elizabeth Mulford, d. 6 Sep 1805.

Jonathan Mulford, b. 29 Jul 1747 and Lewse (Louisa) Smith, b. 20 Mar 1748 m. 24 Jun 1767.

John Bereman and Sarah Bateman m. 29 Mar 1757 and their children: Mary Bereman, b. 16 Feb 1758; Zerviah Bereman, b. 5 Jan 1760; Thomas Bereman, b. 9 Dec 1761; Jonathan Bereman, b. 23 Feb 1766; Ephraim Bereman, b. 16 Mar 1768.

Daniel Maskell, son of Thomas and Marcy Maskell, b. 15 Oct 1728 and Elizabeth Garison, his 2nd wife, b. 12 Mar 1730 m. 28 Dec 1756 and their children: Clemmens Maskell, b. 6 Oct 1757; Hannah Maskell, b. 26 Oct 1759; Constant Maskell, b. 28 Nov 1761, d. 4 Aug 1762; Mary Maskell, b. Almedia Maskell, b. 3 Mar 1765, d. 8 Dec 1766; Thomas Maskell, b. 18 Feb 1767.

Thomas Maskell and Bythia Parsons m. 1658.

Thomas Maskell, son of Thomas and Bythia Maskell m. Marcy Stathem, dau of Thomas and Ruth (Udell) Stathem.

Thomas Maskell, son of Thomas and Marcy Maskell, b. 1721 m. Esther Fithian, dau of Jeremiah and Martha (Carll) Fithian and their children: Abijah Maskell, b. 1773; Sarah, no date; Hannah Maskell, no date.

Thomas Maskell, son of Thomas and Marcy Maskill, d. 9 Sep 1803.
Esther Maskell, wife of Thomas Maskell, d. 11 Sep 1805.

John Grimes and Temperance Bennet, m. by Rev. Andrew Hunter 1766.
Rev. Andrew Hunter was ordained in Greenwich congregation 1 Sep 1746 and m. Amy Stockton, 11 Oct 1748.
Rev. Daniel Lawrence and his children: Deborah Lawrence, b. 7 Nov 1761; Daniel Lawrence, b. 21 Jul 1764. Under his care, Ann

Lawrence, b. 27 1753; Benjamin Lawrence 26 Apr 1757 and four negroes viz: Sila, Vilat, Charity and George.

James McNight and Rebecca Pery and their children: Hannah McNight, b. 8 Aug 1736; John McNight, b. 12 Jan 1738; Samuel McNight, b. 1 Jan 1742; Rebeca McNight, b. 7 Jan 1744; Elizabeth McNight, b. 1 Aug 1741, d. 1742.

Rebeca McNight m. 2nd to John Finlaw and their children: David Finlew, b. 28 Aug 1749; Sarah Finlaw, b. 3 Mar 1751; Nathan Finlaw, b. 2 Jan 1754.

Samuel McNight m. Mercy Smith 10 Sep 1766 and their child: John McNight, b. 9 Aug 1767.

Lot and Judith Fithian m. 17 Dec 1752: and their children: Clover Fithian, b. 20 Sep 1753; Israel Fithian, b. 13 Aug 1755; Isaac Fithian, b. 20 Feb 1757; Elis Fithian, b. 20 Nov 1758, d. 1 Sep 1759; Elis Fithian, b. 21 Mar 1761, d. 18 May 1764; Elizabeth Fithian, b. 18 Mar 1764.

Selas (Seeley) Mills and Elizabeth Reed m. 31 Jan 1739 and their children: Sarah Mills, b. 1 Jan 1740, d. May 1753; John Mills, b. 26 Jun 1742, d. 20 Mar 1746; Mary Mills, b. 22 Aug 1744, m. Jerymiah Mills 3 Jul 1759; Elizabeth Mills, b. 13 May 1747; Rumah Mills, b. 18 May 1749, d. Sep 1753; Jane Mills, b. 12 Aug 1752; Sarah Mills, b. 10 Jan 1756, d. Jan 1759; Theodisia Mills, b. 9 Sep 1757; Thomas Mills, b. 19 Oct 1760, d. Mar 1761; Naomi Mills, b. 15 Dec 1761.

Thomas Brown, b. 22 Nov 1740 and Martha Peek, b. 21 Nov 1740 m. 29 Dec 1762 and their child: Thomas Brown, b. 2 Aug 1764.

Thomas Brown m. 2nd wife, Sarah Fithian, dau of Samuel and Phebe Fithian and their child: Samuel Fithian Brown, b. 3 Jan 1779.

Sarah Brown, wife of Thomas Brown, d. 23 Nov 1779.

Thomas Brown and his 3rd wife, Rebecca Fithian, dau of Joseph and Hannah Fithian m. 5 Jan 1778. (This is evidently an error on the part of the recorder.) and their children: Hannah Brown, b. before 1780; Amos Brown, b. 4 Jul 1792; Enoch Brown, b. 13 Oct 1795.

Lydia Woodruf, b. 13 Oct 1742 m. Joseph Buck of Cape May, 19 Jan 1766. Joseph Buck, d. 2 Jun 1768.

Daniel Clark, b. 25 Jul 1740 and Anna Holmes, b. 23 Oct 1739 m. 19 Aug 1761 and their children: Mary Clark, b. 29 Mar 1762; Charles Clark, b. 7 Feb 1764, bapt 16 Jun 1765; Anna Clark, b. 21 May 1766, bapt the same year; Phebe Clark, b. 19 Sep 1767, bapt; Abijah Clark, b. 22 Jan 1769, bapt and, d. 4 Feb 1770; Daniel Clark, b. 20 Feb 1771, bapt.

Anna Clark, wife of Daniel Clark, d. 18 Apr 1772

Daniel Clark and 2nd wife, Rachel Fithian, b. 7 Jul 1743 m. 19 Nov 1772 by Rev. Andrew Hunter and their child: Charles Clark, b. 19 Oct 1773, bapt.
Daniel Clark, d. 13 Dec 1774; Rachel, relict of Daniel Clark and dau of Samuel Fithian, Esq and his wife Sarah, d. 22 Oct 1822.
Joshua Ewing, fifth son of Thomas and Mary Ewing, b. 17 Nov 1736 and Hannah Harris, youngest dau of Nathaniel and Elizabeth Harris, b. 5 Sep 1739 m. 10 Dec 1760 and their children: Artemas Ewing, b. 30 Oct 1761; Pelmis Ewing, b. 31 Jan 1763; Joshua Ewing, b. 25 May 1765; Ruth Ewing, b. 22 Jan 1768, d. 26 Mar 1776; James Ewing, b. 3 Aug 1770; Robert Ewing, b. 2 Apr 1773; Elizabeth Ewing, b. 18 Jan 1776; Anna Ewing, b. 24 Aug 1779.

Entries made by Dr. Fithian.

Jeremiah Bacon, of Greenwich, Salem County, Taylor deeded to Henry Joyce and Thomas Maskell of the same place one acre of land on which the First Presbyterian Church was erected.

Rev. Andrew Hunter, pastor, d. 28 Jul 1775 aged 60 years.
Rev. George Faitoute commenced his services in 18 Aug 1781, was installed as pastor 8 Apr 1782. Rev. Faitoute resigned 1788 or 1789 and was installed as pastor of the church at Jamaica, Long Island, 15 Dec 1789.
Rev. William Clarkson was installed as pastor of the United Churches of Greenwich and Bridgeton 4 Nov 1794.

Marriages from the year 1781 to 1789 at the Greenwich Presbyterian Church.

John Woodruff m. Catherine Keen 4 Dec 1781.
Bartholomew Hunt m. Eleanor Whitsnack, 7 Jan 1782.
George Shimp m. Mary Folk 19 Mar 1782.
Sylvanus Smith m. Sarah Heritage 20 Mar 1782.
James Booth Hunt m. Sarah Ewing 13 May 1782.
Joel Miller m. Mary Reeves 25 Jun 1782.
John Buck m. Priscilla Padgett 9 Jul 1782.
Daniel Brown m. Mary Donaldson 11 Jul 1782.
Jeremiah Leake m. Susannah Harris 24 Aug 1782.

GREENWICH PRESBYTERIAN CHURCH 105

John Jacquett m. Mary Pierson 10 Oct 1782.
Nathaniel Johnson m. Phebe Smith 4 Dec 1782.
Henry Lawrence m. Mary Waithman 13 Jan 1783.
Thomas Remington m. Sarah Waithman 29 Jan 1783.
Isaac Hall m. Abigail Mulford 10 Mar 1783.
Jonathan Moore m. Miriam Hinchman 19 Mar 1783.
John Harris m. Elizabeth Bacon 8 Apr 1783.
Levi Leake m. Mable Reeves 30 Jul 1783.
Ebenezor Woodruff m. Mary Smith 12 Aug 1783.
Ezekiel Mulford m. Mary Parker 28 Aug 1783.
John Mills m. Elizabeth Stretch 20 Oct 1783.
Benjamin Russell m. Mary Whitaker 26 Nov 1783.
Thomas Karrell m. Elizabeth Donnell 8 Dec 1783.
Enos Ewing m. Rachel Ewing 9 Dec 1783.
Samuel Watson m. Hannah Skellinger 31 Dec 1783.
Moses Platts m. Hannah Lupton 6 Apr 1784.
David Evans m. Lovisa Bennett 20 Apr 1784.
Aaron Parvin m. Lovisa Stacks 29 Jun 1784.
John Brooks m. Judith Robinson 19 Sep 1784.
George Kellor m. Elizabeth Shimp 23 Nov 1784.
Isaac Patrick m. Phebe Corrington 28 Dec 1784.
Doctor Benjamin Peck m. Sabra Woodruff 5 Jan 1785.
Benoi Dare to Rachel Sheppard m. 17 Jan 1785.
David Casto m. Amy Biggs 16 Mar 1785.
Lott Randolph m. Phebe Mulford 21 Mar 1785.
Charles Mills m. Dorcas Stathem 12 Apr 1785.
Jonah Terry m. Reuma Lupton 25 Apr 1785.
Daniel Bishop m. Eunice Reeves 31 May 1785.
Abel Corson m. Hannah Royal 2 Jun 1785.
Peter Carroll m. Rachel Parke 15 Aug 1785.
Daniel Moore to Rachel Parke, 22 Sep 1785.
Joseph Lummis m. Rachel Parke, 22 Sep 1785
(The above marriage are from the records.)
John Ewing m. Naomi Stathem 10 Jan 1786.
--- Hathorn to --- Smith 1 Jun 1786.
John Davis m. Lois Mills 9 Oct 1786.
Ephraim Carll m. Hannah Sharp 12 Oct 1786.
Joseph Miller m. Hannah Davis 26 Dec 1786.
James Parke m. Phebe Fithian 21 Mar 1787.
John Shimp m. Lydia Fix 3 Apr 1787.
William Mulford m. Sarah Ewing 5 Apr 1787.

Jonathan Hood m. Rebecca Finley 17 Apr 1787.
Aaron Stathem m. Sarah Van Winkle 18 Apr 1787.
Joseph Brewster m. Lucinda Carll 30 1787.
Stephen Miller m. Hannah Burgin 8 May 1787.
William Davis m. Eunice Harris 24 Dec 1787.
John Watson m. Abigail Fryant 27 Dec 1787.
Job Gifford m. Sarah Toconsen 22 Jan 1788.
Srimathea Waithman m. Lydia Bacon 29 Jan 1788.
Robert Moore m. Rebecca Caruthers 19 Feb 1788.
Jonathan Moore m. Mary Maskell 4 Mar 1788.
Seth Bowen m. Rebecca McClung 18 Mar 1788.
Adam Youngs m. Miriam Fix 25 Mar 1788.
Jonathan Smith m. Rachel Maul 2 Apr 1788.
Uriah Davis m. Rumah Davis 14 Apr 1788.
John Page m. Naomi Read 16 Apr 1788.
Gamaliel Dare m. Sarah Padgett 29 Apr 1788.
Israel Davis m. Hannah Stephens 25 Jun 1788.
--- Benson m. Jane Potter 19 Jul 1788.
Nathan Finlaw m. Lavinia Dare 12 Aug 1788.
Enos Woodruff m. Mary Foster 26 Aug 1788.
Jonathan Bereman m. Hannah Miller 18 Nov 1788.
David Bowen m. Jane Potter 6 Dec 1788.
Israel Stathem m. Sarah Eldridge 9 Dec 1788.
David Royal m. Mary Bishop 31 Dec 1788.
James Burch m. Sydnea Scott 3 Feb 1789.
Capt. William Ferguson m. Susannah Ewing m. 2 Apr 1789.
Nathan Grandy m. Lovisa Fithian 7 Apr 1789.
Doctor Hugh McKee m. Mary Woodruff 18 May 1789.
Daniel Elmer Ray m. Rachel Wood 2 Jun 1789.

Following records of baptisms in the handwriting of Rev. George Faitoute.

Charles and Buckley Carll Allen, sons of Charles Allen; Rachel and Rebecca Parke; a child of Stephen Lupton 1781.
James Lupton, son of John Lupton 17 Feb 1782.
Israel Ewing, son of Samuel Ewing and Enos Woodruff, son of Abner Woodruff 3 Mar 1782.
Abigail, wife of Israel Miller and their son, Samuel 7 Apr 1782.
James Dicson Parke 5 May 1782.
Ephraim Holmes, son of Col. Abijah Holmes 10 May 1782.

GREENWICH PRESBYTERIAN CHURCH 107

William Reeves, son of Thomas Reeves, Jr. 2 Jun 1782.
Sarah Harris, wife of Noah Harris and their dau, Hannah 23 Jun 1782.
Richard Caruthers, son of Mr. Caruthers 23 Jun 1782.
Ephraim Stathem, son of Thomas Stathem 21 Jul 1782.
William Sink 22 Sep 1782.
Eunice Bennet, dau of James Bennet 7 Nov 1782.
Sabra Woodruff Nov 1782.
Lydia Faitoute, second dau of Rev. George Faitoute by Rev. Daniel McCalla 1 Dec 1782.
Harriet and Henrietta Potter, daus of Col. Potter 24 Jan 1783.
Maskell Mills Carll, son of Phineas Carll 26 Jan 1783.
Lemuel Reeves, son of Johnson Reeves 23 Feb 1783.
Sarah Ewing, dau of George Ewing 23 Mar 1783.
Samuel Reeves, son of Joshua Reeves 6 Apr 1783.
Philena Mills, dau of Jeremiah Mills 1 Jun 1783.
Zacharias Allen, son of Charles Allen 1 Jun 1783.
Sarah and James Read, children of David Read 22 Jun 1783.
Esther Allen, adult of Stow Creek 3 Jul 1783.
Stephen Lupton, son of Stephen Lupton 17 Aug 1783.
Charles Beatty Fithian, son of Joel Fithian 24 Aug 1783.
Ewing Woodruff, son of Abner Woodruff 21 Dec 1783.
John Miller, son of Israel Miller 28 Mar 1784.
Hannah Maskell, dau of Thomas Maskell 11 Apr 1784.
Wife of Doctor Peck 10 May 1784.
Richard Grier, son of George Grier of Stow Creek 13 Jun 1784.
David, James, Noah and Amy Woodruff, children of David Woodruff 20 Jun 1784.
William Harris, son of Thomas Harris 8 Aug 1784.
James Faitoute, son of Rev. George Faitoute 5 Sep 1784.
Ephraim Reeves, son of Johnson Reeves 26 Sep 1784.
Philip Stathem Dare, son of William Dare 31 Oct 1784.
Sarah Reeves, dau of Thomas Reeves, Jr. 10 Apr 1785.
Enoch Brown, son of Thomas Brown 23 Apr 1785.
Reuben Hunt, son of James Hunt 23 Apr 1785.
Amy Ewing, dau of Enos Ewing 23 Apr 1785.
Elizabeth Reeves, dau of Joshua Reeves 15 May 1785.
John Lupton, son of John Lupton 14 Aug 1785.
Thomas, David and Elizabeth Sink, children of William Sink 29 Oct 1785.
Samuel Fithian, son of Joel Fithian 29 Oct 1785.
Sarah Allen, dau of Charles Allen 15 Jan 1786.
David James, son of --- James 29 Jan 1786.

Ruth Harris, dau of Thomas Harris 12 Mar 1786.
Oliver Miller, son of Joel Miller, farmer 30 Apr 1786.
Hannah Stathem, dau of Thomas Stathem 30 Apr 1786.
Rhoda Bishop, granddaughter of Daniel Bishop 10 Jun 1786
Nathan Leake, Enas and Joseph, children of Joseph Reeves 10 Jun 1786.
Deborah Lawrence, dau of Benjamin Lawrence 18 Jun 1786.
Susannah Swinney, wife of Valentine Swinney on her death bed, also their son, Joseph 29 Aug 1786.
George Whitfield Faitoute, son of Rev. George Faitoute 17 Sep 1786.
Charles Allen Moore, son of Daniel Moore 6 Oct 1786.
Ephraim Dayton Lummis, son of Joseph Lummis 6 Oct 1786.
John Potter, son of Col. David Potter 5 Nov 1786.
William Carll, son of Phineas Carll 12 Nov 1786.
Smith Mills, son of Jeremiah Mills 25 Feb 1787.
Benjamin Donnell, son of Major Donnell 1 Apr 1787.
Philip Fithian, son of Joel Fithian 15 Apr 1787.
Rhoda Lupton, dau of Stephen Lupton 10 Jun 1787.
Benjamin, Rachel, and Mary, children of Dr. --- Peck 17 Jun 1787.
Rachel Parvin, dau of David Parvin 28 Jun 1787.
Benjamin Stratton Reeves, son of Joshua Reeves 1 Jul 1787.
Sarah Hunt, dau of James Hunt 1 Jul 1787.
Mary Ewing, dau of Enas Ewing 1 Jul 1787.
Joel Read, son of David Read 8 Jul 1787.
A child of Noah Harris 9 Sep 1787.
Clemens and Jane Sheppard, children of Nias Sheppard's widow.
Jane, a negro woman of Ebenezer Elmer 7 Oct 1787.
Nancy Reeves, dau of Johnson Reeves 30 Dec 1787.
Priscilla Bacon, an adult 10 Feb 1788.
Thomas Watson James, son of David James 10 Feb 1788.
Abigail Bishop, dau of Daniel Bishop 9 Mar 1788.
Martha Brown, dau of Thomas Brown 17 May 1788.
Horatius Brewster, son of Dr. Joseph Brewster 18 May 1788.
Euphemia Faitoute, dau of Rev. George Faitoute 27 Jul 1788.
Thomas Mulford, son of William Mulford 10 Aug 1788.
Daniel Lawrence, son of Benjamin Lawrence 17 Aug 1788.
Elizabeth Ewing, dau of David Ewing 7 Sep 1788.
William Elmer, son of the Honorable Jonathan Elmer 21 Sep 1788.
Martha Potter, dau of Col. David Potter 30 Nov 1788.
David Parke, son of James Parke 14 Dec 1788.
John Gibbon McCalla, son of Sulay McCalla 25 Dec 1788.
Thomas Reeves, son of Joshua Reeves 5 Apr 1789.

Virgil David, son of Mr. David, a student in Divinity 19 Apr 1789.
John Peck, son of Dr. --- Peck 12 Jul 1789.
The above baptisms were attested 10 Jul 1789 by the Rev. George Faitoute, V.D.M.

From a loose leaf in the book is the following:

Birth or bapt of Peter McClain 1770-1773. (McClain is also written McClean, McLane, McLean)
Marriage of Andrew McClain and Amy Means. Amy Means bapt 1748-1752.
Burial or Death of Andrew McClain 1777-1780.
Marriage, second of his widow Amy (Means) McClain to James Nelson.

MARRIAGE LICENSES FROM NEW JERSEY ARCHIVES

Benjamin Acton, Salem Co. and Hannah Randolph, Nov 24 1773.
Charles Allen and Rebecca Dare, Apr 8 1778.
James Anderson and Theodosia Elmer, Aug 1 1761.
Moses Ayar and Sarah Pettet, July 16 1777.
Caleb Ayers and Amy Dunn, July 30 1760.
Amos Bacon and Elizabeth Mills, Nov 22 1769.
David Bacon and Sarah Barker, Mar 7 1786.
Edmond Bacon and Mary Eldredge Cape May Co., Mar 28 1766.
Isaac Bacon and Mary Sayre, Feb 29 1764.
Jeremiah Bacon, Jr. and Rachel Shepherd, Apr 10 1757.
Philip Bacon and Sarah Ward, Mar 1 1768.
Richard Bacon and Martha Devine, Salem Co., Feb 24 1774.
Richard Bacon and Sarah Marshall, Dec 1 1779.
Samuel Bacon and Mary Fitzgerald, Apr 2 1767.
Jonathan Ballinger and Rachel Conner, Dec 26 1769.
Isaac Barber and Phebe Tomlinson, May 19 1778.
John Barber and Abigail Scott, Feb 20 1770.
Richard Barber and Mary Scott, Jan 30 1782.
Wade Barber and Hannah Sayre, Aug 18 1768.
Wade Barber and Hannah Sears, Salem County, Feb 23 1779.
William Barber and Hannah Fithian, Apr 10 1766.
Levi Barnes and Sarah Cleves, Jun 20 1780.
John Barns and Rebecca Haynes, Jan 25 1759.
Jonathan Barns and Damaris Garrison, Mar 24 1762.
Amos Bateman and Jane McChesney, Oct 16 1779
John Bateman and Judith Hand, Cape May Co., July 27 1771.
William Bateman and Victorinia Saunders, Aug 15 1780.
David Bennet and Dillilah Thompson, Apr 12 1780.
James Benson and Abigail Whitecar, May 13 1774.
William Bevan and Alisa Moon, Mar 27 1781.
Daniel Benson and Rhoda Platts, Feb 9 1762.
Joseph Bishop and Anna Harris, Mar 3, 1757.
Joseph Bishop and Priscilla Loyd, Salem Co., Apr 21 1761.
Preston Bishop and Ester Woodruff, May 19 1761.
John Blizard, Jr. and Susannah Taylor, Jun 4 1776.
Levi Bond and Rebekah Burr, Jan 7 1782.
Dan Bowen and Sarah Stiles, Mar 28 1766.
Dan Bowen and Elizabeth Kelsay, Dec 20 1780.

Dan Bowen and Ruth Swinney, Apr 6 1785.
David Bowen and Lucy Shepherd, Sept 16 1763.
David Bowen and Zeruiah Hughes, Cape May Co., Nov 11 1775.
David Bowen, Jr. and Jane Potter, Dec 6 1788.
Elijah Bowen and Rachel Harris, Feb 18 1771.
Jeremiah Bowen and Sarah Stathem, Dec 20 1769.
Jonathan Bowen and Rebecca Shepperd, Dec 4 1758.
Jonathan Bowen and Rachel Pennington, Nov 8 1760.
Joseph Bowen and Mary Bacon, Dec 22 1761.
Samuel Bowen and Ann Chester, July 11 1768.
Samuel Bowen and Rebecca Glaspey, Oct 30 1771.
Smith Bowen and Mary Hand, Jan 24 1786.
Stephen Bowen and Rhoda Stratton, Jun 13 1786.
Michael Bowers and Catherine Sleesman, Aug 3 1779.
Elias Boys, Gloucester Co. and Sarah Shaw, July 14 1760.
James Breaser and Sarah Dare, Aug 22 1754.
Daniel Brewster and Prudence Reeves, Apr 10 1780.
Francis Brewster and Rebecca Peck Jan 6 1758.
Ephraim Brick and Ruth Gallasby, Mar 14 1764.
Joshua Brick and Ruth Rumsey, July 26 1737.
Joshua Brick and Lydia Peters, Aug 5 1771.
Joshua Brick and Mary Fithian, Mar 28 1786.
William Brick, Salem Co. and Rachel Dare, Jan 4 1768.
David Brooks and Elizabeth Parker, Dec 11 1778.
John Brooks and Mary Jenkins, Dec 16 1778.
John Brown and Hannah Scott, May 4 1774.
Thomas Brown and Bathnithcoth Ogden (wid.), Apr 17 1760.
Thomas Brown and Martha Peck, Dec 28 1762.
Thomas Brown and Rebecca Fithian, Jun 29 1780.
Ephraim Buck and Abigail Ogden, Sept 27 1769.
John Buck and Lorainia Whitticar, Jun 17 1761.
Joseph Buck and Ruth Dalen, Mar 15 1779
James Burch and Sidnea Scott, Feb 3 1789.
James Burck and Sarah Elmer, May 9 1785.
John Burgin and Elizabeth Abel, Salem Co., Mar 2 1761.
Reuben Burgin and Deborah Bowen, Nov 28 1787.
James Burns and Abigail Haze, Mar 18 1745/6.
Aaron Butcher and Mary Ireland, Jul 23 1762.
Aaron Butcher and Phebe Moor, Apr 2 1778.
Francis Byram and Christian Liester, Mar 19 1773.
Phineas Carll and Rachel Mills, Oct 7 1760.

William Carll and Sarah Hewing, May 24 1773.
James Caruthers, Salem and Lydia Roberts, Cohansie, Dec 6 1733.
Obadiah Caruthers and Elizabeth Venables, 1768.
Richard Caruthers and Mary Ewing, Dec 16 1780.
Reuben Cheesman, Gloucester Co. and Sarah Ogden, Nov 29 1759.
Charles Clark and Ruth Scott, Nov 21 1769.
Daniel Clark and Anna Holmes, Aug 11 1761.
James Clark and Sarah Ogden, Jun 29 1769.
Joshua Clark and Eunice Devall, Oct 24 1759.
Stephen Clark and Tabitha Nixon, Oct 28 1761.
John Clever and Jemima Draper, Nov 11 1780.
Lawrence Corn and Mary Smith, Nov 27 1781.
John Corson, Cape May Co. and Mary Goff, Dec 19 1761.
Richard Wheat Craven and Rhoda Shephard, Oct 10 1766.
Eli Daniels and Polly Woolson, Cape May Co., Mar 20 1776.
John Daniels and Lydia White, Aug 22 1759.
John Daniels and Mary Newcomb, Jan 30 1770.
Benjamin Dare and Mary Dare, Apr 7 1773.
Benone Dare and Clemens Withman, May 9 1760.
David Dare and Ruth Peck, Dec 15 1778.
Reuben Dare and Rhoda Stevens, Dec 6 1760.
Isaac Davis and Mary Anna David, Salem Co., Sep 23 1767.
Jonathan Davis and Ammi Davis, Jan 8 1783.
Ephraim Dayton and Ruhama Elmer, Dec 29 1747.
Edward Dennis and Jean Cook, Mar 22 1786.
Joseph Dickinson, Salem, and Hannah Smith, Jul 18 1765.
Francis Dixon and Elizabeth Benton, Jul 11 1763.
Daniel Dixson and Ann Dayton, Oct 30 1770.
Jonathan Dolles and Susanna Clarke, Jun 1 1787.
Joseph Donelson and Temperance Fithian, May 23 1774.
Nathaniel Donnell, Jr. and Sarah Forrees, Jun 25 1784.
John Dowdney and Sarah Howell, Nov 20 1773
Nicholas Dowdney and Sarah Worrel, Dec 18 1771.
Samuel Dowdney and Martha Reed, Oct 27 1783.
Abraham DuBois, Salem Co., and Elizabeth Preston, Dec 1 1761.
Jacob Duffel and Ann Ireland, Dec 16 1773.
Benjamin Donn, Piscatawey and Edith Davis Mar 28 1758.
Thomas Eastburn and Abigail Jones, Aug 23 1799.
Thomas Eddis and Ann Johnson, Jun 12 1780.
Daniel Eldredge and Dorcas Bacon, Jan 30 1789.
Daniel Elmer and Mary Shaw, Sep 28 1761

Eli Elmer and Jane Thompson, Feb 13 1781.
Eli Theophilus Elmer and Abigail Lawrence Sep 3 1765.
George Ewing and Rachel Harris, Hunterdon Co., Aug 7 1778.
James Ewing and Martha Boyd, Oct 15 1778.
Remington Ewing and Phebe Ewing, Jan 30 1784.
Samuel Ewing and Mary Miller, Feb 19 1763.
John Flier, Jr. and Sarah Worton, 3-6-1759.
James Farrill and Elizabeth Sheckels, Jul 24 1780.
Morgan Frent and Dorcas Moore, Jun 9 1762.
Henry Fox and Barbary Ruff, Nov 26 1767.
Jeremiah Foster, Jr. and Priscillia Preston, Dec 16 1784.
Jeremiah Foster and Sarah Smith, Oct 19 1778.
Francis Flitcraft and Jemima Leeds, Jan 28 1784.
Ephraim Fithian and Atteliah Gaston, Sep 4 1780.
George Fithian and Sarah Murford, Feb 9 1782.
Joel Fithian and Elizabeth Fithian, Feb 2 1780.
John Fithian and Eunice Johnston, Dec 10 1759.
John Fithian and Mary Brown, Sep 26 1765.
Jonathan Fithian and Isabel Eustace, Mar 25 1780.
Samuel Fithian and Abigail Moore, Oct 26 1750.
William Fithian and Mary Tomlinson, Nov 17 1785.
Thomas Galping and Ruth Gland, Jan 15 1749.
David Gandy and Phebe Blizard, Sep 3 1761.
Thomas Gandy and Naomi Blizard, Feb 23 1779.
Gamaliel Garrison, Salem Co. and Christiana Keen, Oct 2 1762.
William Garrison, Salem Co. and Elizabeth Powell, Jan 28 1769.
John Gibbon and Esther Seeley, Mar 31 1761.
James Gorrel and Sarah Jackson, Oct 27 1768.
Anthony Gould and Phebe Lummis, Mar 6 1781.
Philip Grace and Suria Morris, Oct 12 1782.
Abner Hall and Sarah Shepherd, Aug 15 1774.
George Hall and Ann Elkinton, Burlington Co., Jun 20 1775.
Peter Halter, Salem Co and Dorcas Irelan, Feb 17 1770.
Joseph Hancock and Elizabeth Butcher, Apr 25 1785.
Aaron Hand and Ann Lowring, May 10 1777.
William Hand, Cape May Co. and Hannah Garrison, Nov 17 1776.
Preston Hannah and Bathsheba Moore, Sep 6 1777.
Samuel Hannah and Lydia Sayre, Jan 19 1768.
Daniel Harris and Martha Ogden, Feb 28 1770.
Isaac Harris Salem Co. and Anne Moon, Aug 27 1772.
Jacob Harris and Rachel Bacon, Feb 29 1780.

Moses Harris and Phebe Brooks, Nov 26 1779.
Noah Harris and Mary Aplen, Gloucester Co., Jul 23 1761.
Noah Harris and Sarah Carll, Apr 18 1781.
Samuel Harris and Rachel Hood, Aug 27 1761.
William Harris Cape May Co. and Elizabeth Iszard, Oct 27 1750.
Isaac Hawthorn and Hannah Smith, May 18 1786.
Levi Heaton and Phebe Cook, Nov 19 1777.
Samuel Heaton and Rhoda Terry, May 12 1783.
Joseph Hildreth and Alice Shaw, Nov 12 1777.
Jeremiah Hines and Mary Hann, Apr 26 1776.
Amariah Hogbin and Mercy Simpkin, Aug 16 1757.
Jacob Hollingshead and Sarah Rice, Apr 17 1779.
Samuel Hollingshead and Mary Eldredge, Sep 13 1785.
Adam Hoshel and Phebe Parvin, Oct 6 1763.
Michael Hoshel and Rachel Peck, Jun 14 1773.
Obed Hudson and Phebe Miller, May 23 1786.
John Hunt and Annie Brewster, May 28 1779.
Andrew Hunter and Ann Riddle, Oct 2 1775.
Joseph Irelan and Judith Johnson, Apr 24 1776.
Micajah Irelan and Prudeuce Bacon, May 1 1776.
Joseph Ireland and Phebe Ireland, Nov 9 1762.
David James and Philathea Watson, Dec 6 1784.
Joseph James and Margaret Butler, Feb 1 1748.
Isaac Jenkins and Phebe Brooke, Apr 4 1780.
Isaiah Johnson and Lettitia Miller, Oct 4 1781.
Jeremiah Johnson and Rhoda Townsend, Jun 2 1789.
James Johnston and Elizabeth Hunt, Sep 23 1778.
John Jones and Sarah Hall, Oct 28 1777.
Jacob Keen and Sarah Mulford, Mar 28 1779.
Thomas Keen and Mary Mack, Dec 11 1777.
Reuben Kellogg and Mary Bray, Jan 1 1781.
Edward Ketchem and Rhoda Woodland, Apr 3 1773.
Ebenezer Kiging and Sarah Denton, Nov 27 1759.
Reuben Kimsey and Ruth Vanemon, Jun 8 1779.
Stephen Kirby and Mary Lore, Oct 30 1773.
Stephen Kirby and Margaret Whitaker, Dec 26 1778.
Abraham Lake and Abigail Heaton, Mar 19 1781.
Samuel Lake and Elizabeth McQueen, Feb 14 1769.
John Laning and Ann Ewing, Mar 10 1785.
John Laning and Rhoda Izard, May 20 1773.
Nathan Lawrence and Elizabeth Johnston, Aug 18 1769.

Samuel Leake and Elizabeth McQueen, Feb 14 1769.
George Leawert and Elizabeth Burrows, Oct 27 1778.
Nathan Leek and Hannah Fithian, Dec 27 1761.
Levi Leek and Mabel Reeves, Jul 28 1783.
Stephen Lester and Susannah Smith, Nov 24 1773.
Ansell Long and Margaret Finlaw, Dec 10 1750.
Constant Long and Unis Shepperd, Jun 16 1778.
David Long and Kerenhappuck Shepperd, Jan 10 1757.
Joseph Long and Elizabeth Vanhook, Aug 27 1785.
Jonathan Long and Martha Hand, Cape May Co., Sep 5 1769.
William Lock and Sarah Parent, Dec 1 1778.
Nathaniel Love and Rachel Cook, Sep 28 1778.
Seth Love and Abigail Whitecar, Jun 8 1778.
William Love and Ellener Forgison, May 5 1763.
Jacob Ludlam and Rachel Worthington, Jan 21 1784.
Norton Ludlam and Pbebe Bacon, Nov 8 1779.
Edward Lummis and Polly Elmer, Apr 16 1786.
Manoah Lummis and Mary Elmer, Aug 5 1779.
Parsons Lummis and Hannah Diament, Jul 5 1779.
Benjamin Lupton and Amy Garrison, Aug 25 1761.
Stephen Lupton and Rhoda Garrison, Oct 21 1778.
James Marshall and Ruth Brick, Nov 21 1791.
Daniel Maskell and Mary Vaughn, Jan 15 1749.
Daniel Maskell and Sarah Woodruff, Aug 6 1775.
Thomas Maskell and Ester Fithian, Mar 27 1768.
Thomas Massey and Jameson Lawrence, Mar 8 1780.
Caleb Matlack and Mary Wilie, Dec 18 1777.
Luke Matox and Rebecca Wheeler, Apr 27 1787.
Aulay McCalla and Hannah Gibbon, Apr 9 1787.
Samuel McClintock and Rebecca Garrison, Jan 12 1779.
Hugh McKee and Polly Woodruff, Jun 15 1789.
Israel Miller and Abigail Miller, Nov 16 1779.
Joel Miller and Polly Newell, Apr 10 1787.
John Miller and Phebe Irelan, Jul 31 1777.
Noah Miller and Mary Mills, Nov 16 1762.
Benoni Mills and Lydia Hand, Apr 10 1769.
Isaac Mills and Rebecca Campbell, Mar 1 1762.
Samuel Mills and Mary Chessney Apr 27 1779.
Anthony Montgomery and Elizabeth Powell, Oct 21 1778.
Enoch Moore and Mary Ware Apr 16 1752.
Enoch Moore and Rachel Hutson, Nov 22 1762.

116 EARLY RECORDS OF CUMBERLAND CO.

Hampton Moore and Mary Westcott, Apr 17 1783.
John Morrow and Jane Randolph, Mar 28 1771.
Benjamin Mulford and Mary Sheppard, Oct 4 1760.
Benjamin Mulford and Hepsebeth Wheaton Dec 20 1770.
Benjamin Mulford and Hannah Barker, Dec 19 1771.
Ephraim Mulford and Rebeckah Weilding, Dec 7 1778.
Furman Mulford and Rhoda Johnson, Apr 29 1780.
John Mulford and Clemona Maskell, Apr 2 1776.
John Mulford and Levice Waithman, Apr 3 1781.
Lewis Mulford and Mary Barker, Oct 4 1773.
Moses Mulford and Rachel Moore, Apr 25 1758.
William Mulford and Prudence Maskell, Feb 22 1762.
William Mulford and Sarah Coningham Apr 11 1768.
Robert Munnion and Anne Williams, Dec 27 1748.
Robert Murphy and Damaris Sayre, Mar 1 1780.
Uriah Nail and Emily Fowler, Oct 18 1779.
John Potts Neide and Edith Furniss, Jan 26 1790.
Rebuen Newcomb and Edith Barratt, Jun 9 1779.
Silas Newcomb and Martha Savage, Oct 22 1784.
William Newcomb and Pleasant Long, Jul 31 1759.
Jeremiah Nixson and Mrs. Hannah Jones, Aug 8 1763
Daniel Ogden and Rachel Moore, Jul 6 1768.
David Ogden and Mary Bateman, Sep 13 1759.
Nathaniel Ogden and Jane Hand, Cape May Co., Apr 24 1761.
Thomas Ogden and Violetta Harris, Aug 5 1760.
Thomas Ogden and Sarah Westcote, Mar 1 1761.
William Oldaker and Prudence Powell, Oct 1 1784.
James Ord and Hannah Genkens, Gloucester Co., Oct 30 1754.
John Orin and Mary Hutchinson, May 2 1742.
Daniel Packer and Catharine Fight, Sep 21 1771.
William Paday and Abigail Bishop, Aug 6 1754.
David Padgett and Priscilla Reed, Jan 16 1752.
Thomas Padgett and Annie Lupton, Apr 7 1761.
Aaron Padgitt and Hope Smith, Mar 16 1768.
Ambrose Page and Sarah Shaw, Jan 20 1784.
David Page and Mary Read, Jul 30 1763.
Jonathan Page and Bathier Nixon, Jan 15 1773.
Clarence Parvin and Amy Mayhew, Pittsgrove, Jul 8 1776.
Whitlock Paulen and Sarah Ireland, Dec 4 1778.
William Payday and Mary Tyler, Jun 8 1785.
Benjamin Peck and Martha Powell, Apr 11 1775.

Joseph Peck and Ruth Hannah, Dec 24 1773.
Dan Perry and Hannah Hand, Jan 6 1780.
Aaron Peterson and Martha Hollingshead, Mar 25 1779.
Daniel Peterson and Priscilla Iszard, Jun 30 1760.
Frederick Peterson and Ellener Lore, Nov 3 1775.
Hance Peterson and Rachel Simmons, Cape May Co., Sep 19 1750.
John Peterson and --- Shropshire. Sep 24 1760.
William Peterson and Elizabeth McGlaughlin, May 18 1782.
Andrew Pierce and Mary Jay, Mar 16 1793
Azel Pierson and Mary Siden, Salem Co., Dec 4 1762.
John Pierson and Elizabeth Mulford, Nov 17 1783.
David Platts and Letitia Gilman, Jan 4 1763.
John Potts and Hannah Tyler, Oct 19 1782.
David Randolph and Darkis Ayars, Nov 8 1775.
William Ramsey and Sarah Seeley, Feb 20 1759.
George Adam Rasure and Catharine Ward, Mar 6 1760.
Charles Read and Esther Eldridge, Jan 14 1788.
Israel Read and Sarah Reeves, Jan 29 1787.
Henry Reed and Phebe Ludlam, Cape May, Oct 31 1765.
Abraham Reeves and Christina Shykels, Sep 20 1787.
John Read and Marthew Austin, Nov 19 1777.
Johnson Read and Sevia Bereman, Dec 28 1777.
Moses Rementon and Sarah Walling, Feb 5 1768.
Moses Remington and Theodocia Sayre, Jul 30 1778.
John Richards and Susannah Hewit, Gloucester Co., Mar 7 1770.
Joseph Richardson and Arabella Seagrave, Dec 30 1751.
Joseph Riley and Rachel Ware, Aug 28 1773.
Obediah Robins and Rachel Shepherd, Feb 28 1754.
James Robinson and Elizabeth Dare, Jun 29 1759.
William Robinson and Sarah Woodruff, Jul 9 1759.
William Robinson, Jr. and Mary Youngs, Jun 20 1772.
Bartholomew Rudolph and Sarah Ewing, Sep 20 1779.
John Rulon and Sarah Burt, Dec 10 1782.
Joseph Ryley and Judith Moore, May 26 1774.
Jacob Samson and Mary Harding, Sep 24 1778.
William Sayers and Mary Fithian, Jr., May 25 1762.
Abraham Sayre and Rachel Meake, Jan 15 1779.
Samuel Scudder, Alloways Creek and Leah Sockwell, Jan 8 1761.
John Scullard and Hannah Mulford, Jan 4 1762.
David Seeley and Mary Merscillier, Aug 20 1781.
Ebenezer Seeley and Mary Clark, Mar 30 1783.

Henery Seeley and Hannah Dare, Oct 6 1762.
Isaac Sharp and Rachel Mulford, Apr 9 1764.
Abiah Shaw and Abigail Bucke, Jun 23 1778.
John Shaw and Judith Payday, Oct 8 1786.
Nathan Shaw and Abigail Fithian, Jul 17 1754.
Nathan Shaw and Mary VanMeter, Mar 15 1760.
Nathan Shaw and Mary Jones, Jan 16 1769.
Richard Shaw and Abigail Westcoat, Feb 18 1755.
Furman Shyherd (Shepherd) and Hannnh Maskell, Dec 20 1780.
Ephraim Simpkins and Hannah Stathem, May 4 1784.
William Sink and Esther Bishop, Nov 18 1784.
Asbury Smith and Lydia Hand, Mar 8 1757.
Ebenezer Smith and Sarah Finlaw, Nov 17 1772.
Elisha Smith and Rebekah Bowen, May 2 1778.
Elisha Smith and Laetitia Johnson, Mar 13 1787.
Isaac Smith and Sarah Mulford, Nov 2 1768.
Isaac Smith and Cynthus Walling, Jan 28 1772.
John Smith and Sarah Gruff, Salem Co., Jul 23 1767.
Lewis Smith and Ruth Watson, Jan 5 1769.
Samuel Smith and Sarah Carll, Sep 29 1760.
David Sneathen and Sarah McPeters, Feb 2 1763.
James Snethen and Margaret Gillingham, Alloways Creek, Sept 29 1766.
Jonadab Sockwell and Anne Bowen, Jun 5 1762.
John Souter and Margaret Miller, Alloways Creek, Mar 9 1771.
Benjamin Southward and Abigail Hewitt, Apr 21 1773.
Henry Sparks and Catherine Stratton, Mar 23 1762.
Caleb Stackhouse and Eleanor Long, Aug 22 1767.
Aaron Stathem and Priscilla Pooler, Oct 11 1760.
Aaron Stathem and Susannah Leach, Feb 2 1786.
Isaac Stathem and Mary Watson, Oct 11 1760.
Iaaac Stathem and Lydya Anderson, Newcastle, Del., Nov 27 1769.
James Stephenson and Marcy Hosea, May 10 1778.
Richard Stephenson, Sr. and Isabel Sharp, Jan 5 1778.
John Stidham and Elizabeth Powell, May 19 1779.
James Stratton and Anne Harris, Jul 15 1779.
Joseph Stiles and Elizabeth Channel, May 2 1785.
Elisha Swinney and Eunice Jenkins, Feb 12 1771.
James Sweatman and Mary Price, 8-24-1787.
Benjamin Thompson and Elizabeth Cleaver, Dec 4 1778.
Ephraim Tarry and Judith Platt, Sep 9 1761.

MARRIAGE LICENSES FROM N.J. ARCHIVES

Butler Tarry and Hannah Foster, Jan 26 1779.
George Tomlinson and Anne Ware, May 6 1778.
Jeremiah Towser and Elizabeth Kimme, Apr 20 17-.
John Trenchard and Theodosia Ogden, Jun 25 1770.
Job Tyler and Rachel Sayre, Oct 21 1782.
Jonas Venaman and Christiana Souder, Aug 8 1785.
John Vanderford and Catharine Shull, Jan 29 1778.
Henry Vanhook and Mary Furnis, Jun 3 1784.
William Waithman and Mary Moore, May 22 1763.
William Waithman and Sarah Bacon, Oct 11 1775.
Ladis Walling and Ruth Brewster, Sep 25 1776.
John Walling and Anna Tullis, Mar 26 1761.
Jonathan Walling and Rachel Bacon, Mar 2 1774.
Philip Walters and Mary Brown, Oct 18 1777.
Samuel Ward and Deborah Brewster, 17-.
Elnathan Ware and Marcy Moore, Apr 30 1760.
John Ware and Margaret Newton, Cape May Co., May 22 1783.
Latin Ware and Ann Fithian, Feb 15 1768.
Latin Ware and Elizabeth Barker, Jul 30 1782.
Isaac Watson and Elizabeth Powell, Oct 2 1760.
William Watson and Mary Mulford, Nov 11 1764.
Foster Wescote and Abigail Fraser, May 31 1748.
Jonathan Wheaton and Hannah Woodhouse, Aug 23 1764.
Robert Wheaton and Sarah Whittal, Salem Co., Oct 2 1765.
Jehiel Wheeler and Elizabeth Preston, Dec 9 1751.
George White and Martha Borden, Penns Neck, Nov 7 1772.
Ambrose Whitacar and Rachel Leak, Salem Co., Oct 3 1772.
Joseph Whitacar and Tabitha Davis, Mar 4 1780.
Richard Whitacar and Elisabeth Husted, Dec 7 1756.
Thomas Whitacar and Bertha Brown, Nov 12 1761.
Thomas Whitacar and Rachel Daniels, Feb 16 1780.
David Wood, Salem Co. and Prudence Roberts, Jul 9 1777.
John Wood, Upper Alloways Creek and Martha Sayce (Sayre), Mar 20 1776.
John Wood and Lucia Mulford, Jan 18 1786.
Samuel Wood, Alloways Creek and Sarah Dare, Oct 27 1767.
Amos Woodruff and Mary Walling, Apr 19 1775.
Constant Wothman and Lediah Robins, Jan 10 1754.
Nathan Wright and Ann Wright, Gloucester Co., Jan 31 1764.

INDEX

-A-
AARONS,
 Martha, 3
 Michael, 68
ABEL, Elizabeth, 100, 111
ABRAHAMS, Lewis, 71
ACTON,
 Benjamin, 110
 Letitia, 71
ADAMS,
 Abraham, 80, 81
 Bridger, 80
 Bridget, 81
 Mary, 80
 Michael, 68
 Priscilla, 81
ADOESSON, Ann, 65
ALBERTSON, Elizabeth, 12, 14
ALBRIGHT,
 Henrich, 47
 Johannes, 47
ALBROCHT, Johannes, 47
ALDERMAN,
 Hannah, 32
 Sarah, 32
ALLEN,
 Buckley Carll, 106
 Charles, 106, 107, 110
 Esther, 107
 Isaac, 63
 Mary, 73
 Sarah, 107
 Thomas Elliot, 28
 Zacharias, 107
AMBLER,
 Anne, 12, 14, 15, 18, 19, 20, 25
 Hannah, 16
 John, 15, 16, 17, 18, 19, 20, 23, 25
 Phebe, 17

Rebecca, 18, 25
 Ruth, 20
 Thomas, 19
ANDERSON,
 James, 88, 110
 Joseph, 61
 Lydya, 118
APLEN, Mary, 114
ATKINSON, Isaac, 30
AULD, John, 32
AULS, William, 89
AUSTEN, Cornelius, 3
AUSTIN,
 Marthew, 117
 Sarah, 67
AUSTON, Ruhanna, 1
AVERY,
 Anne, 18
 Charles, 18
 Jemima, 12, 14, 18
 John, 18
 Nathan, 18
 Samuel, 18
 Simeon, 18
AVISE,
 Ann, 82
 George, 78, 79, 80, 81, 82
 Hannah, 81
 James, 79
 Jane, 78, 79, 80, 81
 Joseph, 80
 Rachel, 82
 William, 78
 Zaccheus, 80
AYAR, Moses, 110
AYARS,
 Burgan, 2
 Caleb, 72
 Darkis, 117
 Enoch, 68
 Joshua, 74
 Kesiah, 63
 Margaret, 73

Mary, 70
 Rachel, 65
 Sarah, 71
 Stephen, 63
AYERS, Caleb, 110

-B-
BACHTLER,
 Catherine, 34
 Juliana, 35
 Margaret, 34, 35
 Simon, 34, 35
BACKLEY, William, 73
BACON,
 Abel, 6
 Amos, 110
 Benjamin, 1
 Daniel, 41, 70
 David, 110
 Davis, 102
 Dorcas, 112
 Edmond, 110
 Elesabeth, 4
 Elizabeth, 63, 102, 105
 Enos, 3, 66
 Hannah, 5
 Isaac, 110
 Jeremiah, 1, 104, 110
 Jesse, 71
 Lydia, 41, 106
 Margaret, 41
 Martin, 41
 Mary, 1, 63, 65, 111
 Nathan, 2
 Phebe, 115
 Philip, 3, 110
 Philothea, 5
 Priscilla, 108
 Prudence, 114
 Rachel, 3, 63, 113, 119
 Rebecca, 6
 Richard, 110
 Samuel, 70, 110
 Sarah, 5, 102, 119

Tabitha, 7
BAILEY, Rachel, 52
BAKEN, Isac, 61
BAKER,
 Benjamin, 67
 Chas. C.D., 33
 Polly, 12
BAKN, Daniel, 41
BALLANGER, William, 65
BALLINGER, Jonathan, 110
BANER,
 Cassandra, 53
 Elisha, 53
 Elizabeth, 53
 Hannah, 53
 Isaac, 53
 Jacob, 53
 Lydia, 53
 Mark, 53
 Nathan, 53
 Rachel, 53
 Ruth, 53
BANNETT, Rebecca, 67
BANST, Jonathan, 59
BARACLIFF, George, 67
BARBER,
 Isaac, 110
 John, 110
 Mary, 4
 Richard, 110
 Wade, 110
 William, 110
BARKER,
 Elizabeth, 32, 119
 Hannah, 12, 14, 116
 John, 69
 Martha, 63
 Mary, 14, 68, 116
 Richard, 4, 5
 Ruth, 65
 Sarah, 110
BARNES, Levi, 110
BARNS,
 John, 110

Jonathan, 110
Phebe, 1
BARRAT, Violet, 63
BARRATT, Edith, 116
BARRETT,
 Joshua, 72
 Mary, 64
 Sarah, 64, 70
 Silvia, 65
BARROT, Sarah, 90
BARTON,
 Ellener, 61
 Miriam, 71
 Mordici, 61
BATEMAN,
 Abigail, 71
 Abigal, 61
 Amey, 70
 Amos, 58, 110
 Burgin, 59
 Daniel, 56
 David, 73
 Elizabeth, 59
 Esther, 73
 Job, 25
 Joe, 58
 John, 58, 71, 110
 Jonathan, 73
 Julia, 60
 Levina, 67
 Lovina, 29, 31
 Lydia, 1, 58
 Mary, 116
 Phebe, 69
 Reuben, 59
 Rubon, 59
 Ruth, 6
 Sarah, 69, 102
 Seviriah, 73
 Susa, 59
 Susannah, 67
 Thomas, 56, 58, 70
 William, 29, 59, 110
BATTON, Moses, 32
BAUER,
 Conrad, 47

Hannah, 66
Johann Micheal, 47
BAUR, Johann Michael, 47
BAWEN, Ebenezer, 59
BEACON, Sarah, 5
BEATTY,
 Ann, 99
 Charles, 99
 Elizabeth, 99
BECKLER, Beuler, 71
BEDENT,
 Abigal, 87
 John, 88
BEE,
 Elizabeth, 30
 Mary, 30
BEESLEY, Jno., 67
BELDING, ---, 22
BENDER, Hans George, 47
BENET, Daniel, 58
BENNET,
 David, 31, 110
 Eunice, 107
 James, 107
 Samuel, 30
 Temperance, 102
BENNETT,
 Betsey, 73
 David, 71
 Dorcas, 67, 102
 Eunice, 102
 Freelove, 66
 Isaac, 59
 James, 62, 102
 Jerymiah, 97
 John, 29
 Jonathan, 59, 60, 61
 Joseph, 60
 Leonard, 97
 Lois, 63
 Lovisa, 105
 Lovise, 97
 Mably, 67
 Nathan, 73

INDEX

Sarah, 97
Unis, 102
BENSON,
---, 106
Daniel, 110
James, 110
BENTLY,
Elizabeth, 94
Gardner, 94
Hannah, 94
John, 94
Lydia, 94
BENTON, Elizabeth, 112
BEREMAN,
Ephraim, 102
John, 102
Jonathan, 106
Mary, 102
Sarah, 102
Sevia, 117
Thomas, 102
Zerviah, 102
BERIMAN,
Parthenia, 100
Sarah, 97
Zeruriah, 100
BERNARD, Elizabeth, 30
BERRIMAN,
Aaron, 27
Hannah, 20
James, 20
James Glasby, 26
Joel, 11, 13, 20, 26, 27
Mary, 30
Rebecca, 12, 14, 20, 26, 27
Thomas, 20
BETCHNER,
Catherine, 34
Christina, 36
Juliana, 35
Margaret, 34, 35, 36
Simon, 34, 35, 36
BETTY, Elizabeth, 30
BEVAN, William, 110
BICHESS, Icabud, 59

BIGGS,
Aaron, 16
Amy, 105
Ephraim, 22
Hannah, 22
Jeremiah, 16
John, 26
Rachel, 10
Rhoda, 29
William, 16
BISHOP,
Abigail, 108, 116
Anne, 96
Daniel, 97, 105, 108
Elesabeth, 5
Ephraim, 97
Esther, 101, 118
Isabel, 59
Jeremy, 67
Jerymiah, 96
Jos, 110
Joseph, 22
Mary, 106
Nathaniel, 23, 29
Phebe, 67, 97
Polly, 63
Preston, 101, 110
Rachel, 101
Rhoda, 108
Rodah, 97
BITTER, John Jacob, 47
BITTERS,
Elisabeth, 39
Heinrich, 39
Johannes, 39
BLACK, Judith, 52
BLACKMAN,
Jemina, 29
Mary, 2
Ruth, 61
BLACKWOOD,
Dalia, 72
John, 63
BLANJA, Hannah, 68
BLEW,
Elizabeth, 30

John, 64
Sarah, 25
Selah, 25, 31, 66
BLISARD,
John, 89
Levy, 89
BLIZARD,
Daniel, 70
John, 110
Naomi, 113
Phebe, 113
Susanna, 63
Tabitha, 68
BLIZZARD,
Abiah, 91
Benjamin, 87
Elizabeth, 91
John, 58, 60
Mary, 68
Naomy, 87
BOEN,
Enock, 89
Enos, 59
Mason, 60
BOND, Levi, 110
BOOEN, Gate, 69
BOON, Rebekah, 1
BORDEN, Martha, 119
BORDON, Anne, 51
BOWEN,
Anne, 63, 118
Charity, 5
Christiana, 25
Dan, 22, 29, 110, 111
Daniel, 1, 70
David, 5, 67, 106, 111
Deborah, 111
Elijah, 3, 111
Enoch, 71
Ephraim, 25
Jane, 69
Jeremiah, 111
Jonathan, 2, 3, 111
Joseph, 70, 111
Lucy, 3
Mark, 70

Mary, 1, 3, 71
Miraim, 25
Miriam, 4
Moses, 3, 6
Noah, 65
Phebe, 29
Priscilla, 22
Rachel, 3, 30
Rebekah, 118
Rhoda, 68
Ruth, 63
Samuel, 3, 111
Sarah, 3
Seth, 1, 68, 106
Smith, 69, 111
Soviah, 5
Stephen, 111
BOWER,
 Ebenezer, 57
BOWERS,
 Ebinzar, 62
 Eli, 61
 Elizabeth, 67
 Jaid, 65
 Michael, 111
 Nancy, 27
BOWLES, Mrs., 67
BOWMEN, F. W., 75
BOWN, David, 2, 4
BOX, Widow, 22
BOYD,
 Amy, 17
 James, 17, 85, 97
 Martha, 97, 113
 Mary, 85, 97
 William, 23
BOYS, Elias, 111
BRACKNEY, William, 63
BRADBILLER, John, 80
BRADFOOT, Silas, 89
BRADFORD,
 Amos, 64, 90, 91
 Anna, 91
 Cathrine, 91
 Elias, 91

Hary, 91
James, 59
Jeams, 60
Mary, 91
Phebe, 90
Silas, 30, 88, 91
Temperance, 90
BRAGG,
 John, 87, 88
 Mary, 87
BRAGNER, John, 29
BRAINERD,
 J., 10, 17
 John, 8
BRAINOR, Mr., ?63
BRANAGAN, William, 4
BRANDFORD, Cattren, 90
BRASIER, Sarah, 30
BRAY, Mary, 114
BRAZIER,
 Rachel, 17
 Sarah, 17
BREASER, James, 111
BRENDSHOLTZ,
 Adam, 34
 Anna Maria, 34
 Heinrich, 34
BRENISTHOLBY,
 Henry, 65
BREWSTER,
 Abijah, 100
 Amee, 100
 Anna, 95, 101
 Annie, 114
 Benjamin, 95
 Daniel, 100, 111
 Deborah, 119
 Ebenezar, 95
 Eunice, 100
 Francis, 95, 100, 101, 111
 Francis Gilbert, 31, 65, 95
 Hannah, 95
 Horatius, 108

Jonathan, 100
Joseph, 8, 11, 13, 18, 20, 21, 95, 106, 108
Lucinda, 12, 14, 18, 20, 21
Mary, 95, 100
Rebecca, 95, 101
Ruth, 18, 95, 119
Samuel, 20, 95
William, 21
BRICK,
 Abegail, 72
 Ephraim, 3, 111
 Hannah, 55
 Joshua, 55, 111
 Mary, 58
 Rachel, 2, 3
 Ruth, 4, 115
 Samuel, 3
 William, 2, 111
BRIGGS, Rachel, 74
BRIGHT, William, 89
BRINESHOLTZ,
 Adam, 34, 35
 Anna Maria, 34
 Heinrich, 34
 John Adam, 47
 Maria Catherine, 35
BRINESTHOLD,
 Barbary, 71
BRINISHOLTS, Henry
BROOKE, Phebe, 114
BROOKFIELDS, John, 68
BROOKS,
 Abegail, 3
 Abigail, 68
 Alpheus, 3
 David, 111
 Dorcas, 4
 Eleanor, 1
 Enoch, 63
 Ephraim, 2
 Hannah, 2
 Ira, 70
 Jeremiah, 3

John, 10, 13, 15, 24, 105, 111
Juda, 24
Judah, 15
Martha, 3
Mary, 70
Noah, 24
Phebe, 28, 114
Ruth, 28
Sarah, 30, 70
Seth, 1
Widow, 23
Zebulon, 28
Zebulun, 5
BROULAS, Nanse, 59
BROWN,
Abagail, 71
Amos, 103
Anna, 72
Bertha, 119
Daniel, 74, 104
Elezabeth, 4
Enoch, 103, 107
Hannah, 103
Harry, 67
Jacob, 3, 5
John, 72, 111
Joseph, 73
Margery, 67
Martha, 103, 108
Mary, 68, 113, 119
Sarah, 103
Thomas, 72, 103, 107, 108, 111
BRUCKS(BROOKS),
Bucks, 58
BRYAM, Francis, 111
BRYSELIUE, Paul, 80
BRYZELIUS,
P. D., 82
P.D., 81
Paul Daniel, 82
BUCHALOD, James, 52
BUCK,
Abigail, 72
David, 31, 72

Ephraim, 56, 111, ?63
Henry, 19, 20, 27, 29, 31, 73
Jeremiah, 56, 57
John, 23, 104, 111
Joseph, 103, 111
Judith, 85
Lurina, 68
Lydia, 103
Mary, 19, 27
Patty, 32
Sarah, 12, 14, 19, 20, 27, 61
Susannah, 20
BUCKE, Abigail, 118
BUDD,
Anne, 52
Eli, 52
Wesley, 52
BURCH,
James, 86, 106, 111
Sarah, 86
Theophilus, 86
Timothy, 70
BURCK, James, 111
BURDON, Isaac, 32
BURGIN,
Elizabeth, 100
Enoch, 72
George, 100
Gilbert, 100
Hannah, 100, 106
John, 100, 111
Reuben, 100, 111
Ruth, 100
Zeruriah, 100
BURK, John, 29
BURKE, Silvia, 70
BURNE, Patrich, 89
BURNETT,
Esther, 98
Josiah, 98
Priscilla, 98
William, 98
BURNS,
Elizabeth, 90

James, 111
BURR,
Noar, 59
Rebekah, 110
BURROUGHS, Thomas, 23
BURROWS, Elizabeth, 115
BURT,
Daniel, 61
Jesphus, 59
John, 59, 62
Richard, 59
Ruth, 69
Sarah, 117
BURTON, John, 61
BUSHBY, Prudence, 68
BUSBY, Mary, 72
BUSY, Mary, 72
BUTCHER,
Aaron, 111
Elizabeth, 113
Jonathan, 65
BUTLER, Margaret, 114
BUTTON, Thomas, 31, 69
BUZBY,
Daniel, 55
Isaac, 54, 55
Joseph, 55
Martha, 54, 55
Melicent, 54
Naomy, 55
Nathaniel, 54
Rachel, 55
Rebecca, 54
Sarah, 54, 55
William, 54
BYRCELIUS, Paul Daniel, 76

-C-

CAKE,
Betsy, 32
Henry, 32
Peggy, 31, 71

EARLY RECORDS OF CUMBERLAND CO.

Philip, 30
CAMBELL, Sarah, 64
CAMBLE, John, 69
CAMBORN,
  Hannah, 51
  John, 51
CAMBURN,
  DeLucy, 51
  Margaret, 51
  Nancy, 51
CAMEL,
  Elizabeth, 90
  Rachel, 90
CAMP, Elizabeth, 64
CAMPBELL,
  Anne, 64
  Charles, 100
  Elizabeth, 68, 100
  James, 52, 100
  Jean, 100
  John, 68
  Nicholas, 100
  Peter, 90
  Rebecca, 69, 100, 115
  Sarah, 100
CAMPBLE,
  Mary, 90
  Thomas, 90
CANDELL, Elizabeth, 31
CAREL,
  Elizabeth, 95
  Ephraim, 95
  Phineas, 95
  Rachel, 95
CARL, John, 68
CARLE,
  Burton, 95
  Elizabeth, 92
  Issable, 95
  Jeremiah, 95
  Lusinda, 95
  Mary, 63
  Pamela, 95
  Rebecca, 95
  William, 95
CARLL,

Abraham, 25
Elizabeth, 22
Ephraim, 105
Henry, 22
Lucinda, 106
Martha, 102
Maskell Mills, 95, 107
Phineas, 107, 108, 111
Rachel, 28
Sarah, 114, 118
William, 108, 112
CAROTHERS,
  Deliverance, 93
CARRELL, Isaac, 69
CARROLL, Peter, 105
CARROW, Aaron, 68
CARTER, Jeremiah, 70
CARUTHERS,
  Deliverance, 92
  Hannah, 94
  James, 112
  Mary, 95
  Obadiah, 112
  Obediah, 95
  Philenah, 95
  Rebecca, 95, 106
  Richard, 31, 64, 95, 107, 112
  Richard Ewing, 95
CARYLY, Susannah, 23
CASE, Herre, 59
CASPER,
  Eliza, 45
  Johannes, 45
  Lawrence, 45
  Lorenz, 46
  Lorenzo, 41, 46
  Margaret, 45
  Phebe, 45
  Susan, 46
  Susanna, 41
CASTO,
  David, 87, 105
  Jacob, 16
  John, 28
  Phebe, 87

Thomas, 74
William, 16, 68
CAUSON, Judith, 66
CHAMPNEYS,
  Benjamin, 63
CHAND, Benjamin, 57
CHANNEL, Elizabeth, 118
CHARD,
  Elizabeth, 73, 90
  Joab, 66
  Joal, 69
  Samuel, 30
  William, 69
CHARLES, Henry, 31, 66
CHEASMAN, Sarey, 64
CHEESMAN,
  Reuben, 89, 112
  Thomas, 71
CHESSNEY, Mary, 115
CHESTER, Ann, 111
CHOATE, Joseph, 30
CHTTEN, Beulah, 55
CHURCH, Silas, 88
CLARK,
  Abijah, 103
  Amos, 60
  Ananias, 23
  Ann, 54
  Anna, 99, 103, 104
  Bathsheba, 6, 69
  Charles, 103, 104, 112
  Daniel, 99, 103, 104, 112
  David, 69
  James, 15, 59, 61, 112
  Joel, 6, 66
  John, 64, 86
  Joshua, 22, 112
  Lavicy, 66
  Mary, 23, 67, 103, 117
  Phebe, 103
  Polly, 72
  Rachel, 23, 104
  Ruhannah, 15
  Sally, 31, 64

INDEX

Samuel, 23, 24, 28
Sarah, 104
Stephen, 88, 112
CLARKE, Susanna, 112
CLARKSON, William, 104
CLEAVER, Elizabeth, 118
CLEMENTS,
  Elizabeth, 53
  Jacob, 53
CLEMONS, John, 30
CLEVER, John, 112
CLEVES, Sarah, 110
CLIFTON, Tabitha, 67
CLUN,
  Charles, 86
  Mariah, 86
  Rachel, 86
COALS, Sarah, 4
COBB,
  Caroline, 77
  Catherine, 76, 77
  Constant, 52
  Elizabeth, 64
  Samuel, 76, 77
  William, 61, 77
COBURN, David, 73
COCKE, Felix, 67
COCKS(COOK), Gabriel, 61
CODINGTON, Rhoda, 67
COFFEE,
  Hannah, 92
  Isaac, 92
COFFIN, Sarah, 3
COKE, Sally, 72
COLEMAN, Mary, 28
COLES, Sarah, 5
COLLETT,
  Hester, 51
  Margaret, 51
  Silas, 51
COMPTON, William, 74
CONEY, Ruth, 63

CONINGHAM,
  Alexander, 1
  Sarah, 116
CONKLIN(G),
  David, 30, 64
  Hannah, 28
CONKLYN, Joseph, 72
CONNER,
  George, 30
  Rachel, 110
  Tabitha, 91
CONNOR, William, 69
CONRAD, George, 47
CONVENOVER, Peter, 29
COOK,
  David, 63
  Eldad, 1
  Eunice, 6
  Jean, 112
  Phebe, 114
  Rachel, 6, 115
  Ruth, 74
COPE, John, 52
CORDWALL, John, 28
CORN, Lawrence, 112
CORNWALL,
  Jonathan, 29
  Sarah, 30
CORNWELL, Philop, 72
CORRANT, Nancy [Mary?], 70
CORRINGTON, Phebe, 105
CORSON,
  Aaron, 54
  Abel, 105
  Barbery, 68
  Edith, 54
  James, 54
  Jesse, 53
  John, 112
  Juda, 68
  Lydia, 68
  Martha, 53
  Peter, 53

Priscilla, 68
Rebeccah, 53
Rem, 54
Sarah, 52
COUCH,
  Catherine, 38
  Hans George, 38
  Heinrich, 38
  John George, 47
  Joseph, 73
  Micheal, 47
COUNOVER, Isaiah, 2
COUTS, Catharine, 63
COVENHOVEN,
  William, 66
COWNOVER, Sarah, 6
COX, Prudence, 29
CRAMER,
  Anna Margaret, 43, 44
  Anna Maria, 44
  Charity, 43
  Mathias, 43, 44
  Salome, 43
CRANDLE, Rachel, 52
CRAVEN, Richard
  Wheat, 112
CRAWFORD, Mary, 95
CREAMARCH, Mary, 29
CREAMER,
  Charity, 35, 36
  Johan George, 47
  Mathias, 47
CREDIS, Joseph, 65
CREMARCH,
  Catharine, 28
  Charity, 29
CREMER, George, 63
CRIPSING, William, 52
CRONEBERGER, John
  Peter, 47
CROSLEY, Moses, 4
CROWELL, Joshua, 63
CRUM,
  Abigail, 32
  Heman, 31
  Henry, 69

CRUMRINE, Geo
Lenhart, 47
CUNNINGHAM,
Anna Maria, 38
Johann, 38
Rebecca, 38
CURTIS, Samuel, 64

-D-
DALEN, Ruth, 111
DALTON,
Hannah, 68
John, 63
DAMARIES, John, 61
DANIEL,
Damaris, 16
Rhoda, 52
DANIELS,
Eli, 52, 112
John, 89, 112
Joseph, 58
Ogden, 66
Rachel, 119
Randal, 88
Samuel, 90
Sarah, 91
Susanna, 69
DANTZEBECHER,
Freidrich, 47
DANZEBAKER,
Catherine, 33
Chas. C.D., 33
DANZEBECHER,
Catherine, 33
Johann Ludwig, 33
DANZENBAKER,
Anna, 46
Cathere, 35
Catherine, 34, 36, 37, 38, 40, 41, 46
Elisabetha, 38
Elizabeth, 46
Freidrich, 47
George, 40
Heinrich, 46
Henry, 46

Johann, 40
Johann George, 36
Johann Heinrich, 34
Johann Jacob, 35
Johann Ludwig, 34, 35, 36, 37, 38, 42, 46
Maria, 40
Susan, 46
Susanna, 37, 41
DARE,
Anne, 24
Benjamin, 112
Benoi, 105
Benone, 112
Damaras, 4
David, 5, 24, 27, 68, 112
Eleanor, 2
Elizabeth, 67, 117
Gabriel, 72
Gamaliel, 106
Hannah, 11, 14, 16, 24, 72, 118
James, 5
John, 63, 71
Lavinia, 106
Ludlum, 24
Mary, 112
Philip Stathem, 107
Rachel, 111
Rebecca, 110
Reuben, 112
Robert, 16, 17, 22
Ruth, 5, 14, 24
Ryneer, 23, 29
Sarah, 72, 111, 119
Tamzen, 63
William, 107
DATEN,
Abigail, 85
Ann, 85
David, 85
Eli, 85
Joseph, 57, 85
Prudence, 85
DATON, Ephrain, 60
DAVENPORT,

Elizabeth, 12, 13
J., 11, 12
John, 8
Mr., 11, 14, 18, 24, 30
DAVID,
Mary Anna, 112
Mr., 109
Othaniel, 9
Virgil, 109
DAVIS,
Aaron, 19
Abigail, 17, 64
Abishac, 25
Alfred, 20
Ami, 6
Ammi, 112
Amos, 16, 17
Anna, 68
Arthur, 8, 18, 23, 30
Benjamin, 11, 13, 18, 19, 20, 26, 31, 69
Broadway, 9, 11, 13, 16, 18, 19, 21, 24, 25, 31, 32, 66
Damaris, 16
Daniel, 11, 13, 14, 16, 17, 18, 26, 31, 32, 70
David, 67
Deborah, 1, 4
Edith, 112
Edward, 66
Elijah, 9, 13, 16, 18, 31, 65
Elizabeth, 6, 9, 14, 16, 26, 30
Enos, 32
Ester, 10
Esther, 13
Esther Preston, 18
Eunice, 6, 12, 14
Gilbert, 21
Hannah, 11, 14, 19, 26, 105
Harriet, 18
Isaac, 25, 112
Israel, 106

INDEX

Jacob, 71
James, 11, 14, 18, 26
Jane, 18
Jemima, 31, 65
Jemina, 65
Joanna Wilkins, 66
John, 13, 17, 105
Jonathan, 29, 112
Joseph, 22
Levi, 18
Lot, 16
Lydia, 24, 25
Margaret, 73
Mary, 68
Molly, 72
Nancy, 18, 30, 64
Nathan, 6
Othniel, 13
Patience, 9, 13
Phebe, 13, 14, 16, 17, 19, 27, 32
Priscilla, 18
Rachel, 31, 71
Rebecca, 19
Reumah, 12, 14, 19, 20, 22, 25, 27
Rhoda, 12, 13
Richard, 19
Rufush, 22
Rumah, 106
Ruth, 12, 14, 18, 19, 20, 24, 65
Sally, 31, 69
Samuel, 73
Sarah, 10, 13
Stephen, 63
Susannah, 20
Tabitha, 119
Tamson, 26
Thomasin, 26
Thomazine, 18
Titus, 59
Uriah, 10, 11, 13, 14, 16, 17, 19, 20, 22, 23, 25, 27, 106
William, 6, 106

Zebadiah, 71
DAY, Michael, 22
DAYTON,
  Ann, 112
  Charles, 24
  Ephraim, 112
DEAL,
  Anna Margaret, 34, 35
  George, 34, 35
  Jacob, 34
  Maria, 35
DEAR,
  James, 5
  Marion, 6
  Mary, 6
DELSHOFER,
  Johannes, 34
  Maria Anna, 34
DEMARIS,
  Charlotte, 67
  Peter, 73
DENNIS,
  Edward, 112
  Sarah, 98
DENSELBECK,
  Anna Margaret, 42
  Freidrich, 42
  Johannes, 42
DENTON,
  Elinor, 101
  Sarah, 114
DEVALL, Eunice, 112
DEVINE, Martha, 110
DIAMENT,
  Hannah, 115
  James, 56, 57
  Johnathan, 57
  Jonathan, 56
  Lois, 85
  Nathaniel, 8, 11, 13, 56, 57, 85
  Priscilla, 12, 13
  Ruth, 70
DICKENSON,
  John, 2
  Mary, 2

DICKINSON, Joseph, 112
DICKSON, Ann, 4
DIEH,
  Anna Margaret, 34
  George, 34
  Jacob, 34
DIEL,
  Anna Margaret, 35
  George, 35
  Maria, 35
DIENGER, Catherine, 33
DILLSCHAFFER,
  Elizabeth, 36
  Jacob, 36
  Johannes, 36
DILLSCHOFFER,
  Maria Elisabeth, 41
  Michael, 41
DILSHAVER,
  Anna Maria, 38
  Caroline, 43
  Christiana, 71
  Elisabeth, 36
  Elizabeth, 36
  Jacob, 29, 36, 38
  Johann Micheal, 43
  Johannes, 34, 36, 43
  Margaret, 40
  Maria Ann, 46
  Maria Anna, 34, 40
  Maria Catherine, 43
  Maria Elisabeth, 41, 43
  Michael, 41
  Micheal, 43
  Philip, 40, 65
  Simon, 43
  Susanna, 38
  Susannah, 31, 65
DIMON,
  Josiah, 59
  Ruth, 61
DISHAVER,
  Johannas, 37
  Margaret, 37
  Maria Anna, 37

EARLY RECORDS OF CUMBERLAND CO.

DIXON,
  Anna Barbara, 38
  Daniel, 64
  Francis, 7, 112
  Hannah, 58
  Issable, 95
  Johann George, 38
  Johannes, 38
  Rachel, 93
  Urban, 69
  Urben, 58
  Urbin, 59, 60, 61
DIXSON,
  Ann, 5
  Daniel, 112
  Francis, 5
DOFFEL,
  Catherine, 33
  Elisabeth, 33
DOLE,
  Hannah, 53
  Isaac, 53, 55
  John, 55
  Mary, 55
  Rachel, 53, 55
  Sarah, 55, 65
DOLLAS, Rebecca, 54
DOLLASS, Anee, 66
DOLLES,
  Jonathan, 112
  William, 87, 88
DOLLIS,
  Mary, 90
  Rebeccah, 54
  Sussannah, 91
  William, 87, 88
DONALDSON, Mary, 104
DONELSON,
  Joseph, 112
  Samuel, 39
  Susanna, 39
DONN, Benjamin, 112
DONNELL,
  Benjamin, 108
  Elizabeth, 105

  Major, 108
  Nathaniel, 112
DONNELLY,
  George, 52
  John, 52
DORMAN, Claford, 58
DOWDNEY,
  John, 1, 112
  Nicholas, 112
  Samuel, 112
  Tabitha, 1
DRAGSTON, Jessey, 72
DRAPER, Jemima, 112
DUBOIS,
  Abraham, 112
  Anne, 69, 31
  Solomon, 69, 31
  William, 32
DUBOS, Benjamin, 32
DUFF,
  Elizabeth, 29
  John, 22
  Thomas, 29
DUFFEL,
  Deborah, 32
  Jacob, 112
  John, 18
  Peter, 29
  Susannah, 12, 14, 18
  William, 18
DUFFIELD,
  Catherine, 33
  Elisabeth, 33
  Elizabeth, 70
DUFFILE, David, 65
DUNHAM, Ephraim, 65
DUNN, Amy, 110
DUVALL, Susannah, 2

-E-
EAEMMELL,
  Johann Mathias, 38
  John Martin, 38
  Rosina Catherine, 38
EARE, Nathian, 59
EARLS,

  John, 73
  Thomas, 58
EASTBURN, Thomas, 112
EBERT,
  Hannah, 55
  Jeremiah, 55
  Mary, 55
EDDIS, Thomas, 112
EDWARDS,
  Curtis, 73
  David, 63
  Martha, 5
  Temperance, 30
EGBERT,
  Jacob, 51
  jacob, 52
  Lotitia, 51
  Mary, 51
EIREIGH, Susannah, 29
ELDREDGE,
  Daniel, 112
  Mary, 110, 114
  Susanna, 65
ELDRIDGE,
  Esther, 117
  Sarah, 106
ELKINTON, Ann, 113
ELLASS,
  Daniel, 69
  Job, 69
ELMAN, Theodores, 58
ELMER,
  Abigail, 85
  Daniel, 57, 85, 112
  David, 56
  Ebenezer, 108
  Eli, 113
  Eli Theophilus, 113
  Hannah, 85
  J., 85
  John, 64, 73
  Jonathan, 70, 108
  Mary, 85, 115
  Polly, 115
  Ruhama, 112

Sarah, 67, 111
Theodosia, 73, 110
Theodotia, 85
Thoephilus, 85
Timothy, 85
William, 108
William Ramsey, 85
ELMORE,
Daniel, 59
John, 61
Jonathan, 60, 61
ELWELL,
Catharine, 32
Cornelius, 4, 5
David, 4, 5, 7
Hannah, 2, 5
Isaac, 25, 64
Sarah, 4, 5
Yocominetie, 6
Yocomintine, 63
EMBERSON, John, 67
EMMEL,
Anna Maria, 35
Caroline Catherine, 39
Elisabeth, 33, 35, 37
Emuel, 41
Ester, 41
Estor, 41
Isaac, 41, 45
Johann, 41
Johann Martin, 36, 39
Johann Mathias, 38
Johann Micheal, 36
Johanna Henrich, 36
John, 45
John Martin, 38
Lydia, 41, 45
Peter, 33, 35, 37, 41
Rosina, 37
Rosina Catherine, 36, 38, 39
Rudy, 41
Sara Ann, 41
EMMON, Jacob, 63
EMUL,
Elisabeth, 33

Peter, 33
ENGANFULL,
Jane, 87
Joseph, 87
ENGLISH, John, 2
ERL, Thomas, 60
ERNSDOFF,
Elisabeth, 37
Heindrich, 37
Heinrich, 37
ERRICKSON, John, 69
EUSTACE, Isabel, 113
EVANS,
David, 64, 105
Lott, 47
Mary, 65
EWELL, Jacob, 2
EWING,
Abigail, 93, 94
Abner, 67
Ame, 94
Amy, 107
Ann, 114
Anna, 104
Artemas, 104
Charles, 97
Charolette, 38
Daniel, 38
David, 94, 108
Dixon, 93
Elizabeth, 104, 108
Enas, 108
Enos, 105, 107
George, 93, 107, 113
Hannah, 4, 93, 104
Harriet, 94
Harriet Seeley, 94
Hope, 93
Israel, 106
James, 97, 104, 113
James Josiah, 94
Joel, 93
John, 97, 105
Joshua, 97, 104
Lydia, 73
Martha, 97

Mary, 93, 94, 95, 97, 100, 104, 108, 112
Maskell, 94, 95, 97, 100
Micheal, 38
Pelmis, 104
Phebe, 93, 94, 113
Rachel, 93, 94, 105
Rebeca, 93
Remington, 113
Robert, 104
Ruth, 104
Samuel, 97, 106, 113
Samuel Fithian, 94
Sarah, 93, 94, 100, 104, 105, 107, 117
Susan, 100
Susanna, 94
Susannah, 106
Thomas, 52, 93, 94, 97, 104
William Belford, 94
EWINGS, Barzillar, 29

-F-
FAHEN, Lat, 61
FAITONTE, Mr., 11
FAITOUTE,
Euphemia, 94, 108
Geo, 94
Geo., 101, 102
George, 96, 104, 106, 107, 108
George Whitfield, 108
James, 94, 107
Lydia, 94, 107
Mr., 92
FALCK,
Adam, 43
Elisabeth, 43
FALK,
Catherine, 45
Elisabeth, 36
Elizabeth, 36
FARRILL, James, 113
FAUVERN, Barbara, 28

FELLAS(FELLOWS),
John, 60
FELLERS, Widow, 61
FERGUSON, William,
106
FICHIAN, Daniel, 59
FIECHER, Hans Geo, 47
FIGHT,
  Catarina, 68
  Catharine, 116
FILAR, David, 31, 65
FILE, John, 24
FILE(FILES OR FILER),
Hannah, 22
FILER,
  Anna, 46
  Hannah, 66
  John, 24, 68
  Margaret, 67
  Martha, 63
  Mary, 68
  William, 29
FILES, John, 24
FINLAW,
  David, 103
  John, 103
  Margaret, 115
  Nathan, 103, 106
  Rebeca, 103
  Sarah, 103, 118
FINLEW,
  Elenor, 97
  Elizabeth, 97
  Finlaw, 97
  John, 97
  Sarah, 97
FINLEY,
  MAry, 65
  Rebecca, 106
FINNAMAN, Joseph, 72
FISCHER,
  Anna Maria, 43
  George, 43
  Margaret, 43
FISH,
  Asa, 73
Jonathan, 31, 66
Samuel, 22
FISHER,
  Adam, 35, 36
  Anna Maria, 43
  Benjamin, 52
  Christina, 35, 36
  Elisabeth, 36
  George, 29, 43
  Hans Geo, 47
  Margaret, 29, 43
  Susanna, 35
FISHTER,
  Adam, 35
  Christina, 35
  Susanna, 35
FISMIRE, Mary, 63
FISTHER,
  Adam, 36
  Christina, 36
  Elisabeth, 36
  Philip, 36
FITHEN, Ephiam, 58
FITHIAN,
  Abigail, 94, 118
  Amos, 97
  Amy, 98
  Ann, 119
  Anne, 99
  Athele, 10, 13, 14
  Betsey, 64
  Charles B., 99
  Charles Beatty, 96, 107
  Clover, 103
  David, 56, 85
  Deliverance, 93
  Deliverane, 92
  Dr., 104
  Elis, 103
  Elizabeth, 72, 92, 96, 99,
  103, 113
  Enoch, 97
  Ephraim, 26, 71, 98, 113
  Erkurius B., 99
  Ester, 115
  Esther, 72, 92, 98, 102
George, 4, 92, 113
George R., 92
Gervas Reeves, 92
Glover, 67
Hannah, 92, 97, 98, 103,
110, 115
Hope, 92
Ira, 26, 98
Isaac, 92, 103
Israel, 103
James, 92
James Carothers, 92
Jeremiah, 92, 98, 102
Job, 92
Joel, 96, 99, 107, 108,
113
John, 32, 98, 113
Jonathan, 67, 97, 113
Joseph, 97, 98, 103
Josiah, 97
Judith, 103
Karenhappuch, 92
Lot, 103
Lovisa, 106
Margaret, 98
Martha, 93, 98, 102
Mary, 1, 2, 26, 92, 99,
111, 117
Mathias, 92, 93, 98
Phebe, 98, 103, 105
Philip, 97, 99, 108
Philip Vicars, 30
Priscilla, 92, 98
Rachel, 98, 99, 104
Rebecca, 97, 103, 111
Rhoda, 63, 92
Ruth, 67, 99
Samuel, 94, 98, 99, 103,
107, 113
Sarah, 4, 92, 94, 99, 103
Seeley, 67, 99
Temperance, 98, 112
Thomas, 97
William, 72, 92, 93, 98,
113
FITZGERALD,

INDEX

Lewis, 51
Mary, 110
FIX,
  Adam, 33
  Elisabeth, 33
  Lydia, 105
  Maria Anna, 33
  Miriam, 106
FIXEN,
  Catharine, 30
  Eva, 28
FLEETWOOD, Eve, 69
FLIER, John, 113
FLITCRAFT, Francis, 113
FOLK, Mary, 104
FORGISON, Ellenor, 115
FORREES, Sarah, 112
FORSMAN, Daniel, 69
FOSER, Ezekiel, 8
FOSTER,
  Christina, 37
  Daniel, 19
  Ebenezer, 17
  Ephraim, 16, 17, 25, 31, 66
  Esther, 25
  Ezekiel, 10, 11, 15, 18, 19
  Hannah, 9, 11, 13, 15, 16, 18, 19, 119
  Heinrich, 37
  Jeremiah, 8, 113
  Jonathan, 17, 23, 29
  Lydia, 12, 15, 70
  Mary, 14, 25, 106
  Mr., 11
  Nathaniel, 17
  Peter, 37
  Ruth, 25, 72
  Sarah, 15
FOWLER,
  Emily, 116
  Thomas, 65
FOX,
  Adam, 33, 43

  Anna Maria, 38
  Catherine, 43
  Charolette, 44
  Elisabeth, 33, 43
  Eva Maria, 43
  Freidrich, 38
  Henry, 113
  Johan Adam, 47
  Maria Anna, 33
FOY, Temperance, 27
FRASER, Abigail, 119
FRENT, Morgan, 113
FREVEL,
  Anna Margaret, 37
  Catherine Elisabeth, 37
  Johannes, 37
FRIES,
  Anna Margaret, 34, 42
  Elisabeth, 34, 36
  Frederick, 30
  Hannah, 41
  Jacob, 17, 34, 36, 39, 42, 43
  Johannes, 42
  Margaret, 34, 42
  Maria Ann, 39
  Mary, 17
  Philip, 39
FROSTER,
  Christina, 37
  Heinrich, 37
  Peter, 37
FRY, Henry, 32
FRYANT, Abigail, 106
FUCH, Johan Adam, 47
FUCHS,
  Adams, 43
  Anna Maria, 38
  Catherine, 43
  Elisabeth, 43
  Eva Maria, 43
  Freidrich, 38
FULK, Elizabeth, 29
FULSE, Jacob, 64
FURMAN, Judah, 61
FURNIS, Mary, 119

FURNISS, Edith, 116

-G-
GALL, Rebecca, 67
GALLASBY, Ruth, 111
GALPING, Thomas, 113
GAMBOLD,
  Ann, 80
  E., 81
  Eleanor, 80
  Ernest, 80
GANDE,
  Nathan, 61
  Nathaniel, 59, 61
GANDY,
  Abbia, 87
  Abiah, 88
  Aron, 88
  David, 89, 113
  Mary, 70
  Sheppard, 66
  Thomas, 113
GANGER, Johan Conrad, 48
GARDNER,
  Rebecca, 70
  William, 67
GARISON,
  Elizabeth, 102
  Enos, 26
  Lawrence, 26
  Rhoda, 26
  Susannah, 72
GARRISON,
  Abraham, 15, 23, 28, 66, 89
  Abram, 90
  Amy, 115
  Andrew, 69
  Ann, 66, 97
  Anne, 4, 31, 96
  Catherin, 87
  Christiana, 12, 14, 20, 21
  Corneliius, 88
  Cornelis, 89

Damaris, 110
Daniel, 14, 16, 17, 27
Daniel Davis, 21
David, 13, 17, 20, 21, 23, 24, 30, 31, 69, 89
Elanor, 91
Eleanor, 6
Elener, 90
Eliza, 20
Elizabeth, 17, 21, 25, 69
Ephraim, 71
Gamaliel, 113
Garrard, 29
Garrett, 88
Hannah, 13, 16, 21, 31, 63, 65, 113
Isaac, 88
Jacob, 87, 88, 89, 90
James, 31, 65
Jemina, 2
Jeremiah, 90
Joel, 20, 21
John, 8, 11, 13, 15, 20, 23, 31, 59, 66, 67, 69, 72, 83, 87, 88, 89
Jonathan, 13, 14, 28, 71
Jonathan Thompson, 21
Jonathon, 9
Joseph, 65, 73
Joshua, 91
Judith, 70
Levi, 15, 16, 17, 23
Lewis, 73
Lydia, 15, 18
Margaret, 66
Mary, 9, 14, 26, 29, 90, 91
Mathias, 27
Neoma, 91
Omy, 90
Phebe, 14, 17, 20, 23, 66
Powel, 16
Rachel, 30, 87
Rebecca, 32, 87, 115
Rhoda, 16, 115
Ruth, 10, 14, 26, 63, 90

Sarah, 20, 21
Stephen, 16
William, 8, 9, 10, 13, 15, 16, 17, 20, 26, 31, 69, 87, 89, 113
GARTEN, Ephraim, 64
GARTON,
Daniel, 17
David, 17, 59, 63
Israel, 17
Jonathan, 15, 17, 22, 24, 61
Mary, 17
Nancy, 69
Phebe, 15
GASTON, Atteliah, 113
GENKENS, Hannah, 116
GENTRY, Naomi, 68
GIBBON,
Ephraim, 95
Ester, 95
Hannah, 95, 115
John, 95, 113
Leonard, 95
Nicholas, 95
GIFFORD,
Job, 106
John, 31, 66
William, 61
GILL,
Catherine, 76
Christiana, 79
Deborah, 77
Elizabeth, 80
Magadalene, 79
Magdalen, 76
Magdalene, 76, 78, 81
Magdene, 77
Mary, 78, 79
Matthew, 76, 77, 78, 79, 80
GILLINGHAM, Margaret, 118
GILLMAN, Daniel, 74
GILMAN,
Alethea, 30

Letitia, 117
GILMON,
David, 4
Lydia, 4
GLAN,
Forazor, 72
Gabril, 89
GLAND, Ruth, 113
GLANN, Gabriel, 83, 88
GLASBEY, Mary, 72
GLASCOM, Polly, 67
GLASPEY,
Job, 66
Rebecca, 111
GLASPY, Sarah, 5
GOFF,
Jeremiah, 87, 88, 89
John, 68
Joseph, 89
Lidia, 52
Mary, 112
GOLDAN,
John, 2
Joseph, 1
Rebekah, 2
GOLDEN,
Lydia, 63
William, 87
GOLDIN, Mary, 87
GORREL, James, 113
GOTTSHALK,
M., 77
Matthew, 76
GOULD,
Anthony, 113
Ruma, 64
GRACE, Philip, 113
GRACEBERRY,
William, 76
GRACEBURY,
Ann, 78
Mary, 78
William, 78
GRAHAM, Elizabeth, 31, 66
GRANDY, Nathan, 106

INDEX

GRANT, Martha, 68
GRAVESTON,
  Elizabeth, 53
  Job, 53
  Lucinda, 53
  Millicent, 53
  Rachel, 53
  Rebecca, 53
  Reuben, 53
  Samuel, 53
  Townsend, 53
GRAY, Sarah, 52
GRAYDON, Alexander, 68
GREEN,
  Ann, 17
  Charles, 17
  E., 9, 10, 17
  Enoch, 8, 15, 16, 22, 28
  William, 16
GREENMAN, Nehemiah, 93
GRIER,
  George, 107
  Richard, 107
GRIFFARD, John, 66
GRIMES, John, 102
GROOM, Peter, 71
GROSS,
  Anna Maria, 43
  Elisabeth Margaret, 43
  Theobald, 43, 48
GRUFF, Sarah, 118
GUEST,
  Catherine, 78
  Christiana, 79, 81, 82
  Christina, 76, 77, 78
  Isaac, 76
  Joseph, 77
  Mary, 79
  Nathaniel, 77
  Sarah, 81
  William, 76, 77, 78, 79, 81, 82
GUMIN, Christopher, 66
GUNNELL, Anna, 68

-H-
HACKETT, Sarah, 71
HAHN,
  Anna Maria, 44
  Margaret, 44
  Nichols, 44
HAISHT, Georg, 30
HALL,
  Abba, 6
  Abner, 113
  Ebenezer, 69
  George, 113
  Hannah, 64
  Isaac, 105
  Ruth, 65
  Sarah, 114
HALTER,
  David, 71
  Hans Martin, 47
  Johanna George, 43
  Peter, 113
  Sophia, 29
HAMBLETON, John, 90
HAMILTON, Edward, 65
HAMPTON,
  Doctor, 60
  Masse, 60
  Mercy, 64
  Thomas, 70
HANCOCK, Joseph, 113
HAND,
  Aaron, 113
  Daniel, 60
  Fanny, 70
  Hannah, 117
  Jane, 116
  Jonathan, 89
  Judith, 110
  Lydia, 115, 118
  Martha, 90, 115
  Mary, 111
  William, 61, 113
HANN,
  Jonathan, 70
  Mary, 114
HANNAH,

  Bathsheba, 12, 15
  David, 17
  James, 22
  Joseph, 64
  Lydia, 22
  Preston, 10, 15, 113
  Ruth, 29, 117
  Samuel, 113
  Silas, 22
HANNAN,
  Adam, 45
  Anna Maria, 37
  Catherine, 37
  George, 37
  Joseph, 64
  Susanna, 45
HAPPENER, Johannes, 47
HARDEN,
  John, 71
  Jonathan, 63
HARDING, Mary, 117
HARDMAN, John, 29
HARIS, Jeremiah, 60
HARKER,
  Kathrine, 2
  Samuel, 2
HARLAND, John, 64
HARMER, Mary, 71
HARRIS,
  Abigail, 93
  Abijah, 72
  Amariah, 59
  Anna, 110
  Anne, 118
  Bathsheba, 67
  Catharine, 26
  Caty, 70
  Daniel, 3, 5, 113
  David, 66
  Delamore, 71
  Ebenezer, 8, 10, 13, 18, 19, 30
  Ebenzer, 26
  Eleanor, 12, 14, 19, 20, 26

Elizabeth, 17, 18, 29, 70, 104
Enoch, 31
Enos, 25
Ephraim, 56, 60
Eunice, 106
George, 26
Hannah, 12, 14, 18, 19, 30, 72, 85, 104, 107
Isaac, 85, 113
Israel, 27
Jacob, 4, 6, 113
Jalin, 59
James, 63
Jeremiah, 58, 63, 67, 85
Joel, 17, 19, 20, 26
Johanthan, 26
John, 16, 59, 70, 105
John Applin, 15, 22
Jonathan, 16, 17, 18
Joseph, 69
Josiah, 17, 24
Judah, 19
Lydia, 69
Margaret, 4
Mary, 3, 4, 5, 7, 19, 71
Miss, 67
Moses, 4
Moss, 114
Nathaniel, 23, 93, 104
Noah, 13, 15, 16, 107, 108, 114
Pamely, 101
Peason, 59
Phebe, 4
Priscilla, 22
Rachel, 4, 63, 66, 69, 93, 111, 113
Rebeccah, 101
Rev. Mr., 21
Robert, 4, 7, 30
Rodha, 61
Ruth, 108
Samuel, 1, 3, 114
Sarah, 1, 16, 18, 70, 107
Susanna, 85

Susannah, 3, 85, 104
Thomas, 20, 57, 85, 101, 107, 108
Violetta, 116
Widow, 23
William, 107, 114
HARTMAN,
Catherine, 41
Catherine Friedenia, 34
Christopher, 34, 37
Clara, 40
Estor, 40
Heinrich, 48
Jane, 41
Johann, 40, 47
Johannes, 40
Lillian, 40
Margaret, 40
Maria Margaret, 37
Martin, 41
Peter, 40
Susanna, 34, 37, 40
Wilhelm, 40
HATEN, Ephraim, 61
HATHORN, ---, 105
HAUTZ, Hans George, 48
HAWKINS, William, 52
HAWTHORN, Isaac, 114
HAY, Patrick, 52
HAYNES, Rebecca, 110
HAZE, Abigail, 111
HEAPPNAR,
Anna Maria, 39
Johann, 39
Margaret, 39
HEATON,
Abigail, 114
Betsey, 71
Epheraim, 4
Gideon, 87, 88
Levi, 3, 114
Mary, 4
Phebe, 70, 90
Samuel, 87, 88, 114
HECTOR,
Casper, 30

Elizabeth, 31, 66
HEIER,
Conrad, 47
Kunrad, 47
HEINE,
Johannes, 39
Rosina, 39
Wilhelm George, 39
HEINRICH, Peter, 48
HEMINGTON, Jacob, 65
HEMPLE,
Anna Barbara, 41
Elisabeth, 44
Johan Nicklaus, 48
Maria Barbara, 41, 44
Metrus Nicholous, 41
Nichols, 44
HENARD, John, 66
HENDERSON, Amey, 72
Anney, 72
Thomas, 52
HENDRICKSON, Mary, 2
HENNERY, John, 58
HENRY, Marey, 74
HEPNER,
Anna Maria, 39, 40
Betsy, 40
Joahnes, 48
Johann, 39, 40
Margaret, 39
HEPPEL,
Elisabeth, 44
Maria Barbara, 44
Nicholas, 44
HEPPOL,
Anna Barbara, 41
Maria Barbara, 41
Metrus Nicholous, 41
HERITAGE,
Benjamin, 21
Enoch, 21
Ester, 12
Esther, 14, 21
Forman, 21
Maria, 21

Nancy, 74
Sarah, 104
HERKIN, Anna Margaret, 42
HERRINGTON, Jacob, 66
HESTON, Samuel, 87
HEUARD, Ruth, 14
HEUSTED, Moses, 56
HEVERSON,
  Ezebel, 91
  Richard, 91
HEWARD,
  Ephraim, 21
  Isaac, 21
  John, 31
  Lydia, 21, 31
  Ruth, 21, 28
  Sarah, 21
  Zeboriah, 28
HEWARD(KENNARD),
  Joseph, 23
HEWET,
  Nathaniel, 88
  William, 88
HEWETT, Rebekah, 2
HEWING, Sarah, 112
HEWIT, Susannah, 117
HEWITT, Abigail, 118
HEWS, Esther, 2
HEYER,
  Christina, 37
  Conrad, 37
  Johanna, 37
HICHNER,
  Andrew, 68
  Salome, 33
HIEFFER,
  Daniel, 51
  George, 51
  Lydia, 51
HIGH,
  Hannah, 68
  Jacob, 26
  Joseph, 70
  Mary, 26

Rebecca, 26
HIGUENEL,
  Anna Maria, 34
  David, 34
HILDRETH, Joseph, 114
HILER, Eunice, 30
HILGERT,
  Christina, 38
  Heinrich, 39
  Henrich, 38
  Jacob, 39
  Johann Philip, 39
  Salome, 39
  Salomne, 38
HILLARD,
  Christina, 38
  Heinrich, 39
  Henrich, 38
  Johann Philip, 39
  Salome, 39
  Salomne, 38
HILLIARD,
  Heinrich, 39
  Jacob, 39
  Johann Heinrich, 37
  Salome, 37, 39
HILLMAN, Patty, 66
HILMAN(HILLMAN),
  John, 62
HILYARD,
  Johann Heinrich, 37
  Johann Henrich, 37
  Salome, 37
HINCHMAN, Miriam, 105
HINES, Jeremiah, 114
HINNE,
  Andreas, 39
  Bathasar Schmidt, 35, 36, 39
  Catherine, 35, 36, 39
  Christina, 35
  Johannes, 36
HINNER,
  Bathasar Schmidt, 35
  Catherine, 35

Jacob, 35
HINNIN,
  Anna Maria, 37
  Catherine, 37
  George, 37
HIPPEL, Johan Nicklaus, 47
HIRES,
  Christina, 37, 38
  Conrad, 37, 38
  Conrad (Kunrad), 48
  Johanna, 37
HITCHENOR,
  Christiana, 28
  Jacob, 30
  Maudlin, 29
HITCHER,
  Catherine, 43
  Jacob, 43
  Maria Magdalene, 43
  Salome, 35
HITCHNER,
  Anna Maria, 39, 40, 41
  Catherine, 40
  Christina, 38, 43
  Hans Jacob, 41
  Heinrich, 41
  Jacob, 39, 43, 44
  Johannes, 40
  Magdalene, 37, 39, 44
  Maria Barbara, 44
  Maria Magdalena, 44
  Maria Magdalene, 43
  Peter, 40
  Salome, 37, 39
  Susanna, 41
HITSCHNER, Peter, 48
HITZLER,
  Catherine, 40
  Johannes, 40
  Peter, 40
HIX, Josiah, 64
HODSON, Obed, 4
HOFFMAN,
  Abraham, 78
  Ann, 77

EARLY RECORDS OF CUMBERLAND CO.

Anna Margaret, 37
Benjamin, 82
Catherine, 76, 78, 79, 81
Deborah, 76
Drusilla, 66
Elizabeth, 77, 80, 81
Frederick, 78, 81
Johannes, 37
John, 75, 77, 79, 80, 81
Laurance, 76
Lawrence, 81, 82
Levisa, 69
Lorens, 76
Margaret, 81
Mary, 76, 77, 81
Peter, 76, 77
Rebecca, 81
Samuel, 77
Sarah, 70, 81, 82
HOGBEN,
  Joseph, 25
  Miriam, 25
HOGBIN, Amariah, 114
HOLETON, Rebecca, 66
HOLIDAY, John, 88
HOLL, Jane, 60
HOLL(HOWELL),
  Charles, 61
HOLLINGSHEAD,
  Jacob, 114
  Martha, 117
  Samuel, 114
  William, 97
HOLLOCHEIT,
  Adam, 41
  Anna Elisabeth, 41
  Christina, 41
  Justus, 41
HOLMES,
  Abijah, 99, 106
  Anna, 99, 103, 112
  Anne, 99
  Ephraim, 99, 106
  Eunice, 99, 100
  Jonatha, 99
  Jonathan, 72, 99

Mary, 99
Phebe, 99
Rachel, 99
Samuel, 68
Sarah, 99
HOLSEIT,
  Adam, 41
  Anna Elisabeth, 41
  Christina, 41
  Johanna Micheal, 42
  John Adam, 48
  Justus, 41
HOLSTEIN,
  Andrew, 81
  Lawrence, 78, 79, 81, 82
  Lorenze, 78
  Margaret, 79, 82
  Mary, 78
  Susanna, 79
HOLSTIN,
  Lawrence, 82
  Margaret, 82
  Sarah, 82
HOLSTINE,
  John, 79
  Lawrence, 78, 79, 80
  Lorenze, 78
  Margaret, 79, 80
  Mary, 78
  William, 80
HOOD,
  James, 68
  Jonathan, 106
  Rachel, 1, 114
HOOVER, Jacob, 48, 69
HOPMAN,
  Abraham, 78
  Catherine, 78, 79, 83
  David, 78
  Elizabeth, 78, 79
  Frederick, 78
  John, 78, 79, 83
  Lorenz, 76
HOPPNER,
  Anna Maria, 40
  Betsy, 40

Johann, 40
HORN,
  Anna, 42
  Christina, 42
  George, 42
  Johannes, 48
  Micheal, 42
HORSHELS, Adam, 23
HOSEA, Mary, 118
HOSEL, Michael, 29
HOSHALL,
  Michael, 22
  Ruth, 22
HOSHEL,
  Adam, 114
  Michael, 114
HOSHELL,
  Lydia, 30
  Michael, 24
HOSMAN, Prudy, 67
HOUSE, Ann, 87
HOUSEMAN, William, 65
HOWARD,
  Hannah, 73
  Lydia, 69
  Ruth, 13
HOWEL,
  Abigail, 73
  Ebenezer, 3
HOWELL,
  Charles, 61, 64
  John, 32
  Sarah, 112
HUDSON,
  Ann, 4
  Jedidia, 2
  Obed, 114
HUET,
  Eligah, 89
  William, 89
HUGER, Conrad, 28
HUGHES,
  Martha, 93
  Theophilus, 67
  Zeruiah, 111

INDEX

HULER, Lotitia, 52
HUMPHREYS, Susanna, 71
HUNG,
  Charolette, 38
  Daniel, 38
  Michael, 38
HUNIGAL,
  Anna Maria, 34
  David, 34
HUNT,
  Amy, 102
  Andrew, 102
  Anna, 101
  Bartholomew, 100, 101, 104
  E., 67
  Eleanor, 104
  Elizabeth, 101, 114
  Esther, 101
  Garner, 89
  James, 107, 108
  James B., 100
  James Booth, 100, 101, 104
  John, 101, 114
  Margaret, 100, 101
  Reuben, 100, 101, 107
  Richard, 101
  Sarah, 100, 108
  Susan, 100
  Thomas Ewing, 100
  William, 101
  William Ferguson, 100
HUNTER,
  A., 17
  Andrew, 8, 9, 114
  Andrews, 104
  Isaac, 66
  Jacob, 67
HUSBANDS, Vayer, 70
HUSTEAD, Moses, 57
HUSTED,
  Aaron, 62, 65
  David, 56
  Elisabeth, 119

  Elizabeth, 71
  Henry, 67, 73
  Joll, 61
  Letitia, 65
  Liddah, 59
  Mary, 12, 15
  Mrs., 58
  Philip, 7
  Rachel, 59
  Rhoda, 29
  Zebniah, 58
HUTCHINSON, Mary, 116
HUTSON, Rachel, 115
HYAT, Jaid, 67
HYDE,
  Mr., 10, 11
  Simeon, 8

-I-
INGERSOLL, Rebecca, 10, 13
INGERSON, Sarah, 73
INGERSUNN, Daniel, 66
IRELAN,
  Dorcas, 113
  Joseph, 114
  Micajah, 114
  Phebe, 115
IRELAND,
  Amos, 56
  Ann, 112
  Davis, 70
  Esther, 15
  John, 72, 74
  Joseph, 114
  Mary, 4, 111
  Phebe, 70, 114
  Phila, 32
  Sarah, 116
  Silas, 22
IRVIN, Rachel, 67
IRWIN, Sally, 69
ISZARD,
  Elizabeth, 114
  Priscilla, 117

  Rhoda, 3
  Samuel, 83
IZARD,
  Catherine, 75
  Gabriel, 75
  Martha, 75
  Rhoda, 114

-J-
JACKSON, Sarah, 113
JACOBS, Burton, 67
JACQUETT, John, 105
JAGGER,
  David, 24
  Elizabeth, 23
  John, 27
  Lorana, 27
JAGGERS,
  John, 68
  Jonathan, 66
JAMES,
  David, 2, 11, 13, 15, 107, 108, 114
  Joseph, 114
  Lewis, 16
  Patience, 9, 13
  Philothea, 5
  Rachel, 26
  Tamsin, 26
  Thomas Watson, 108
  Thomasin, 14
  Thomazine (Tamsin), 10
  Thomazine(Tamsin), 14
JAMMISON, Naome, 59
JANSON,
  Ann Catherine, 42
  Anna Maria, 33
  Hans, 42
  Jan. Stoll, 42
  Johann, 33
  Johanna, 33, 42
  Johannes, 42
  Peter, 33, 42
  Petrus, 42
  Philip, 42
  Priscilla, 58

JARMAN,
 Reuben, 68
 Ruth, 3
JARRELL, Isaac, 60
JAY,
 Elizabeth, 90
 Jacob, 90
 Mary, 117
JEFFERS, Phebe, 52
JELLEY, Henry, 2
JENKINS,
 Ann, 1, 5
 David, 1
 Eunice, 118
 Isaac, 114
 Mary, 73, 111
JERELL, Sarah, 73
JERMAN, Richard, 73
JERRILL, Zechariah, 66
JESS,
 Henry, 54
 James, 54
 Keziah, 54
 Maurice, 54
 Zula, 54
JESSUP,
 Anna, 14
 Anne, 10, 15
 Daniel, 22
 Isaac, 9, 13, 15, 17, 30
 John, 15, 16
 Judith, 15, 17
 Laurania, 17
 Lorana, 68
 Rachel, 16
 Stephen, 16
JINKINS, Mary, 90
JOCELIN,
 Daniel, 20
 Ester, 12
 Hannah, 17, 20, 28
 Hosea, 20
 Jacob, 9, 14, 16, 26
 Jane, 10, 13, 20, 28
 Jedidiah, 13, 20, 26
 John, 25

 John Nichols, 21
 Jonathan, 13, 20, 21, 28
 Jonathan Worrel, 20
 Lydia, 30
 Mary, 20, 26
 May, 14
 Phebe, 12, 14, 20, 21, 25, 28
 Samuel, 9, 13, 16, 17, 20, 28
 Sarah, 20
 Susannah, 16
 William, 16, 22
JOCELINE, Widow, 22
JOHN, Jedediah, 59
JOHNSON,
 Abigail, 4
 Ann, 112
 Anna Catherine, 42
 Anna Maria, 33
 Barbara, 35
 Bathsheba, 57
 Daniel, 1, 71
 David, 35, 63
 Elisabeth, 44
 Enos, 66
 Ethniel, 69
 George, 35, 71
 Hans, 42
 Isaac, 23
 Isaiah, 114
 Jan. Stoll, 42
 Jeremiah, 114
 Job, 73
 Johann, 33
 Johanna, 33, 42
 Johannes, 42, 44
 Judith, 114
 Laetitia, 118
 Mabel, 93
 Maj., 57
 Nathaniel, 105
 Nicholas, 5
 Paul, 44
 Peter, 33, 35, 42
 Petrus, 42

 Philip, 42
 Rebeckah, 116
 Rhoda, 1, 116
 William, 29
JOHNSTON,
 Elizabeth, 114
 Eunice, 113
 James, 114
JONES,
 Abigail, 112
 Abraham, 77, 78, 80, 81, 83
 Andrew, 70, 82
 Ann, 82
 Elizabeth, 31, 64, 80, 82
 Gunla, 77
 Hannah, 116
 Jacob, 82
 Jane, 78, 80, 81
 John, 77, 114
 Jonah, 76
 Jonathan, 55
 Joseph, 76, 78, 80, 81, 87
 Lidia, 101
 Lydia, 83
 Margaret, 41, 76, 78, 80, 81, 87
 Mary, 55, 78, 82, 118
 Owen, 55
 Priscilla, 83
 Rebecca, 77
 Robert, 41
 Samuel, 81
 Sarah, 72, 78
 Stephen, 77
 William, 41
JOSELIN,
 Ephraim, 18
 Jacob, 18
JOSLANE, Thomas, 56
JOSLEN, Ehpram, 72
JOSLIN,
 Jacob, 64
 Joseph, 67
 Lois, 61

William, 62, 63, 69
JOYCE, Henry, 104
JUNG,
  Johann Philippus, 50
  Jonas, 34
  Louisa, 34
JUSTIS, Margaret, 82

-K-
KAISER, Thomas, 45
KANDLE,
  Anna Maria, 35, 36, 39
  Elisabeth, 37
  Heinrich, 35, 36, 39
  Johann Adam, 39
  Joseph, 37
  Margaret, 36, 37
  Peter, 35
KARNS, Elizabeth, 63
KARRELL, Thomas, 105
KATS,
  Anna, 82
  Anna Dorthea, 82
  Barbara, 80, 81, 82
  Dorthea, 82
  Jacob, 80, 81, 82
  Marianna, 82
  Martin, 81, 82
  Mary, 80
  Michael, 80
  Rosina, 80
KATTS,
  Elizabeth, 26
  Hannah, 26
  Michael, 26
KAUCHER,
  Catherine, 38
  Eva Maria, 42
  George, 42
  Hans George, 38
  Heinrich, 38
  Maria, 42
KAUTZ,
  Ann, 40
  Anna Maria, 34, 36, 37, 40

Barbara, 38
Catherine, 36
Christina, 37
Elisabeth, 37
Jacob, 36
Johann George, 36, 37, 38, 40
Johannes, 34, 36, 38
Johannes George, 34
Maria, 36
Philip, 37
KEADEL,
  Anna Maria, 35
  Heinrich, 35
  Peter, 35
KEEN,
  Abraham, 77
  Benjamin, 25
  Catherine, 76, 77, 78, 104
  Eric, 76, 77, 78
  Jacob, 114
  John, 76, 77
  Lodema, 71
  Mary, 76
  Rachel, 29, 76
  Thomas, 78, 114
KELLOGG, Reuben, 114
KELLOR, George, 105
KELSAY,
  Elizabeth, 110
  Hezia, 6
  John, 4
  Kesiah, 6
  Miriam, 1
  Robert, 1, 2
  Sarah, 4, 65
  William, 5
KELSEY,
  Gartey, 17
  Michael, 17
  Polly, 72
  Sary, 90
KEMBLE,
  Samuel, 63
  Tasse, 74

KEMP,
  Andrew, 78
  Jane, 78
  Paul, 78
KENARD, Benjamin, 11, 15
KENN, Christiana, 113
KERMANN, Anna Elisabeth, 34
KERNAN,
  Anna Elisabeth, 34
  Jacob, 34
KETCHEM, Edward, 114
KIGING, Ebenezer, 114
KIMBLE, Ruth, 55
KIMME, Elizabeth, 119
KIMSEY, Elizabeth, 71
  Hannah, 4
  John, 66
  Reuben, 114
KING, Andrew, 65
KINNEY, Stephan, 88
KIRBY, Stephen, 114
KIRNSEY, Elizabeth, 71
KNAPPER, Catharine, 30
KNARRY,
  Anna Maria, 34
  Larynx, 34
  Maria Eva, 34
KNARY,
  Anna Maria, 33, 34
  Catherine, 33
  Larynx, 33, 34
  Maria Eva, 34
KOOCH, John George, 47
KOTLER, Johanna George, 43
KRAMER,
  Johan George, 47
  Mathias, 47
KREAMNOR,
  Anna Margaret, 43
  Charity, 43
  Mathias, 43
  Salome, 43

KROGSTRUP,
 C. O., 82
 C. Otto, 81
KRUMREIN, Geo
 Lenhart, 47
KUNKLEMAN,
 Anna Maria, 35
 Christopher, 35
 Johann Heinrich, 35
KYN,
 Catherine, 76
 Eric, 76
 George, 82
 Margaret, 82

-L-
LACY, Thomas, 52
LADOW,
 Ambrose, 70
 Mary, 72
 Peter, 73
 Phebe, 91
LAHMONT,
 Catherin Elisabeth, 35
 Freidrich, 35
 Sarah, 35
LAKE,
 Abraham, 114
 Samuel, 114
LAMMOND,
 Catherine Elisabeth, 34
 Fredrich, 34
 Johannes, 34
LAMONT,
 Catherin Elisabeth, 35
 Catherine Elisabeth, 34
 Freidrich, 34, 35
 Johannes, 34
 Sarah, 35
LANG, Joat, 48
LANGLEY, Richard, 1
LANGSTAFF,
 Amy, 54
 Deborough, 54
 Elizabeth, 54
 George, 54

Hannah, 54
 James, 54
 Mallachi, 54
 Mary, 54
 Rhoda, 54
 Samuel, 54
 Thomas, 54
 William, 54
LANING, John, 114
LANNING, Isaac, 73
LARENCE, Norton, 60
LARRANCE, Norton, 61
LARRENCE, Norton, 59
LARSAN, Beniaman, 61
LATON, Sarah, 65
LAURENCE,
 Christina, 40
 George, 40
 Nosten, 58
LAUTENBACH,
 Conrad, 81
 Elizabeth, 81
LAUTENSCHLAGER,
 Hans
 Micheal, 48
LAUTERBACH,
 Adam, 80
 Conrad, 79, 80
 Elizabeth, 79, 80
 Mathias, 80
 Peter, 79
LAUTESBACH,
 Elisabeth, 34
LAVERY,
 Isaac, 55
 John S., 55
 Margaret, 55
 Marget, 55
LAW, Mary, 66
LAWRENCE,
 Abigail, 113
 Ann, 103
 Asa, 19
 Benjamin, 103, 108
 Daniel, 102, 108
 Deborah, 102, 108

Henry, 105
 Jameson, 115
 John, 11, 14, 19, 24, 25
 Nathan, 114
 Polly, 24
 Sally, 19
 Sarah, 19, 24, 32
 Zachariah, 68
LAWS, Rebeca, 90
LAYCOCK, Samuel, 67
LEACH, Susannah, 118
LEAK, Rachel, 119
LEAKE,
 Abraham, 22
 Amy, 27
 David, 30
 Eleanro, 30
 Elizabeth, 9, 13
 Ephraim, 16
 Jeremiah, 104
 John, 13, 24
 Levi, 11, 13, 18, 105
 Lewis, 18
 Mabal, 11, 14, 18
 Nathan, 16, 18
 Phebe, 31, 69
 Rebecca, 31, 69
 Recomenpence, 9
 Recommence, 28
 Recompence, 8, 14
 Ruth, 18
 Samuel, 115
 Susannah, 31, 70
LEAMAN, Jeremiah, 89
LEANERD, Patrick, 66
LEAWERT, George, 115
LEDEU, Ambros, 90
LEE,
 Benjamin, 39
 Elezabeth, 3
 Elisabeth, 39
 Juliana, 39
 Millicent, 65
 Susanna, 65
LEEDS,
 Catharine, 54

INDEX

Jemima, 113
John, 54, 66
Judith, 54
Noah, 54
Samuel, 63
Sarah, 54
Vincent, 54
Warren, 54
LEEK,
  Hannah, 4
  Levi, 115
  Martha, 1
  Nathan, 115
LEIG,
  Benjamin, 39
  Elisabeth, 39
  Juliana, 39
LEISTER, Christian, 111
LESTER, Stephen, 115
LIDENIUS, Abraham, 78
LINN, John, 64
LINSEY, John, 60
LINZE, Isabel, 61
LIVINGSTON, Elizabeth, 29
LLOUD,
  Bateman, 82
  Jacob, 82
  Lydia, 82
LLOYD,
  Bateman, 80
  Beekman, 80
  Benjamin, 80
  Charity, 79
  Christiana, 80
  Daniel, 81
  Jaconias, 82
  John, 1, 63
  Josiah, 81
  Lydia, 80
  Magdalene, 81
  Matthew, 81
  Obadiah, 79, 80
  Obediah, 81, 82
  Priscilla, 110
  Rebecca, 79, 80, 81, 82

Samuel, 81
William, 80
LOCK,
  John, 76, 77
  Peter, 76
  Priscilla, 76
  Rebecca, 76, 77
  William, 115
LODER,
  Daniel, 29, 73
  Euben, 30
  Rhoda, 29
LOGAN,
  James, 27, 28
  Lydia, 11, 14, 27
LONG,
  Ansell, 115
  Bathseba, 21
  Bathsheba, 13, 14
  Constant, 90, 115
  David, 2, 4, 115
  Dorcas, 5
  Eleanor, 118
  Eunice, 90
  Grace, 1
  Jonathan, 115
  Joseph, 115
  Malichia, 5
  Pleasant, 116
  Sarah, 60
  Thomas, 31
  Unes, 64
  Uriah, 60
LOOMIS,
  Ebenezer, 8, 11, 13, 14, 28
  Edward, 56
  Ephraim, 8, 9, 13, 17
  Hannah, 29
  Lovisa, 12, 14, 32
  Lydia, 11, 14
  Polly, 31, 66
LOPER,
  Abraham, 17
  Benjamin, 22
  Daniel, 90, 91

James, 24
Mary, 29
Rachel, 30
Sarah, 29
Uriah, 22, 30
LOPPER, Elizabeth, 90
LORANCE, Jonathan, 56
LORANCO, Jonathan, 85
LORE,
  Ann, 88
  Dan, 88
  Daniel, 88, 89
  David, 89
  Elizabeth, 75, 90
  Ellener, 117
  Esekiah, 87
  Hezekiah, 75
  John, 90
  Jonathan, 87, 88
  Mary, 114
  Nathaniel, 89
  Rachel, 90, 91
  Richard, 88
  Ruth, 90
  Seth, 87, 88
  Tabitha, 71
  Temperance, 90
  William, 88
LORING, Rachel, 1
LOVE,
  Anne, 64
  Ichabod, 64
  Isaac, 64
  Nathaniel, 115
  Seth, 115
  William, 115
LOW,
  Margaret, 69
  Robert, 56, 69
LOWRING, Ann, 113
LUBIAN, Ephrim, 58
LUDENSLACKER, Hans
  Micheal, 48
LUDLAM,
  Jacob, 115
  Norton, 115

Phebe, 117
Priscilla, 65
Providence, 3, 5
Sarah, 3
LUDLEY, Lydia, 72
LUISE, Joseph, 60
LUMIS, Noer, 58
LUMMIS,
  Amy, 64
  Edward, 115
  Ephraim, 65
  Ephraim Dayton, 108
  Joseph, 105, 108
  Manoah, 115
  Parsons, 115
  Phebe, 113
LUPTON,
  Amee, 100
  Annie, 116
  Benjamin, 96, 115
  Daniel, 29
  Esther, 96
  Hannah, 100, 105
  James, 106
  John, 100, 107
  Keziah, 73
  Nathan, 100
  Phebe, 100
  Phineas, 69
  Prudence, 63, 69
  Rachel, 100
  Reuma, 105
  Rhoda, 67, 108
  Ruman, 100
  Stephen, 100, 106, 107, 108, 115
  Susannah, 100
  Widow, 72
LUTZ,
  Anna Maria, 34
  Johannes, 34
  Maria Barbara, 34
LYNMEYER,
  Ann, 76, 77, 78, 80, 82
  Christina, 77

Christopher, 76, 77, 78, 80
Nicholas, 78
Sarah, 76

-M-

MCCALLA,
  Aulay, 115
  Daniel, 107
  John Gibbon, 108
  Sulay, 108
MCCALLS, Daniel, 94
MCCHESNEY, Jane, 110
MCCLAIN,
  Amy, 109
  Andrew, 109
  Peter, 109
MCCLEAN, Peter, 109
MCCLINTOCK, Samuel, 115
MCCLUNG, Rebecca, 106
MCDONAL, Elick, 71
MCGILLARD,
  Hannah, 99
  James, 99
  John, 99
MCGILLIARD, James, 71
MCGLAUGHLLIN,
  Elizabeth, 117
MACHANEY, William, 52
MACHESEY, Sally, 73
MACHESNY, Sally, 73
MACHGAY,
  Acory, 37
  Maria, 37
  Robert, 37
MACK, Mary, 114
MCKEE,
  Hugh, 106, 115
  Mary, 67
MACKEY,
  Acory, 37
  Maria, 37

Robert, 37
MCKIMM, Mary, 30
MCKNIGHT, Nicholas, 67
MCLANE, Peter, 109
MCLEAN, Peter, 109
MCLONG,
  H., 73
  James, 65
MCNIGHT,
  Elizabeth, 103
  Hannah, 103
  James, 103
  John, 103
  Mercy, 103
  Rebca, 100
  Rebeca, 103
  Rebecca, 103
  Samuel, 103
MCPETERS, Sarah, 118
MCPHERSON, Mary, 71
MCQUEEN, Elizabeth, 114, 115
MADKIFF, William, 89
MADON, George, 68
MAGEE, Ephraim, 31, 71
MAHN,
  Johannes, 47
  Micheal, 47
MAIN, Mary, 91
MAINES, Mary, 63
MALL,
  Abigail, 28
  Benjamin, 15, 23, 24
  David, 32
  Hannah, 23
  John, 23
  Uriah, 23
  Urial, 30
MARIS, Johnathan, 60
MARSHALL,
  James, 115
  Mary, 32
  Sarah, 110
MARTIN,
  Johann Peter, 37

Johanna Martin, 37
Johannes, 48
Rosina Catherine, 37
MARTS, Zappaniah, 65
MASKELL,
  Abijah, 102
  Almedia, 102
  Bythia, 102
  Clemmens, 102
  Clemona, 116
  Constant, 102
  Daniel, 102, 115
  Elizabeth, 102
  Esther, 102
  Hannah, 102, 107, 118
  Marcy, 102
  Mary, 97, 102, 106
  Prudeence, 116
  Sarah, 102
  Thomas, 102, 104, 107, 115
MASKILL, Abigiah, 72
MASLANDER,
  Elizabeth, 77
  William, 77
MASON,
  David, 91
  Juda, 90
  Lyddea, 90
  Phebe, 91
  Sarah, 91
  William, 6, 89
MASSEY, Thomas, 115
MATCLIFF, Reeves, 65
MATERSON, Joseph, 69
MATHES, John, 67
MATHEWS,
  Temperance, 70
MATLACK, Caleb, 115
MATOX, Luke, 115
MATTHEWS, Richard, 66
MATTISON, Sarah, 6
MAUER, Johann Adam, 48
MAUL,

Daniel, 73
Rachel, 106
MAY,
  Elisabeth, 36, 37, 39
  Heinrich, 38
  Johann Jacob, 37
  Johann Micheal, 36
  Johann Philip, 39
  Philip, 36, 37, 39
MAYHEW,
  Amy, 116
  David, 3
  Dorcas, 32
  Hannah, 66
  Isal, 69
  John, 2
  Jona, 2
  Sanford, 32
MAYHEY, William, 32
MEAD, Margaret, 32
MEAKE, Rachel, 117
MEAL, George, 72
MEANS, Amy, 109
MECRAY, Jeams, 61
MEDELBEEKS, Robert, 73
MEEK,
  James, 21
  Mary, 21
  Rachel, 21
  William, 85
MEGRINE, James, 61
MEGUMERY, Mary, 61
MEGUMMERY, Robert, 62
MENSCH,
  Christina, 37
  Peter, 37
MEPIX, Clinton, 71
MEREDITH, Jude, 67
MERIOTT, Jonathan, 73
MERSCILLIER, Mary, 117
MEY,
  Elisabeth, 36
  Johann Micheal, 36

Philip, 36
MEYERS,
  George, 48
  Jacob, 48
MICHEAL, Christina, 39
MICHEL, Hannah, 60
MICKEL,
  Daniel, 60
  Thomas, 60
MICKELL, Joseph, 63
MICKELSON, William, 61
MICKLE,
  Daniel, 63
  Polly, 64
MICKLESON, William, 68
MIDDLETON, Mary, 68
MIKENER, John, 74
MILES,
  Jeremiah, 59
  Sarah, 3
MILLER,
  Abigail, 106, 115
  Abraham, 72
  Anna Barbara, 42
  Anna Maria, 35, 37
  Barbara, 33, 35
  Bathsheba, 29
  Catharine, 30
  Catherine, 33, 37
  Daniel, 72
  Ephraim, 96, 101
  Eunice, 96
  Experience, 101
  Hannah, 106
  Hans Michael, 41
  Hans Micheal, 48
  Isaac, 70
  Israel, 101, 106, 107, 115
  Jacob, 33, 37, 48
  Joel, 101, 104, 108, 115
  John, 64, 96, 107, 115
  Joseph, 32, 66, 105
  Keziah, 96

Lettitia, 114
Lovice, 101
Lydia, 28
Margaret, 41, 118
Mary, 101, 113
Michael, 37, 41
Nathan, 1, 6
Noah, 101, 115
Oliver, 101, 108
Phebe, 114
Rachel, 96
Rebecca, 96
Sally, 73
Samuel, 96, 101, 106
Sarah, 3
Simon, 32
Stephen, 106
Susanna, 45
William, 67
MILLS,
Ann, 97
Benjamin, 52
Benoni, 115
Charles, 100, 105
Daniel, 96
David, 63, 97
Elizabeth, 103, 110
Hannah, 97
Isaac, 100, 115
Jane, 103
Jeremiah, 107, 108
Jerymiah, 103
John, 103, 105
Letitia, 71
Lois, 100, 105
Mary, 101, 115
Naomi, 103
Philena, 107
Philenah, 95
Rachel, 95, 96, 111
Rebecca, 67, 100
Rumah, 103
Samuel, 115
Sarah, 65, 92, 96, 103
Seeley, 103
Selas, 103

Smith, 108
Theodisia, 103
Thomas, 103
MILS, Samuel, 89
MINCE, Bets, 60
MINCH,
Adam, 48
Christina, 37
Peter, 37
MINE, Adam, 59
MINTY, Elizabeth, 64
MISSE, Betz, 61
MISSEY, Hannah, 73
MITCHELL, Charles, 68
MITCHNER,
Hans George, 48
Hans Jacob, 48
Martin, 48
Peter, 48
MONTGOMERY,
Anthony, 115
Sally, 71
MOON,
Alisa, 110
Anne, 113
MOOR,
Hope, 95
Mary, 91
Phebe, 111
MOORE,
Abigail, 113
Alexander, 99
Amey, 10, 14
Ann, 99
Azariah, 24
Bathsheba, 113
Betsy, 32
Charles Allen, 108
Damaris, 29
Daniel, 24, 28, 30, 105, 108
David, 17, 24, 25, 28
Dorcas, 113
Edward, 72
Enoch, 64, 115
Eunice, 32

Hampton, 116
Joanna, 25, 27
Joel, 25, 27
John, 16, 18, 22, 26, 27, 28, 32
Jonathan, 105, 106
Joseph, 8, 9, 14, 18, 28
Judith, 117
Lewis, 31, 72
Lois, 16
Lydia, 14, 20, 24, 28, 72
Marcy, 119
Mary, 10, 14, 18, 20, 27, 73, 119
Moses, 14, 25, 27
Phebe, 18, 32
Polly, 25
Rachel, 4, 26, 31, 72, 116
Robert, 106
Ruth, 16
Sally, 12
Samuel, 17, 20
Sarah, 14, 99
Stephen, 27
MORE,
Abigail, 100
Abigil, 99
Azariah, 99
Bathsheba, 100
Jacob, 99, 100
John, 99
Joseph, 99
Martha, 100
Mary, 100
Ruth, 100
William, 89
MORGAN,
Anna, 52
Catharine, 53
Daniel, 36
Elisabeth, 36
John, 70
Mica, 52
Samuel, 2
Siballa, 36

INDEX

MORRIS,
 Ann, 73
 Suria, 113
MORROW, John, 116
MOSLET,
 Anna Maria Barbara, 37
 Elisabeth, 36, 37
 George, 36, 37
 Johanna George, 36
MOSSE, Thomas, 59
MOWERS, Johann
 Adam, 48
MUCHELROY(MCAVA
 Y), Thomas, 59
MUKENTINE, Lydia, 66
MULFORD,
 Abigail, 96, 105
 Benjamin, 1, 116
 Elizabeth, 102, 117
 Enoch, 70
 Ephraim, 116
 Eunice, 3
 Ezekiel, 105
 Furman, 116
 Hanah, 1
 Hannah, 102, 117
 Henry, 4
 Hope, 6, 96
 Isaac, 2
 Jacob, 96, 102
 James Woodburn, 94
 Jean, 96
 John, 116
 Jonathan, 96, 102
 Lewis, 116
 Lewse, 102
 Louisa, 102
 Lovesoe, 96
 Lucia, 119
 Lucy, 5
 Mary, 119
 Maskell, 96
 Moses, 116
 Phebe, 5, 105
 Prudence, 102
 Prudencfe, 96

Rachel, 118
Richard, 31, 69
Sarah, 94, 102, 114, 118
Stephen, 1, 6
Thomas, 108
Thomas Ewing, 94
William, 94, 96, 102,
 105, 108, 116
MULICKA,
 Catherine, 77
 Eric, 77
 John, 77
MULLER,
 Catherine, 33
 Hans Michael, 41
 Hans Micheal, 48
 Jacob, 33
 Margaret, 41
 Michael, 41
MULLICA,
 Eric, 77
 Thomas, 61
MUNNION, Robert, 116
MURFORD, Sarah, 113
MURPHEN, Stephen, 68
MURPHEY,
 Hudson, 55
 Mary, 55
 Prudence, 55
 Richrd, 55
 Steven, 55
MURPHY,
 Isaac, 70
 Phebe, 12, 14, 27
 Rachel, 31, 71
 Robert, 27, 116
 William, 27
MURRAY,
 Mary, 68
 Sarah, 64
MURRY, Kezia, 66
MUSENTINE, Dolla, 65
MUSSENTINE, John, 70
MYER, Mary, 29

-N-
NAIL, Uriah, 116
NEAL, Lydia, 73
NEALSON, Elonar, 2
NECHANEY, ---, 58
NEGRO,
 Charity, 103
 Festus, 67
 George, 103
 Jane, 108
 Philli, 67
 Sila, 103
 Vilat, 103
NEIDE, John Potts, 116
NEISSER,
 George, 82
 Theodore, 82
NELSON,
 Elisabeth, 18
 Elizabeth, 12, 13
 James, 109
 Phebe, 3
NEWCOM,
 Dalton, 58
 David, 62
NEWCOMB,
 Abagail, 64
 Annah, 91
 Baes, 58
 Base, 59
 Butler, 91
 Daniel, 58
 Daton, 64
 David, 60
 Ephraim, 60, 61
 John, 58
 Josiah, 73
 Mary, 112
 Nancy, 66
 Nathan, 89, 90
 Polly, 73
 Prudance, 90
 Prudence, 90
 Rebuen, 116
 Silas, 88, 116
 Webster, 59

William, 1, 87, 88, 116
NEWELL, Polly, 115
NEWMAN,
　Kezia, 73
　Keziah, 31
NEWTON, Margaret, 119
NEWWKIRK, Garret, 32
NICHESON,
　Desire, 2
　Nehemiah, 2
NICHOLLS, Ish,ael, 69
NICHOLS,
　Almeda, 63
　Jonathan, 15
　Miriam, 24
　Rhoda, 30
　Sarah, 68
　Thomas, 24
NICHSON,
　Jeremiah, 56
　William, 56
NICKELS, Sarah, 5
NICKELSON, Ruth, 61
NICKLESON, William, 68
NICKOLS, Hannah, 59
NIXON,
　Abigail, 84
　Bathier, 116
　Ephraim, 67
　Jeremiah, 57, 60, 63
　Polly, 64
　Reuben, 84
　Ruth, 28
　Seaborn Troy, 57
　Tabitha, 112
　William, 57
NIXSON, Jeremiah, 116
NOBLIT, Rachel
　Wheaton, 65
NOESMAN, Gabriel, 78
NOLL,
　Anna, 44
　Hans George, 49
　Micheal, 44
NOLLEN, Elisabeth, 38

NORBERRY, Joseph, 3
NUCOMB, Abigail, 73
NUGEN, Dorcas, 65
NULL,
　Anna, 44
　Hans George, 49
　Micheal, 44
NYBERG,
　Lawrence, 77, 78
　Lawrence T., 75

-O-
OCHSENBECKER,
　Christina, 39
　Henrich, 39
　Michael, 39
OCHSSENBECHER,
　Heinrich, 49
ODEN(OGDEN), John, 58
OGDEN,
　Abdon, 84
　Abigail, 70, 111
　Bathnithcoth, 111
　Beniaman, 61
　Beniamen, 58, 60
　Daniel, 9, 14, 17, 26, 116
　David, 17, 31, 56, 57, 60, 71, 84, 116
　Deborah, 70
　Elmer, 60
　Ester, 66
　Esther, 31
　George, 61
　Hannah, 84
　Harris, 59
　James, 60, 61
　Jedidiah, 59
　Jeremiah, 61
　John, 56, 58, 59, 84
　Jonathan, 13, 17
　Jonathon, 9
　Joseph, 56, 57, 58, 59, 60, 84
　Josiah, 70

　Lewis, 17
　Malachi, 17, 22
　Martha, 113
　Mary, 30
　Nathaniel, 61, 116
　Pashience, 62
　Ruhanne [Ruhame], 69
　Ruth, 17
　Sally, 73
　Samuel, 58
　Sarah, 57, 85, 112
　Susannah, 9, 13, 14
　Temperance, 10, 13, 14
　Theodosia, 119
　Thomas, 56, 57, 85, 116
　Violetta, 84
　Zephanian, 84
O'HARA,
　Deborah, 31
　Mary, 12, 14
　Polly, 32
OLBEN, France, 62
OLDAKER, William, 116
OLIVER,
　Joseph, 68
　Susanna, 3
ONANDER, Eric, 78
ORANGE, Jonathan, 84
ORD, James, 116
ORIN, John, 116
ORR,
　James, 91
　John, 91
　Peggy, 91
　Sopiah, 91
OSBORN, Ethan, 96
OTT,
　Anna Catherine, 34
　Bodo, 49
　Catherine, 36
　Elisabeth, 41
　Elizabeth, 45
　Heinrich, 41
　Henry, 45, 65
　Jacob, 35
　Johann Adam, 35

INDEX

Johann Heinrich, 35
Johann Martin, 35, 36, 49
John Martin, 34, 40, 45
Margaret, 34, 35, 36, 40, 45
Martin, 45
Mathias, 40
Susanna, 35
OTTO,
  Bodo, 33, 42
  Dorthea Catherine, 42
  Freidrich Christopher, 42
O'WARD, Debby, 72
OWEN,
  Hannah, 29
  Joshua, 55
OXEBECHER,
  Christina, 39
  Henrich, 39
  Micheal, 39
OXENBECHER,
  Heinrich, 49

-P-
PACKER, Daniel, 116
PADAY, William, 116
PADGET,
  Andrew, 4
  Mary, 4
PADGETT,
  David, 116
  Dorothy, 94
  Ephraim, 63, 72
  Hannah, 67
  Mary, 94
  Priscilla, 104
  Sarah, 106
  Thomas, 94, 116
PADGITT, Aaron, 116
PADY, Mary, 60
PAGE,
  Ambrose, 116
  Betsey, 64
  David, 28, 89

Grace, 90
James, 69
John, 106
Jonathan, 116
Joseph, 88
Ruth, 84
PAGUE, David, 87
PAINTER, Isaac, 71
PALING, William, 2
PARENT, Sarah, 115
PAREY, Phebe, 65
PARIS,
  Elizabeth, 20
  George, 11, 13, 19, 20
  Jacob, 39
  Lewis, 19
  Mary, 10, 14, 19, 20
  Peter, 39
  Ruth, 19
  Susanna, 39
PARK,
  James, 11, 15, 19
  Phebe, 12, 15, 19
  Sarah, 19
PARKE,
  David, 108
  James, 105, 108
  James Dicson, 106
  Rachel, 105
  Rebecca, 106
PARKER,
  Abigail, 26
  Elizabeth, 29, 32, 111
  Mary, 105
  Moses, 67
  Samuel, 26, 31, 67
PARKS,
  James Dixon, 95
  Rachel, 95
  Rebecca, 95
  Sarah, 95
  Thomas, 95
PARREY, Ami, 3
PARRY, Mary, 2
PARSON, Elenor, 52
PARSONS,

Anna, 82
Bythia, 102
PARVEN, Marcy, 61
PARVIN,
  Aaron, 61, 105
  Ann, 101
  Benaiah, 18, 27, 30
  Benjamin, 84, 96
  Clarance, 101
  Clarence, 116
  David, 96, 108
  Enaus, 61
  Enoch, 65
  Holmes, 30
  James, 32
  Jeffard, 60
  Jeffia, 59
  Jeremiah, 25, 31, 72
  Jonathan, 70
  Josiah, 64
  Lidia, 101
  Lovisa, 101
  Mary, 71
  Mathew, 57
  Peggy, 67
  Phebe, 114
  Rachel, 67, 108
  Rebecca, 18
  Rodah, 60
  Sally, 32
  Sarah, 24
  Silas, 101
  Susannah, 27
  Theophilus, 69
  Thomas, 29, 84
PATRICK,
  Isaac, 105
  Mary, 31, 69
PAULDING,
  Enoch, 32
  Margaret, 28
PAULEN, Whitlock, 116
PAULIN,
  Patience, 87
  William, 87
PAULING,

Catharine, 3
Henry, 2
Patience, 1
William, 4
PAULLIN,
Patience, 87
William, 88
PAVEY, Jason, 63
PAYDAY,
Judith, 118
William, 116
PAYNE, Jasper, 81
PEACOCK, David, 65
PEARCE, Elizabeth, 64
PECK,
Andrew, 26
Benjamin, 95, 105, 108, 116
Constant, 16, 17, 23, 24
Dr., 107, 108
Elizabeth, 23
Hannah, 16, 30, 64
Israel Moore, 19
John, 94, 109
Joseph, 29
Lydia Moore, 19
Margaret, 12, 14, 26
Martha, 111
Mary, 108
Phebe Shoemaker, 19
Rachel, 17, 23, 29, 108, 114
Rebecca, 95, 111
Ruth, 17, 112
Susannah, 23
Susannah Royal, 19
PEDRICK,
John, 65
Paul, 51
PEEK,
Martha, 103
Sarah, 102
PEIRSON,
Betsey, 66
Henry, 56, 57
John, 66

Lydia, 65
Mary, 65
Mrs., 57
Prudence, 70
PENNINGTON, Rachel, 111
PEPPER,
Amos, 69
Jesse, 69
Rachel, 90
Reuben, 73
Ruth, 66
Sarah, 87, 90
William, 64, 87, 88, 89, 91
PERCE,
Andrew, 60
Richard, 59
PERKINS, Mary, 32
PERRY,
Abbie, 37
Abigail, 39
Amy, 70
Benjamin, 22, 29
Dan, 117
George, 37, 39
Hannah, 39
Hester, 1
Ishmael, 70
Ishmael, 64
Mary, 2
PERSON,
Azrial, 60
David, 61
PERSONS, William, 89
PERVIE, Jesse, 68
PERVIS, Wanak, 68
PERY, Rebecca, 103
PETERS, Lydia, 111
PETERSEN,
Christina, 76
Jeremiah, 76
Lawrence, 76
Luke, 76
Magdalene, 77
Susannah, 76

Zachariah, 77
PETERSON,
Aaron, 117
Abigail, 78, 79
Abraham, 77
Anna, 80
Aran, 88
Christiana, 80
Daniel, 117
David, 89
Frederick, 117
Hance, 117
John, 80, 117
Laurence, 77
Lawrence, 78
Lydia, 79
Rebekah, 79
Samuel, 79
Susanna, 77, 78, 79
Thomas, 78, 79
William, 117
PETTESON, Aaron, 58
PETTET, Sarah, 110
PETTIL, Hannah, 72
PETTY,
Hannah, 29
Israel, 56, 84
PHILPOT,
Elizabeth, 76
Nicholas, 76
PIATE, Mary, 102
PICKLES,
Mr., 10, 11
W., 11
William, 8
PIERCE, Andrew, 117
PIERSON,
Azel, 117
John, 117
Mary, 105
PILGRAM,
Anna Maria, 43
Frantz, 43
Johanna, 43
Maria, 40
PILGRIM, Bathsheba, 31

INDEX 151

PLATT, Judith, 118
PLATTS,
  DAvid, 101
  David, 5, 117
  Elezebeth, 101
  Judah, 101
  Judith, 101
  Mary, 101
  Moses, 105
  Phebe, 101
  RAchel, 101
  Rhoda, 110
  Rodah, 97, 101
  Sarah, 101
PLOTTS, Letitia, 4
PLUMBLEY, John, 68
POLHEMUS, John B., 73
POOLER,
  Hester, 1
  Priscilla, 118
POOR, Susannah, 6
POTTER,
  Christina, 39
  Col., 107
  David, 108
  Harriet, 107
  Heinrich, 39
  Henrietta, 107
  Jane, 6, 106, 111
  John, 108
  Martha, 108
  Mary, 69
  Micheal, 39
  Sally, 63
POTTS, John, 117
POWEL, Richard, 57
POWELL,
  David, 84
  Elizabeth, 113, 115, 118, 119
  Elkanah, 32
  John, 56, 57, 59
  Martha, 116
  Priscilla, 57
  Prudence, 116
  Richard, 84

  Rodah, 59
  Rubin, 59
  Samuel, 24
PRESTON,
  Elizabeth, 112, 119
  Ephraim, 66
  Levi, 66, 84
  Priscillia, 113
  Ruth, 64
PRICE,
  Captain, 89
  Mary, 118
  Mrs., 90
PURPLE,
  Abigail, 78
  John, 78
PYRALAEUS, John C., 76
PYRLAEUS, J. C., 77

-Q-
QUIGLY, Robert, 68

-R-
RAEMEL,
  Anna Maria, 38
  Christina, 38
  Heinrich, 38
RAMALL,
  Jacob, 34
  Magdalena, 34
RAMMEL,
  Anna, 39
  Anna Maria, 38
  Christina, 38
  Elisabeth, 39
  Hans George, 49
  Hans Jacob, 49
  Heinrich, 38
  Jacob, 34
  Johann Joseph, 39
  Magdalena, 34
RAMSEY,
  David, 56
  Ephraim, 84
  Sarah, 84

  William, 56, 57, 84, 117
RANDEL, Catherine, 46
RANDOLPH,
  David, 117
  Hannah, 110
  Jacob, 73
  Jane, 116
  Jonathan Fitz, 27
  Lott, 105
  Widow, 73
RANKINS, Hosea, 70
RAOL,
  John, 76
  Margaret, 76
RASURE, George Adam, 117
RAWLINGS,
  John, 76
  Margaret, 76
RAWLINS,
  John, 76
  Margaret, 76
RAWSON, William, 83
RAY,
  Daniel Elmer, 106
  Eleanor, 69
  James, 5
READ,
  Charles, 117
  Daniel, 67
  David, 107, 108
  Experience, 29, 101
  Israel, 117
  Isreal, 26
  James, 107
  Joel, 108
  John, 117
  Johnson, 117
  Naomi, 106
  Rachel, 66
  Sarah, 31, 107
READING, Ann, 99
REAMINGTON,
  Thomas, 6
REAVES, Thomas, 59
REDMOND,

Elizabeth, 21
Henry, 21
REED,
Daniel, 89
David, 94
Elizabeth, 103
Henry, 117
Isaiah, 88
James, 94
Margaret, 97
Martha, 112
Priscilla, 116
Rachel, 94, 96
Sarah, 72, 94
Thoams, 8
REEVE,
Abigail, 25
Cornelius, 32
John, 21
Joseph, 25
Martha, 13, 14, 21
Nancy, 27
Rachel, 13, 15
Ruth, 26, 27, 31, 69
Thomas, 26, 27
William, 26
REEVES,
A., 73
Abigal, 98
Abraham, 93, 117
Ame, 98
Anna, 98
Benjamin Stratton, 108
David, 64
Elijah, 93
Elizabeth, 107
Enas, 108
Enos, 99
Ephraim, 107
Eunice, 93, 105
Hannah, 71, 98, 99
Herbert, 51
Isaac, 88
John, 72, 93, 98
Johnson, 107, 108
Jonson, 93

Joseph, 72, 93, 108
Joshua, 67, 107, 108
Josiah, 98
Juliana, 12, 13
Lemuel, 107
Mabel, 93, 115
Mable, 105
Mary, 98, 104
Nancy, 93, 108
Nathan Leake, 108
Patty, 72
Prudence, 111
Rebecca, 12, 14
Ruth, 63
Samuel, 107
Sarah, 93, 98, 99, 107, 117
Stephen, 93
Thankful, 98
Thomas, 59, 73, 98, 107, 108
Unas, 93
William, 107
REIBELL, Johann George, 49
REIBNEL,
Anna Catherine, 34
Isaac, 36
Johann George, 49
Johannes, 34
Johannes George, 34
John George, 36
Margaret, 36
REID, Sally, 68
REIMMEL, Hans George, 49
REINCKE, Abraham, 75
REINKE,
A., 79, 80
Abr., 77
Abraham, 76, 78
REISS, Christian, 49
REITZ,
Mathew, 79, 80
Matthew, 79
REMENTON,

Moses, 117
Thomas, 4
REMINGTON,
Clementia, 72
Elizabeth, 1
John, 1
Moses, 117
Thomas, 105
REMMINGTON, Mark, 73
REUTZ,
M., 80
Matthew, 75, 79
REVES, Moses, 89
REYNOLDS,
Benjamin, 30
Rhoda, 18
Silas, 71
William, 33
RHEIEL,
Catherine, 34
Johannes, 34
Maria, 34
RHEIL,
Johann Heinrich, 35
Johann Phillip, 35
Johannes, 35
Maria, 35
Susanna, 35
RICE,
Owen, 75
Sarah, 114
RICHARDS, John, 117
RICHARDSON,
John, 88
Joseph, 117
Mary, 3
Richard, 2, 3
RICHMAN,
Jane, 64
Rebecca, 64
RICHMOND,
David, 32
Elizabeth, 12, 14, 21
Henry, 21
Isaac, 31, 71

INDEX

Priscilla, 32
William, 29
RIDDLE, Ann, 114
RIELEY, Sarah, 3
RIGGER, Jacob, 41
RIGHT, Susannah, 5
RILEY,
  Anna, 71
  Charles, 67
  Ephraim, 72
  Hope, 68
  Jonathan, 31
  Joseph, 117
  Levi, 15, 17
  Rachel, 72
  Sarah, 90
RITCHIE,
  Elizabeth, 92
  George, 92
  Lois, 32
RITTENHOUSE, Henry, 72
ROBART, Francis, 32
ROBBINS,
  John, 87, 90
  Temperance, 90
ROBENSON,
  Elezabeth, 3
  Prudence, 4
ROBERSON,
  Dorcas, 90
  Ruema, 68
  Ruhanna, 69
  Silas, 89
  Temperance, 69
ROBERTS,
  Lydia, 112
  Prudence, 119
ROBERTSON,
  Joel, 6
  John, 6
  Rachel, 6
ROBESON, Dorcas, 91
ROBINS,
  Cibel, 88
  John, 88, 89

Lediah, 119
Mary, 87
Obadiah, 1
Obediah, 117
Temperance, 90
ROBINSON,
  Abraham, 29
  Anne, 30
  Dan, 30
  James, 117
  John, 90
  Judith, 105
  Reeves, 66
  Sarah, 87
  Silas, 66, 68
  Temperance, 66
  William, 87, 88, 117
ROBNS, Levin, 52
ROCAN,
  Johann George, 33
  Johann Jacob, 33
  Salome, 33
ROCAP,
  Anna Margaret, 39
  Barbara, 36
  Catherine, 34, 36, 37, 38, 46
  Charity, 35, 36
  George, 39, 68
  Heinrich, 35, 36, 49
  Johann George, 35, 37
  Johann Heinrich, 37
  Magdalena, 35
  Margaret, 35
  Mary, 73
  Salome, 35, 37, 39
ROCAR, Cathere, 35
ROECAP, Henry, 29
ROGERS, John, 89
ROKOP, Heinrich, 49
ROSEN, William, 83
ROSS,
  Adam, 39
  Anna Maria, 35, 39
  Charles, 35
  Mathias, 35

Mathis, 35
Philippina, 39
Susanna, 35
ROTHGAB,
  Johann George, 33
  Johann Jacob, 33
  Salome, 33
ROTHGEB,
  Catherine, 36
  Charity, 35, 36
  Heinrich, 35, 36
  Margaret, 35
ROTTER,
  Catherine, 34
  David, 34
  Jacob, 34
  Maria Elisabeth, 34
  Theobald, 34
ROUTHKEP,
  Barbara, 36
  Charity, 36
  Heinrich, 36
ROWCAP,
  Barbara, 66
  Katharine, 66
ROYAL,
  David, 63, 106
  Hannah, 105
  John, 4
RUDOLPH,
  Bartholomew, 117
RUFF, Barbary, 113
RULON, John, 117
RULONG, John, 60
RUMFORD, Jonathan, 1
RUMSEY, Ruth, 111
RUPELL, Mary, 65
RUSEL, Oliver, 60
RUSSAL,
  Achjah, 4
  Elesabeth, 4
  Ephraim, 3
  Sarah, 3
RUSSEE, Anna, 61
RUSSEL,
  Anne, 28

Edward, 28
RUSSELL, Benjamin, 105
  Mary, 66
RUTHCEP,
  Johann George, 35
  Magdalena, 35
  Salome, 35
RUTTER,
  Catherine, 34
  David, 34
  Jacob, 34
  Maria Elisabeth, 34
  Theobald, 34
RYAL,
  David, 13, 21
  John, 21
  Phebe, 21
  Polly, 21
  Ruth, 13, 21
  Susannah, 21
RYLEY,
  Elizabeth, 63
  Jonathan, 64
  Joseph, 117
  Polly, 63
  Rebecca, 66

-S-
SACKWELL, Eve, 1
SALES, Ebenezer, 60
SAMSON, Jacob, 117
SAP, Elijah, 71
SAUDER,
  Jacob, 34
  Margaret, 34
  Simon, 34
SAUNDERS,
  Victorina, 110
  Victorinia, 110
SAUREN, Christeen, 30
SAUTER,
  Eva Margaret, 33
  Peter, 33
  Philip, 33
SAVAGE, Martha, 116

SAYCE, Martha, 119
SAYER, William, 117
SAYRE,
  Abraham, 56, 117
  Ananias, 93
  Damaris, 116
  David, 84
  Dina, 66
  Elezebeth, 5
  Elizabeth, 5
  Hannah, 110
  Lydia, 113
  Martha, 93, 119
  Mary, 110
  Phebe, 93
  Rachel, 119
  Richard, 101
  Theodocia, 117
SAYRES,
  Abraham, 29
  David, 2
  Ichabod, 22
  Richard, 28
SAYRS, Esther, 70
SCHAUM,
  Julian, 38
  Michael, 38
  Nathan, 38
SCHIMPT,
  Anna Maria, 40
  David, 39
  Elisabeth, 44
  Heinrich, 40
  Johannes, 44
  Johannes Wilhelm, 39
  Maria Magdalene, 39
  Susanna, 40
SCHMICK,
  Anna, 36, 39
  Anna Maria, 36, 39
  Catherine, 36
  Wilhelm, 36, 39
SCHMIDT,
  Catherine Elisabeth, 38
  Edmond, 36
  Elisabeth, 36, 37

  Johann, 38
  Johannes, 37
  Magdalene, 36
  Sophia, 38
  Susanna, 37
SCHNEIDER, Hans George, 49
SCHNELL, Leonard, 75
SCHOOT,
  Anna Maria, 38
  Elisabeth, 38
  Freidrich, 38, 39
  Johann George, 38
  Johannes, 38
  Susanna, 38, 39
SCHUTE,
  Anne, 81
  William, 81
SCHUTZ,
  Joseph, 37, 39
  Louisa, 39
  Lousia, 37
  Maria Barbara, 39
SCHWAM,
  Elizabeth, 39
  Julian, 38
  Julianna, 39
  Micheal, 38
  Nathan, 38, 39
SCHYNER, Sarah, 29
SCOTT,
  Abigail, 110
  Hannah, 111
  Joseph, 74
  Mary, 110
  Ruth, 112
  Sidnea, 111
  Sydnea, 106
SCUDDER, John, 117
SCUDER, Christiana, 68
SCULL,
  Captain, 89
  Captin, 89
  Hannah, 2
  Isaac, 87
  Peter, 2

INDEX 155

Tabitha, 87
SCULLARDS, Polly, 64
SCULLO, Nancy, 32
SEAGER,
  Catherine, 40
  Heinrich, 40
  Peter, 40
SEAGRAVE, Arabella, 117
SEAGRAVES,
  Onifornus, 2
  Sarah, 2
SEARS,
  Aabrin, 61
  Anna, 67
  Hannah, 110
  Jeremiah, 60, 61, 67
  Lemone, 59
  Rhoda, 28
  William, 65
SEELEY,
  D., 73
  David, 117
  Dorcas, 32
  Ebenezer, 117
  Elias, 68
  Enos, 68
  Ephraim, 24, 84
  Ester, 95
  Esther, 113
  Hannah, 58
  Henery, 118
  John, 24
  Joseph, 56, 94
  Josiah, 24
  Leonard, 24
  Lydia, 24
  N., 73
  Polly, 31
  Rachel, 68, 99
  Rebecca, 24, 94
  Richard, 32
  Samuel, 24
  Sarah, 117
  Silas, 18
SEELY,

Keturah, 29
Polly, 65
SEGER,
  Johann George, 49
  Johann Peter, 49
SEGGARS,
  Catherine, 40
  Christina, 40
SELE,
  Ebenezer, 59
  Ggeddedials, 58
  Joseph, 58
  Martha, 58
SEMY(TERRY), Rhoda, 66
SFYN, Joseph, 58
SHAFFER,
  Conrad, 49
  Jacob, 49
  Johannes, 49
SHARER, Catharine, 30
SHARP,
  Hannah, 105
  Isaac, 118
  Isabel, 118
  Rachel, 31, 71
SHAVER, Jacob, 28
SHAW,
  Aaron, 53
  Abiah, 118
  Abigal, 59
  Alice, 114
  Amos, 53
  Carle, 63
  David, 67
  Edmond, 30
  Elie, 53
  George, 88
  Hannah, 71
  Hennery, 59
  Hope, 91
  Jeams, 62
  John, 53, 88, 118
  Jonathan, 69
  Joshua, 53
  Judith, 70

Lenord, 60
Lydia, 66
Mary, 112
Nathan, 118
Peggy, 66
Peter, 53
Polly, 73
Preison, 63
Rachel, 53, 89
Richard, 61, 118
Sarah, 111, 116
SHECKELS, Elizabeth, 113
SHEIDNER, Hans George, 49
SHENSHORE, Phebe, 65
SHEPERD, Jonadab, 1
SHEPHERD,
  Abel, 2
  Ann, 1
  David, 1, 3, 87, 88
  Deborah, 6
  Dickenson, 2
  Eleanor, 1
  Elnathan, 4
  Enoch, 1, 88
  Ephraim, 3
  Furman, 118
  Hannah, 4, 5
  Harvey, 6
  Hope, 5
  Isaac, 6
  James, 3
  John, 1
  Jonadab, 87, 88
  Joseph, 2, 3
  Keziah, 4
  Lucy, 111
  Lydia, 4
  Martha, 5
  Mary, 1, 3, 4, 6, 7
  Milicent, 4
  Nancy, 87
  Nathan, 3
  Owen, 6
  Phebe, 4, 6, 7

Philip, 1, 5, 7
Prissilla, 87
Prudence, 3
Rachel, 110, 117
Rhoda, 112
Ruth, 1, 4, 6
Sarah, 1, 3, 4, 5, 6, 87, 113
Stephen, 1
Temperance, 87
Thomas, 87, 88
SHEPHERED, Thomas, 87
SHEPPARD,
Ann, 73
Anree, 60
Ansee, 60
Clemens, 108
David, 71, 72
Dickeson, 73
Elbonar, 89
Elizabeth, 68, 90
Ephraim, 89
Hannah, 64, 74, 69
Harvey, 68
Hosea, 89
Jane, 108
Job, 65
John, 71
Jonadab, 89
Jonathan, 65, 69
Josiah, 73
Lovice, 70
Marthew, 71
Mary, 65, 116
Nias, 108
Patty, 64
Rachel, 73, 105
Ruth, 73
Sarah, 73
Sillet, 64
Thomas, 89
SHEPPERD,
Hosea, 88
Kerenhappuck, 115
Rebecca, 111

Unis, 115
SHIMP,
Anna Maria, 40
Bastion, 63
Charolette, 44
Christina, 34, 36, 38, 39
David, 29
Elisabeth, 44
Elizabeth, 105
George, 104
Heinrich, 40
Johannes, 44
Johannes Wilhelm, 39
John, 44, 105
Maria Magdalene, 39
Susanna, 40
SHINER,
Catherine, 45
John, 45
Phebe, 45
SHIPSHIRE, Edward, 52
SHINTS, Nancy, 70
SHOEMAKER, John, 68, 72
SHROPHSIRE, ---, 117
Sarah, 74
SHULL,
Catharine, 119
Hannah, 29
Hopwell, 64
Hoshel, 30
Jacob, 26, 30
Samuel, 32
Susannah, 30, 31, 72
William, 24, 28, 31, 71
SHUSTER, Margaret, 68
SHUTE,
Adam, 18, 19, 24, 28
Ann, 80, 81, 82
Anna Maria, 38
Catharine, 24
Charles, 19
Diana, 82
Elisabeth, 38
Elizabeth, 18, 19, 24, 28
Enoch, 96

Freidrich, 38, 39
George, 80
Hannah, 30, 31, 65
Hope, 95
Johann George, 38
Johannes, 38
John, 26
Joseph, 81
Margaret, 95
Mary, 23, 96
Samuel, 96
Samuel M., 67
Sarah, 95
Susanna, 38, 39
William, 80, 81, 82, 95
SHUTES, George, 28
SHYHERD, Furman, 118
SHYKELS, Christina, 117
SIBLY, John, 70
SICKLER,
Anna Maria, 35, 37
David, 39
Dewaldo
  Theobald(David), 37
Elisabeth, 41
Elizabeth, 45, 65
George, 37, 41, 46, 49
Hannah, 41
Hans George, 49
Hosie, 46
Johann, 41
Johannes, 37, 41
Magdalene, 37, 39
Mary, 41
Mosey, 41
Philip, 39
Susan, 46
Susanna, 35, 41
Theobald Dewaldo, 39
Zacharias, 35, 37
SIDEN, Mary, 117
SIFFIN, John, 5
SIGARA,
Catherine, 40
Heinrich, 40

INDEX

Peter, 40
SIGARS,
  Catherine, 40, 41, 45
  Christina, 40
  Joel, 41
  Johann George, 49
  Johann Peter, 49
  John George, 41
  Ludwig, 41
  Margaret, 41
  Peter, 40, 41, 45
SIGLER, Jane, 25
SILVER, William, 52
SIMKINS,
  Alplan, 1
  Ananias, 74
  Dorkies, 66
  Dorkis, 69
  Esther, 29
SIMMONS, Rachel, 117
SIMPKIN, Mercy, 114
SIMPKINS,
  Abnar, 4
  Amos, 4
  Celah, 60
  Daniel, 65
  Ephraim, 118
  Phebe, 69
  Rachel, 4
  Rebeca, 4
SIMPSON, James, 71
SIMS, Temperance, 65
SINK,
  David, 107
  Elizabeth, 107
  Thomas, 107
  William, 107, 118
SIRAK, Ann, 1
SISSEN,
  Abel, 88
  Maiah, 87
SITHEN, Joel, 32
SKELLINGER, Hannah, 105
SKINNER, John, 58

SLEESMAN, Catherine, 111
SMART, Charles, 68
SMICK,
  Anna, 39
  Anna Maria, 36, 39
  Catherine, 36
  Wilhelm, 36, 39
SMIDE, Elazer, 61
SMITH,
  ---, 105
  Aaron, 70
  Abigail, 10, 13, 32
  Abner, 8, 9, 10, 13, 16, 19, 21, 25, 26
  Abraham, 1, 3, 5
  Alderman, 19
  Asa, 17, 20
  Asbury, 118
  Ashbury, 1
  Balthasar, 46
  Catherine, 46
  Constant, 100
  David, 89
  Dorcas, 5
  Ebenezer, 118
  Eleazer, 16
  Elesabeth, 5
  Elisha, 52, 74, 118
  Elizabeth, 26, 67, 71
  Ephraim, 61
  Esther, 29
  Hannah, 15, 16, 31, 68, 71, 100, 112, 114
  Hope, 116
  Hosea, 21
  Isaac, 3, 118
  Jabez, 72
  James, 70
  Jemima, 10, 14, 19, 21, 25, 26
  John, 15, 25, 118
  John Davenport, 26
  Johnathan, 57
  Jonathan, 11, 13, 19, 20, 26, 106

  Joseph, 5
  Lewis, 118
  Lewse, 102
  Louisa, 102
  Margaret, 2, 28
  Mary, 30, 105, 112
  Mercy, 103
  Miriam, 71
  Noah, 29
  Phebe, 1, 4, 6, 105
  Phebe Garrison, 21
  Rachel, 3, 16, 19, 20
  Rebca, 100
  Rhoda, 30
  Robert, 8, 9, 11, 84
  Samuel, 68, 118
  Sarah, 16, 29, 63, 73, 84, 91, 113
  Sary, 90
  Satira, 26
  Sephiah, 2
  Silas, 61
  Snythche, 4
  Susannah, 115
  Sylvanus, 104
  Thomas, 6, 7
  William, 8, 10, 13, 14, 16, 17, 67
  William Garrison, 19
SNEATHEN,
  David, 118
  Jonas, 24
SNETHEN, James, 118
SOCKWELL,
  Eve, 87, 88
  Jonadab, 88, 118
  Jonathan, 70
SOLLEY,
  James, 96
  Margaret, 96
  Marget, 5
  Timothy, 96
SOLLY, Nathan, 71
SOPER,
  Daniel, 58, 59
  Uriah, 62

SORAR, Nicholas, 29
SOUDER,
  Anna Margaret, 38
  Anna Maria, 40
  Barbara, 40
  Catharine, 40
  Catherine, 35, 40, 45
  Christiana, 71, 119
  Christina, 34, 36, 38, 39
  Daniel, 34
  Elisabeth, 38, 39, 45
  Eva Margaret, 33, 34, 35
  George, 40, 45, 68
  Jacob, 34, 40
  Johann, 34
  Johann George, 35
  Johann Wilhelm, 35
  Johannes, 35, 37, 45
  Margaret, 34, 35, 36, 37, 39, 40
  Maria, 38
  Martin, 40
  Mary M., 45
  Peter, 33, 34, 35, 37, 40
  Philip, 33, 36, 38, 39, 40, 45
  Reuben, 23
  Simon, 34, 38, 39, 45
  Susanna, 34
SOUDERS,
  Elizabeth, 72
  John, 90
  Susy, 17
SOULARD,
  Hannah, 102
  John, 102
  Mary, 102
  Peter, 102
  Rachel, 102
SOUTER, John, 118
SOUTHWARD,
  Benjamin, 118
SOWDER, John, 90
SOWDERS, Mary, 6
SPARKS,
  Henry, 56, 84, 118

  Rohada, 84
SPENCER, Mary, 52
SPICELOR, Wido, 89
STACKHOUSE,
  Caleb, 118
  Hannah, 6
  Sarah, 63
STACKS, Lovisa, 105
STAMME,
  Johann Jacob, 38
  Sophia, 38
  Wilhelm, 38
STANDLEY, William, 68
STANGAR, Christian, 49
STANGER,
  Isabelle, 39
  Johan Adam, 49
  Johann, 39
  Johann Philip, 39
STARKY, Phebe, 29
STATEHM, Israel, 106
STATHANS,
  Deliverance, 97
  Dorcas, 98
  Hannah, 97
  Nathan, 98
  Philip, 97
  Rebecca, 97
  Sarah, 97
  Thomas, 97
STATHEM,
  Aaron, 106, 118
  Dorcas, 105
  Ephraim, 107
  Hannah, 30, 108, 118
  Isaac, 118
  Marcy, 102
  Naomi, 105
  Philip, 72
  Ruth, 102
  Sarah, 111
  Thomas, 102, 107, 108
STATHEMS, Margaret, 73
STATTEN, Lewis, 58
STEDDAMS, John, 58

STEDDEMS, Anna, 71
STEDHAM, Elizabeth, 63
STEELMAN,
  Anne, 81
  Charles, 81
  Nancy, 71
  Rebecca, 81
STEGER,
  Christian, 49
  Johan Adam, 49
STEPHANS, William, 59
STEPHENS,
  Ame, 60
  Hannah, 106
STEPHENSON,
  James, 118
  Richard, 118
  Stephen, 52
STEVENS,
  Abigail, 60
  John, 15, 16, 18, 23, 24, 60
  Phebe, 16
  Rhoda, 28, 112
  Sarah, 18, 24
STEVENSON, Lydia, 69
  Richardson, 89
STEWART,
  Archibald, 65
  Frank H., 56
  Ruth, 28
  William, 67
  Zeboriah, 28
STIDHAM, John, 118
STILES,
  David, 71
  Joseph, 118
  Sarah, 110
STILLMAN, Andrew, 52
STITERS, David, 71
STITES,
  David, 73
  George, 28
  Jonathan, 89
  Pleasant, 70
  Prudence, 90

INDEX

STOCKTON,
  Amy, 102
  Samuel, 70
STOLL, Johanna, 33, 42
STOM,
  John, 64
  Lewis, 28
  William, 29
STOMS, Catherine, 68
STRANGER,
  Isabelle, 39
  Johann, 39
  Johann Philip, 39
STRATTEN, Preston, 84
STRATTON,
  Aaron, 17
  Abigail, 16, 30
  Amos, 54
  Benjamin, 56, 84
  Catherine, 118
  Charles, 63
  David, 22, 27
  Eleanor, 11, 14
  Eli, 54
  Elizabeth, 15, 24, 28
  Emily, 21
  Ephraim, 17, 24
  Esther, 23
  Eunice, 54
  Fithian, 15, 17, 52
  Hannah, 21, 54
  James, 118
  Jemima, 12, 14, 21
  Jeremiah, 73
  Joel, 17
  John, 8, 9, 10, 13, 15, 30, 69
  Jonathan, 15, 16, 54, 56
  Joshua, 55
  Lot, 24, 29
  Lydia, 64
  Mary, 55
  Noah, 29
  Phebe, 12, 14, 92
  Preston, 27, 69
  Rachel, 54

  Rebecca, 21, 25
  Rhoda, 111
  Sarah, 15, 27, 29, 54, 84
  William, 21, 25, 31, 65
STRATTPM, Levi, 59
STRENG, Peter, 83
STRETCH,
  Anna Maria, 39
  Elizabeth, 105
  Jacob, 39
  Mary, 64
  Thomas, 39
STRITES, George, 28
STUPHEN, Miller, 67
STUTS,
  Barbara, 46
  Elizabeth, 46
  George, 46
  John Geo, 46
STUTZ, Johannes, 49
SULLIVAN,
  John, 65
  Penninant, 72
SUTPHEN, Miller, 67
SUTTON,
  Mary, 52
  Moses, 30
  Thomas, 65
SWAIN,
  Phebe, 15
  Richard, 52
  Z, 52
SWEATMAN, James, 118
SWEN, Joseph, 60
SWING, Mical, 59, 60
SWINNEY,
  Elisha, 118
  Joseph, 108
  Martha, 1
  Rachel, 72
  Ruth, 111
  Susannah, 108
  Valentine, 108
SYDDEN, Mary, 90
SYDDENS, Rachel, 90

SYEN, Joseph, 58
SYGERS,
  Catherine, 41
  Joel, 41
  Peter, 41
SYMKINS, Ruth, 66

-T-
TALER, Lydda, 90
TARBELL,
  Abraham, 18
  Hannah, 18
TARBLE,
  Abraham, 15, 17
  David, 17
  Holmes, 17
  Priscilla, 15
TARRY, Ephraim, 118
TARYY, Butler, 119
TAVER, Margaret, 65
TAYLOR,
  Daniel, 88
  Frederick, 63
  George, 30
  Jonathan, 73
  Mathias, 64
  Polly, 32
  Sally, 69
  Sarah, 68
  Susannah, 110
  William Bradford, 58
TEAL, Ruth, 66
TEILER,
  David, 15
  John, 15
TEMP, Ruth, 66
TERRIL,
  Adam, 16
  Jeremiah, 16
  Polly, 31
  Ruth, 31
TERRILL, Polly, 71
TERRY',
  David, 89
  John, 87, 88, 89
  Jonah, 105

Jonathan, 89
Jude, 68
Rhoda, 66, 114
Ruth, 87
Sarah, 87
THOMAS, Hope, 70
THOMPSON,
  Benjamin, 57, 118
  Butler, 16
  Dillilah, 110
  Elijah, 66
  Elizabeth, 21, 63
  Jaid, 65
  Jane, 113
  Mary, 69
  Mary Dare, 19
  Newcomb, 16, 18, 19, 23
  Phebe, 18, 20
  Ruth, 12, 14, 19, 20, 21, 27
  Sally, 67
  Samuel, 11, 13, 19, 20, 21, 72
  William, 16
  Zadok, 56
THOMSON, Catharine, 5
THORNE, Widow, 22
THURINGAR,
  Catherine, 34
  Johann Jacob, 34
THURINGER,
  Andreas, 35
  Catherine, 33, 34, 35
  Elisabeth, 33
  Johann, 33
  Johann Jacob, 34
  Johannes, 35
THURINGOR,
  Anna, 42
  Barbara, 42
  Johann, 42
TITUS, Philip, 29
TOCONSEN, Sarah, 106
TOMLINSON,
  George, 119

Mary, 113
Phebe, 110
TOMSON, Beminiam, 62
TONDELSPACH,
  Anna Margaret, 42
  Freidrich, 42
  Johannes, 42
TOWNSEND,
  Daniel, 53
  Elizabeth, 53, 69
  Isaac, 53
  Lydia, 53
  Mark, 53
  Millicent, 53
  Rachel, 53
  Rebecca, 53
  Rebeccah, 53
  Rhoda, 114
  Richard, 53
  Ruth, 53
  Samuel, 53
  Sarah, 53
TOWSER, Jeremiah, 119
TRAYER, Andrew, 29
TRENCHARD,
  Curtis, 70
  John, 119
TRENSHER,
  Bets, 60
  John, 60
TRIBET, Thomas, 72
TRIMNAL, John, 64
TRUELENDER,
  Andreas, 35
  Catherine, 33, 35
  Elisabeth, 33
  Johann, 33
  Johannes, 35
TUBMAN,
  Silvanus, 90
  Silveneous, 89
  Sylvena, 6
  Theodosia, 6
TUCKER, Mary, 70
TULIS, Rachel, 90
TULLIS,

Ann, 101
Anna, 119
Annah, 101
Daniel, 89, 101
Eli, 101
Elinor, 101
Elizabeth, 90
Ellinor, 101
John, 32, 64, 90, 91, 101
Mary, 30
Moses, 25, 29, 101
Phebe, 32
Rachel, 27, 90
Ruth, 101
Sarah, 91
William, 8, 9, 14, 25, 101
TURNER, John, 30
TYLER,
  Hannah, 117
  John, 119
  Mary, 116
TYRELL,
  Adam, 17
  Ruth, 17

-U-

UDELL, Ruth, 102
UGNAY, Owan, 88
ULRICH,
  Augutha Catherine, 43
  Johann Casper, 43
  Maria, 40
  Micheal, 40
  Sarah, 40
ULTZNER,
  Anna Maria, 41
  Heinrich, 41
UNDERWOOD,
  Mary, 64
  William, 30
UTZ,
  Anna Maria, 41
  Hans George, 48
  Hans Jacob, 41, 48
  Heinrich, 41

Martin, 48
Peter, 48
UTZNE,
 Catherine, 43
 Jacob, 43
 Maria Magdalene, 43
UTZNER,
 Hans George, 48
 Hans Jacob, 41, 48
 Martin, 48

-V-
VAIL, Adah, 32
VAN EMMEN, Yerred, 78
VAN HORNE, Catherine, 68
VAN INMEN, Garrett, 77
VAN METER,
 Bathsheba, 32
 Joel, 32
 Mary, 118
VAN VINCLE, Abraham, 67
VAN WINKLE, Sarah, 106
VANAMAN,
 David, 79
 Elizabeth, 79
 Herbert, 51
 Jonah, 79
 Lydia, 79, 83
 Martha, 83
 Mary, 83
 Metachabel, 79
 Samuel, 83
 William, 79
VANDEFORD, Abraham, 68
VANDERFORD, John, 119
VANEMAN,
 Catherine, 79
 Elizabeth, 51
 Isaac, 51
 Luke, 51

Mary, 51
Peter, 79
Rachel, 51
Rebeckah, 51
Thomas, 51
VANEMON, Ruth, 114
VANHOOK,
 Deborah, 51
 Elizabeth, 115
 Henry, 119
VANHORN, P. Peterson, 4
VANMETER, William, 68
VANNEMAN,
 Catherine, 80
 Daniel, 80
 David, 81
 Isaac, 77
 John, 77
 Margaret, 81
 Mary, 77
 Mehitabel, 81
 Peter, 80
 Samuel, 81
 Sarah, 81
VATSON,
 Christian Ludwig, 38
 Johan, 38
 Maria Anna, 38
VAUGHN, Mary, 115
VEAL,
 Nehemiah, 23
 Platts, 5
VENABLES, Elizabeth, 112
VENAMAN, Jonas, 119
VICKERS,
 Hannah, 97
 Hope, 93
 Philip, 1, 93
 Sarah, 93
VINCENT,
 Charles, 30
 Theodorus, 28

-W-
WADE, John, 77, 78
WAIKEL, Jost, 49
WAITHMAN,
 Clemens, 92
 Elisabeth, 92
 Elizabeth, 92
 Levice, 116
 Mary, 92, 105
 Philathea, 92
 Sarah, 105
 Srimathea, 106
 Thomas, 92
 William, 119
WALKER,
 Ambrose, 70
 Marey, 64
WALLACE, Martha, 2
WALLING,
 Abijah, 68
 Cynthus, 118
 George, 95
 John, 119
 Jonathan, 95, 119
 Ladis, 95, 119
 Mary, 2, 69, 95, 119
 Rachel, 74
 Ruth, 95
 Sarah, 117
 Thomas, 84
WALTERS,
 Amelia, 70
 Philip, 119
WALTON, Ann, 63
WARD,
 Catharine, 117
 Debby, 72
 Eunice, 99
 James, 100
 Lovisa, 100
 Mary, 100
 Oliver, 100
 Parthenia, 100
 Plany, 58
 Samuel, 76, 99, 119
 Sarah, 3, 76, 110

162 EARLY RECORDS OF CUMBERLAND CO.

Seth Samuel, 76
WARE,
Anne, 119
Elnathan, 119
Enoch, 97
Hannah, 97
Isaac, 97
John, 119
Latin, 119
Lydia, 97
Margaret, 97
Mary, 115
Priscilla, 97
Rachel, 117
Thomas, 97
WASHINGTON, George, 42
WATSON,
Abigail, 94
Christian Ludwig, 38
Howell, 5
Isaac, 94, 119
Johann, 38
John, 106
Maria Anna, 38
Mary, 118
Philathea, 114
Rebecca, 66
Ruth, 118
Samuel, 105
Sarah, 5
William, 119
WEASTCOAT, David, 71
WEATON, Ann, 68
WEBSTER, Mary, 70
WECKS, Johanna Nickel, 49
WEDENMOYER, Johan George, 49
WEEK, Mary, 30
WEEKS,
Ames, 71
Amos, 27, 31
David, 11, 13, 15
Johanna Nickel, 49
Mary, 12, 13, 15

Naomi, 27
Rachel, 27
WEIDEMEYER,
Elisabeth, 36
Gideon, 38
Johan George, 49
Maria Magdalena, 36
Maria Magdalene, 36, 38
Urbanus, 36, 38
WEILDING, Rebeckah, 116
WELCH, William, 64
WELDIN, Jerisha, 65
WELLDONE, Anthony, 71
WELLS,
Samuel, 23
Varney, 32
WENTZEL,
Adam, 37, 38, 39
Anna Maria, 37, 39
Anna Maria Catherine, 45
Carl, 36, 38, 45
Catherine, 36, 38, 45
Chas, 36, 38, 45
Christina, 37
Daniel, 37, 38, 39, 46
Eliza, 45
Elizabeth, 33
Eva, 35, 39
George, 33
Hannah, 39
Jacob, 36
Johann, 41, 45
Johann George, 50
Johann Philip, 33
Johann Wilhelm, 45, 50
Johannes, 41
John Carl, 50
Levi, 40
Louisa, 38
Margaret, 35
Maria, 38, 40, 45
Mathias, 37
Philip, 39

Sara, 38, 39
Sarah, 37
Susanna, 41
Theodoras, 35
Theodoris, 39
Wilhelm, 45, 46
WENTZELL, Adam, 71
WENZEL,
Elizabeth, 33
George, 33
Johann Philip, 33
WESCOT, Lues, 58
WESCOTE, David, 56
WESCOTT, Lues, 58
WESK, Elizabeth, 71
WESSKET, Forster, 89
WEST, Elizabeth, 71
William, 70
WESTCOAAT, Phebe, 1
WESTCOAT,
Abigail, 118
David, 6
Ezekel, 61
Henry, 5
Phebe, 6
Philip, 5
Rhoda, 69
WESTCOATT, Amus, 60
WESTCOE, Joseph, 56
WESTCOT,
Elizabeth, 84
Mary, 90
WESTCOTE,
Daniel, 56
David, 57, 84
Ezekiel, 84
Foster, 119
Henry, 57
Joseph, 57
Rachel, 84
Sarah, 116
Susannah, 57
WESTCOTT,
Aamus, 59
Amos, 64
Ananias, 66

EARLY RECORDS OF CUMBERLAND CO.

James, 40
Johann George, 43
Johann Micheal, 43
Johanna Peter, 43
John Michael, 37
John Micheal, 37, 40
John Peter, 38
Jonathan, 40
Maria Catherine, 40, 43
Micheal Johann, 40
Samuel, 40
Sophia, 38
WOLF,
Elizabeth, 34
Heinrich, 34
Johann, 34
WOLFF,
Elizabeth, 34
Heinrich, 34
Johann, 34
WOLPERT,
Elisabeth, 38
John Peter, 38
Sophia, 38
WOOD,
Albina, 71
David, 119
Elezabeth, 3
Hannah, 65
Henry, 88
Jackoniah, 82
Jaconias, 82
John, 119
Jonathan, 89, 92
Mary, 92, 100
Mellicent, 92
Polly, 72
Rachel, 106
Richard, 100
Sally, 72
Samuel, 3, 65, 119
Sarah, 64, 66
Temperance, 72
WOODHOUSE, Hannah, 119

WOODLAND, Rhoda, 114
WOODLARD, William, 89
WOODROW, Sarah, 73
WOODRUF, Lydia, 103
WOODRUFF,
Abner, 106, 107
Ame, 92
Amos, 67, 119
Amy, 107
Ann, 68
Catherine, 104
David, 67, 72, 73, 92, 107
Ebenezor, 105
Elizabeth, 73
Enos, 101, 106
Ester, 110
Esther, 101
Ewing, 107
James, 92, 107
John, 92, 104
Mary, 106
Noah, 73, 92, 107
Pheba, 92
Phebe, 73, 92
Polly, 115
Sabra, 101, 105, 107
Sarah, 101, 115, 117
Seabury, 67
Silas, 92
Stratten, 92
Timothy, 30
WOOLSON, Polly, 112
WOOSTON, Elizabeth, 52
WORREL, Sarah, 112
WORTHINGON, Rhoda, 6
WORTHINGTON,
Jane, 70
Rachel, 115
WORTON, Sarah, 113
WOTHMAN, Constant, 119

WRIGHT,
Ann, 119
Nathan, 119
WYATT, Rebecca, 31, 72

-Y-
YAPP,
Elizabeth, 23
Esther, 28
Hannah, 72
Lydia, 27, 29
Samuel, 23
Thomas, 23, 25
YARNELL, Thomas, 80
YATES,
John, 64
Pleasant, 90
YORK, Thomas, 61
YOUNG,
Johan Philippus, 50
Jonas, 34
Louisa, 34
Sarah, 91
YOUNGS,
Adam, 106
Martha, 71
Mary, 70, 117

-Z-
ZIEGLER,
George, 49
Hans George, 49
ZIFLWE, Daniel, 41
ZIGLER,
Anna Maria, 37
Hannah, 41
Johannes, 37, 41
Zacharias, 37
ZIGLIER,
Anna Maria, 35
Susanna, 35
Zacharias, 35
ZIMMERMAN, Hans Adam, 50
ZINGLER, Devald, 29
ZOBELL,

Betsey, 67
Charles, 60
Ephraim, 70
George, 71
Hannah, 58
Hennery, 62
Henry, 70
John, 59
Jonathan, 71
Joseph, 58
Lawrence, 69
Levy, 60
Lydia, 58, 67, 70
Mark, 70
Mary, 58, 65, 116
Phillip, 61
Rachel, 62
Ruth, 61, 70
Sally, 64
Samuel, 58, 59, 61
WETCOTT,
Henry, 62
Mary, 74
WETHERBEE, Jude, 69
WETHERBY, William, 68
WETHMAN,
Aarmathea, 65
Lydia, 3
WHEATON,
Ann, 68
Elizabeth, 1
Hannah, 1
Henry, 30
Hephzibah, 3
Hepsebeth, 116
Isaac, 1, 5
Jonathan, 119
Rebecah, 5
Robert, 119
Ruben, 5
Sarah, 3, 4
WHEELER,
Jehiel, 119
Rebecca, 115

WHITACAAR,
Recompence, 72
WHITACAR,
Ambrose, 119
Hannah, 71
Joseph, 119
Richard, 119
Thomas, 119
WHITAKAR, Urania, 70
WHITAKER,
Abel, 18
Diament, 29
Elias, 28
Joseph, 88
Margaret, 114
Mary, 105
Priscilla, 70
Recompence, 31
Sarah, 18
WHITALL, Sarah, 119
WHITE,
George, 119
Josiah, 72
Lydia, 112
Susanna, 72
Susannah, 22
WHITECAR,
Abigail, 110, 115
Allen, 61
Lemuel, 65
Rachel, 69
Silas, 66
Thomas, 56
WHITIAM, Nethaniel, 59
WHITMAN, Clemens, 112
WHITSNACK, Eleanor, 104
WHITTAKER, Benjamin, 89
WHITTCAR, John, 60
WHITTECAR,
Allen, 59, 61
Azabund, 55
Christen, 60
Ellenailian, 60

John, 61
Joseph, 55
Nathaniel, 59
Rachel, 58
Richard, 60
Ruth, 55
Samson, 61
Silas, 60
Tabitha, 55
WHITTICAR, Lorainia, 111
WHITTIKER,
Deamon, 90
Rachel, 90
WHOW(HOOD), James, 61
WICKARD, Sarah, 29
WILIE, Mary, 115
WILLIAMS,
Alle, 62
Ann, 64
Anne, 116
George P., 64
Mary, 5
Peggy, 66
Polly, 69
Simon, 8
Williams, 66
WILLIAMSON, Thomas, 66
WILLSON, Mary, 2
WILPERT,
Johann George, 43
Johann Micheal, 43
WILSON, David, 63
WINCHESTER, Sarah, 74
WINCKESTER, Sarah, 74
WISEMAN, John, 75
WITTECARE, Joseph, 55
WOLBERT,
Catherine, 43
Daniel, 40
Elisabeth, 38
Eva Rosina, 37

Anna Margaret, 41
Christian, 41

Other Heritage Books by Charlotte Meldrum:

Abstracts of Bucks County, Pennsylvania Land Records, 1684–1723

*Early Church Records of Burlington County, New Jersey
Volumes 1–3*

Early Church Records of Chester County, Pennsylvania, Volume 2
Charlotte Meldrum and Martha Reamy

Early Church Records of Gloucester County, New Jersey

Early Church Records of Salem County, New Jersey

Early Records of Cumberland County, New Jersey

Johnston County, North Carolina Marriages, 1764–1867

Marriages and Deaths of Montgomery County, Pennsylvania, 1685–1800

www.ingramcontent.com/pod-product-compliance
Lightning Source LLC
Chambersburg PA
CBHW050814160426
43192CB00010B/1756